This Is Our Story

A Historical Portrait

of the

Missionary Baptist State Convention of Missouri

This Is Our Story

A Historical Portrait

of the

Missionary Baptist State Convention of Missouri

1978-1999

Dr. Sammie E. Jones, President

William R. Boone, D.Min., Compiler

Sunday Shool Publishing Board
National Baptist Convention, USA, Inc.
Nashville, Tennessee

ISBN: 0-910683-88-3

Copyright © 2002 by Missionary Baptist State Convention of Missouri
All rights reserved. The reproduction of this work in any form by electronic, mechanical or other means now known or hereafter invented, including photocopying or recording, or in any informational storage and retrieval system, is prohibited without written permission from the publisher.

Printed in the U.S.A.
Published by Townsend Press
Nashville, Tennessee

Table of Contents

Preface vi

Acknowledgments vii

Prologue viii

Chapter 1—Our Heritage 1

Chapter 2—Our People 14

Chapter 3—Our Churches 46

Chapter 4—Our Associations 102

Chapter 5—Our Convention 124

Epilogue 190

Bibliography 195

Index 196

Preface

It has been thirty-three years since Pastor David O. and Mrs. Alberta D. Shipley initiated the monumental task of gathering and presenting the history of the Missionary Baptist State Convention of Missouri in a systematic manner. Their work resulted in the publication of the *History of Black Baptists in Missouri* in 1976.

The present work was commissioned by President Sammie E. Jones several years ago. He desired to preserve the noble legacy of the ministry God has and is accomplishing through His servants across the great state of Missouri. The project has been a great challenge in every sense of the word. It appeared that the adversary was blocking us on every side in every conceivable way. Praise be to God that we have prevailed.

The writer is convinced that the constituency of the Missionary Baptist State Convention of Missouri has an exciting and powerful story to tell. It is a story of a determined people learning how to submit, to delight themselves in and rest in the power and mercy of the Lord. We continuously praise God. He has brought us as individuals, churches, associations, and as a state convention with auxiliaries since our genesis in Missouri as churches since the early 1800s. We have existed as a convention since 1888. We are a convention that stretches from Iowa to Arkansas; and from Nebraska, Kansas and Oklahoma to Illinois, Kentucky and Tennessee.

Our story is one of agony and ecstasy, defeat and triumph, division and unity, failures and successes, doubt and faith. The common thread is that God continues to be the unseen force that supplies all of our needs according to His riches in glory.

The following pages are a representation of "Our Story." We will look at the people, churches, and associations that covenanted themselves together as baptized believers in Jesus Christ working faithfully to tell the old, old story about Jesus and His love as a state convention. The story will commence with a message delivered by Dr. Issac C. Peay who departed this life in 1999 and close with the Presidential Address delivered by Dr. Sammie E. Jones during the final session of the 1900s.

William R. Boone

Acknowledgments

This work could not have been completed without the research of Pastors David O. Shipley, W. A. Scott, I. C. Peay, and Socrates Scott (retired); Minister Russ McDonald, Mrs. Galinda Wallace, Colonel Peter Sellers (retired); District Association Moderators, State Convention Officers and the leadership of the National Baptist Publishing Board. A very special thanks is extended to Helen Boone, my wife of thirty years, and our children, my parents, Mr. and Mrs. W. L. Boone, all my siblings, relatives and the greater community of the Baptist church family.

Prologue

Our story is about lessons learned during our one-hundred twenty-one year journey as saints of God serving within the borders of the "Show-Me" state and beyond. We, therefore, start this prodigious journey with a message concerning the value and purpose of lessons delivered by the late Dr. Isaac C. Peay, Sr. at the National Baptist Convention Congress of Christian Education entitled "The Things Which Thou Hast Learned" (2 Timothy 3:14-17).

INTRODUCTION

I assure you that it is a profound pleasure and a signal honor to have this opportunity to come to you on this auspicious and momentous occasion.

I need not use or waste our time telling you that we have a great president of our Sunday School and Baptist Training Union Congress, because we are well aware of the type of personality we have—a man of great strength, courage, and ability.

I do not feel worthy of this honor, therefore, I request your prayers that the Lord through His servant may say something to inspire, commend, and encourage you who have come from every nook and corner of the continental United States, and possibly abroad.

The speaker is well aware and fully conscious of his role at this time—to bring the kind of message that is befitting the occasion. I am to speak to you with an educational sermon.

When we say education, we mean, acculturation, indoctrination, instruction, nurture, polish, prepare, rationalize, strengthen, teach, competence, development, discipline, edification, enlightenment, humanization, inculcation, knowledge, learning, pedagogy, scholastic teaching, training, and refinement.

These are some of the approaches we shall make in connection with this message.

1. The learning process.
2. The lessons which Timothy learned.
3. The things which thou hast learned.
4. What one needs if he is going to use what he has learned.
5. What one may expect if he uses what he has learned.

The speaker is well aware of the tremendous amount of time, energy and effort expended in the preparation for this day. Therefore, he shall not show his ignorance and anxiety by discussing the summit conferences; the UN in the Near East War; the

Middle East disengagement; or the Watergate situation, but shall leave the matters to those who have authority in our government.

I say this, if you are going to maintain your leadership position in the communities in which you live, you need the type of religious education that the National Congress has to offer. You cannot stop now, but must seek more education. For that reason, we call your attention to a very familiar passage of Scripture found in Second Timothy 3:14. Paul said, "But continue thou in the things which thou hast learned and hast been assured of, knowing of whom thou hast learned them."

From this passage, we know somewhat of the background of Timothy: his family or domestic background; his social background; and his religious background. We also see the learning process, "And that from a child thou hast known the holy scriptures, which are able to make thee wise unto salvation through faith which is in Christ Jesus" (2 Timothy 3:15). "Which dwelt first in thy grandmother Lois, and thy mother Eunice" (2 Timothy 1:5).

This is the proper and befitting approach to the learning process, "From a child." This learning process begins in infancy and continues throughout life.

Paul said to Timothy, "All scripture is given by inspiration of God, and is profitable for doctrine (<u>for credence</u>; dogma, logic, philosophy, principle, teaching and theory], for reproof, for correction, for instruction in righteousness: That the man of God may be perfect, thoroughly furnished unto all good works" (2 Timothy 3:16-17).

It seems to the speaker that this is a good passage of Scripture in which to center our thoughts for this memorable occasion.

Paul gives to Timothy part of the learning process when he said, "Study to show thyself approved unto God, a workman that needeth not to be ashamed, rightly dividing the word of truth" (2 Timothy 2:15).

The learning process is very important, for no man can know without studying.

I. **SOME FACETS OF THE LEARNING PROCESS.**
   A. The learning process is domestical.
   B. The learning process is sociological.
   C. The learning process is mechanical.
   D. The learning process is biological.
   E. The learning process is physiological.
   F. The learning process is psychological.
   G. The learning process is prophetic.

H. The learning process is anthropological.
I. The learning process is Christological.
J. The learning process is spiritual.
K. The learning process is soteriological.
L. The learning process is ecclesiological.
M. The learning process is eschatological.
N. The learning process is moral.
O. The learning process is theological.

There is an old saying, "He who knows where he is going will be the leader of the people."

Before a man can really learn what he needs to know, he must learn one thing thoroughly; that is, he must learn how little he already knows. One who learns this well is on his way to the goal of perfect knowledge.

There is an adage which says, "If one knows, he can teach others; but it is possible that one doesn't know enough to know that he does not know, therefore he doesn't know enough to be told."

It is said that a certain man went to a strange city and wanted to mail a letter. He started for town to search for the post office. On his way to town, he came upon a little boy who was playing in the sand. He asked the little boy, "Son, could you tell me where the post office is?" The little boy looked up with sympathetic and apologetic eyes, and said, "I'll try, Mister. Do you know where the big hardware store is on the corner of Main Street?" The stranger said, "No." "Well, do you know where the large drugstore is on the next corner?" "No," he said. "Well Sir, you don't know enough for me to tell you where the post office is."

Paul wanted Timothy to know enough to be told what to do and how to do it.

We believe that knowledge is power and essential to a productive life for everyone, no matter what the nationality, racial background or cultural opportunities. It simply costs too much not to know.

It is told of an engineer on one of the major railroads of this country, who had been on this road for about thirty (30) years and had never been late: never missed a schedule: One day while on his run, his engine became out-of-order. He tried to get it started, but with no success. He used every method he knew, but with no progress. So he decided to search the train for help. In searching, he found a mechanical engineer on board one of the coaches. He asked him to come back to the engine room and check it out to see if he could get it started. He explained that he didn't want to mar his long-time record that he had made. He simply wanted to save his record. Well why not! The mechanical engineer soon discovered the trouble and said he thought he could repair it. The old man told him to repair it and make out a bill to the railroad company. When the mechanic had finished, he made out the bill for $250.00. The train made the run on time and the older man's record was saved. But when the railroad company received the bill, they were furiously upset and demanded an itemized record. The mechanical engineer sat down and wrote: "Gentlemen: on such and such a day, your engineer asked me to repair an engine for which I charged $250.00. The steam valve was stuck thereby preventing the steam from going through. I charged $2.00 for tapping and $248.00 for knowing where to tap." So you see! It is expensive not to know. This illustration may be applied to Christian education as well as to secular education.

II. SOME OF THE LESSONS THAT TIMOTHY HAD LEARNED AND THAT WE NEED TO KNOW.

   A. Timothy learned to form the right estimation of himself. He asked the question, "Who am I?"
   1. What have I to offer to the world?
   2. What have I to offer society?

The sociological aspects of this world need to be developed. What have I to contribute? Is there anything I or we can lend to the development of a more hospitable neighborhood?

Is there anything I or we can do to make things more pleasant? Can we create joviality in a society that is packed and jammed with corruption from top to bottom?

To me, religious education is one of the greatest benefits to mankind. It leaves one in no doubt as to his comparative powers and attainments. His homological experiences are always compatible and non-contradictory. It leaves no room for presumption, arrogance, audacity, conceit, disdain, dogmatism, egocentricity, grandiloquence, loftiness or pompousness. In other words, when one learns the Christ way, he is more trusting than self-confident; he is more cautious than presumptuous; he is more earnest than frivolous; he is more humble than haughty.

   B. The second lesson that Timothy learned was to take a just and not a fanciful estimate of himself. This is what Paul had discovered about Timothy, and this is what we should learn.

   C. He had learned to adapt himself to a variety of persons and circumstances. He never became frustrated or confounded when he met with people who desired to be different.

   D. He learned to have the proper respect for the senior ministers. He had the utmost respect for Paul and Silas, etc. He had respect for those of his class.
   E. Timothy had learned to live a godly life in Christ Jesus.
   F. Timothy had learned to honor his parents and respect other mothers and fathers of his hometown.
   G. He had learned the Holy Scriptures. Paul said, "That from a child thou hast known the holy scriptures, which are able to make you wise unto salvation."

III. CONSIDER THE THINGS WHICH THOU HAST LEARNED.

I am sure they are multiple and varied.

   A. The things which thou hast learned are wholesome things, because they tend to promote:
     1. Healthy bodies.
     2. Sound and logical minds.
     3. Clean character.
     4. A good moral and spiritual life.

This is what is needed in this twentieth century; in this mechanized, electronic, atomic, rocket and missile age in which we live, in this highly scientific and pathological age, we need to know what we are doing as leaders. If we don't know, the people will find it out.

In this high speed jet age, we can no longer expect the people to come and sit for an hour in church or in our class on Sunday morning and listen to nothing more than reiteration of one's personal experiences. Although illustrations of personal experiences have their place in our messages, they are not enough for this time in which we live. They must be told about God and His will for them in their lives.

   B. What thou has learned is *essential*.
     1. Essential because of its *necessity* to promote righteous living.
     2. Essential because of the *unique* place or position you hold in the community in which you live. You are considered light holders.
     3. Essential because it is *indispensable* in a world of trouble because it speaks about Christ.

If this world is to be what God would have it to be—socially, morally, economically, politically, and spiritually—what thou hast learned is essential.

What thou hast learned is knowledge, and knowledge is power.
       a. Knowledge is essential to the development of moral character.

      b. Knowledge is essential to the development of Christian character.
      c. Knowledge is essential to the maintenance of a good domestic status quo.
      d. Knowledge is essential to the development and maintenance of a high social and moral standard in the community in which we live.
      e. Knowledge is essential to the development and maintenance of a good stable economic standard of living.
      f. Knowledge is essential to the strong and just political standard of government.
      g. Knowledge is essential to the development of a strong Christian life and witness.

God said, "My people are destroyed for the lack of knowledge: because thou hast rejected knowledge, I will also reject thee, that thou shalt be no priest to me: seeing thou hast forgotten the law of thy God, I will also forget thy children" (Hosea 4:6).

  C. What thou hast learned is *profitable.*
    1. Profitable for doctrine (teaching).

The word is *didaskalin*, teaching or instruction. There is an old saying, "One cannot lead where he does not go, and cannot teach that which he does not know."

  So what thou hast learned is profitable for teaching.

Paul said, "Study to show thyself approved unto God, a workman that needeth not to be ashamed, rightly dividing the word of truth" (2 Timothy 2:15).

Paul sets out a duty and a worker's responsibility for the preaching and witnessing of Christian ministry in this world.

    2. The Scriptures are not only profitable for doctrine, but also profitable for reproof (Censure, chiding, kindly rebuking, admonishing, reprimanding, criticizing).
    3. What thou hast learned is profitable for correction.

Many lives may be corrected as the results of what you have learned. Many strange and spurious dogmas may be changed as the results of what thou hast learned. Too many opinions of man have been thrust upon our people, and it is your responsibility to correct them. God only is infallible and immutable.

    4. What thou hast learned is profitable "for instruction in righteousness: that the man of God may be perfect thoroughly finished unto all good works" (2 Timothy 3:16-17).
  D. What thou hast learned ***must be used***, and therefore should not be hoarded or

stored away in the secret places of your own vocabulary. What thou hast learned is not a treasure to be kept to yourself, but must be disseminated or propagated to a lost and dying world.

1. What thou hast learned must be used for yourself, first. Although we know that what we have learned must not be kept within ourselves, we also know that we should be the first to benefit from what we have learned. It has been said, "Self preservation is the first law of nature."
   a. What thou hast learned must be used for thyself to guard against the critics of this world.
   b. What thou hast learned must be used to keep thyself from the pitfalls of ignorance and stupidity.
2. What thou hast learned should be used for the benefit of others. Others, Lord, yes others. Paul said, "Let nothing be done through strife or vain glory; but in lowliness of mind let each esteem others better than themselves. Look not every man on his own things, but every man also on the things of others."

OTHERS

Lord, help me live from day to day, in such a self-forgetful way,
That even when I kneel to pray, my prayer shall be for others.
Help me in all the work I do ever be sincere and true,
And know that all I'd do for You must needs be done for others.
Let self be crucified, slain and buried deep and all in vain,
May efforts be to rise again unless to live for others.
Others, Lord, yes others, let this my motto be,
Help me to live for others, that I may live for Thee.

   a. What thou hast learned must be used to benefit others in the domestic area. Thousands of homes are being broken every day. Many of them can be mended, or brought back together.
   More and more now, the medical doctors are referring their patients to their ministers and Christian counselors. One should be ready to help in whatever way possible. The problem is not a physical, nor is it a mental one, but a spiritual problem.
   b. What thou hast learned must be used for others in the areas of society and religion. Society will never be redeemed from its low ebb, until Christianity becomes the religion of the people of this age. There must be a deep sense of responsibility where others are concerned.

(1) Christianity must supplant Judaism with all its rites and customs.
(2) Christianity must supplant Confucianism with all its worship of its dignitaries and ancestors, and its attempt to maintain its five principal relationships of life.

Such as:
  (a) Prince and subject.
  (b) Parent and child.
  (c) Husband and brother.
  (d) Brother and brother.
  (e) Friend and friend.
(3) Christianity must supplant Mohammedanism with all of its superior attitudes and philosophies that are sweeping this country of ours.
(4) Christianity must supplant Buddhism with all its self-denial, virtues, wisdom and attainment of happiness through obedience, and freedom from earthly passion.

E. Finally, what thou hast learned should be used to glorify God. God must be magnified, adored, extolled and honored above everybody and everything in the world.

IV. What One Needs If He Is Going to Use That Which He Has Learned.
A. He needs a sympathetic and compassionate heart.
B. He needs a strong will.
C. He needs a strong determination.
D. He needs courage of conviction.
E. He needs God on his side.

V. What May We Expect If We Tell What We Have Learned?

A. We may expect help from those to whom we preach or teach.
  1. *Moral help:* The kind of help that only church membership can give. Moral support is one of the things that an uncompromising teacher needs more than everything else.
  2. *Financial support:* "Who goeth to warfare any time at his own charges? who planteth a vineyard, and eateth not of the fruit thereof? or who feedeth a flock, and eateth not of the milk of the flock?...For it is written in the law of Moses, Thou shalt not muzzle the mouth of the ox that treadeth out the corn. Doth God take care for oxen?...Do ye not know that they which

minister about holy things live of the things of the temple?...If we have sown unto you spiritual things, is it a great thing if we shall reap your carnal things? Even so hath the Lord ordained that they which preach the gospel should live of the gospel"(1 Corinthians 9:7-14).
3. *Spiritual help:* Spiritual help comes from God through spiritual-minded people. There is no doubt about it, all who serve need this kind of support.

B. *Divine Help:* We also may expect help from our God.

David said, "Our soul waiteth for the Lord: He is our help and our shield" (Psalm 33:20). He further said, "God is our refuge and strength, a very present help in trouble" (Psalm 46:1).
1. God gives strength when we are weak.
2. When we lean, He props us up.
3. When we fall, He picks us up.
4. When we thirst, He gives us water.
5. When we hunger, He feeds us.
6. He helps us to love instead of hate.
7. He gives us peace instead of confusion.
8. He gives us joy instead of sorrow.
9. He gives us heaven instead of hell.

C. We need the help that comes from anticipation.

"And I saw a new heaven and a new earth: for the first heaven and the first earth were passed away; and there was no more sea. And I John saw the holy city, new Jerusalem, coming down from God out of heaven, prepared as a bride adorned for her husband. And I heard a great voice out of heaven saying, Behold, the tabernacle of God is with men, and he will dwell with them, and they shall be his people, and God himself shall be with them, and be their God. And God shall wipe away all tears from their eyes; and there shall be no more death, neither sorrow, nor crying, neither shall there be any more pain: for the former things are passed away...And he carried me away in the spirit to a great and high mountain, and showed me that great city, the holy Jerusalem, descending out of heaven from God, Having the glory of God: and her light was like unto a stone most precious, even like a jasper stone, clear as crystal; And had a wall great and high, and had twelve gates, and at the gates twelve angels, and names written thereon, which are the names of the twelve tribes of the children of Israel: on the east three gates; on the north three gates; on the south three gates; and on the west three gates. And the wall of the city had twelve foundations, and in them the names of the twelve apostles of the Lamb. And he that talked with me had a golden reed to measure the city, and the gates thereof, and the wall thereof. And the city lieth foursquare, and the length is as large as the breadth: and he measured the city with the reed, twelve thousand furlongs. The length and the breadth and the height of it are equal. And he measured the wall thereof, an hundred and forty and four cubits, according to the measure of a man, that is, of the angel. And the building of the wall of it was of Jasper: and the city was pure gold, like unto clear glass. And the foundations of the wall of the city were garnished with all manner of precious stones. The first foundation was jasper; the second, sapphire; the third, a chalcedony; the fourth, an emerald; the fifth, sardonyx; the sixth, sardius; the seventh, chrysolite; the eighth, beryl; the ninth, a topaz; the tenth, a chrysoprasus; the eleventh, a jacinth; the twelfth, an amethyst. And the twelve gates were twelve pearls; every several gate was of one pearl; and the street of the city was pure gold, as it were transparent glass. And I saw no temple therein: for the Lord God Almighty and the Lamb are the temple of it. And the city had no need of the sun, neither of the moon, to shine in it: For the glory of God did lighten it, and the Lamb is the light thereof. And the nations of them which are saved shall walk in the light of it: and the kings of the earth do bring their glory and honor into it. And the gates of it shall not be shut at all by day: for there shall be no night there. And they shall bring the glory and honor of the nations into it. And there shall in no wise enter into it any thing that defileth, neither whatsoever worketh abomination, or maketh a lie: but they which are written in the Lamb's book of life" (Revelation 21:1-4, 10-27).

BEAMS OF HEAVEN

"Beams of heaven, as I go, Thro' this wilderness below,
Guide my feet in peaceful ways, Turn my midnights into days;
When in the darkness I would grope, Faith always sees a star of hope,
And soon from all life's grief and danger, I shall be free some day.

Burdens now may crush me down, Disappointments all around,
Troubles speak in mournful sigh, Sorrow through a tear-stained eye:
There is a world where pleasure reigns, No mourning soul shall roam its plains,
And to that land of peace and glory, I want to go some day."

Chapter 1

Our Heritage

HAM'S DISPERSAL

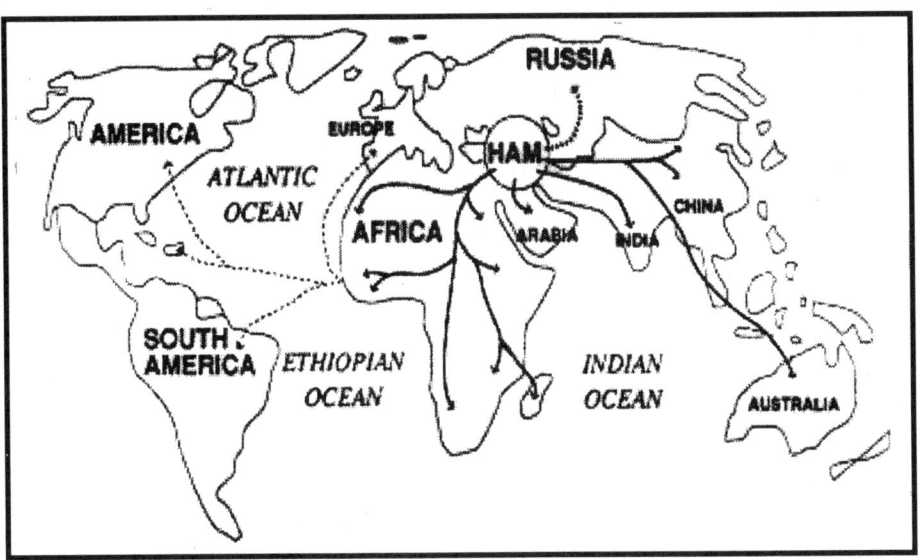

Settlement of the Ark   (HAM)

Temporary Settlement . . . .
Permanent Settlement . . . .
Later Settlement . . . .

AFRICA   **HAITI-ST. DOMINQUE**   **MISSOURI**

AFRICAN AMERICAN (BLACK) HISTORY MONTH

This past week my daughter excitedly approached me about some new information that she had discovered relative to our heritage in the February issue of *Ebony* magazine. She exclaimed, "Dad! Did you know that there were hundreds of black entrepreneurs in America before the American Revolution? They were merchants, plantation owners, shipping company owners, inventors, etc." I smiled and did not immediately respond to her excitement. I mused, isn't it great to live in a country that ultimately provides people with the opportunity to celebrate their uniqueness and pursue truth?

I am excited about living in this rural cosmopolitan area. I would readily put our surface human relations profile in competition with any area in the world. I am sure that the military has played a significant role in a lot that we experience here today. People of all races move freely from church to church, housing area to housing area, business to business, and school to school. All is not perfect. However, the potential for greatness is certainly here. For, each of us brings to this sacred community the richness of our historicity and culture. We are truly blessed by our diversity.

Hence, I would like to enlighten some and remind others this month about the history of Americans of African ancestry. The articles that will come from a variety of sources are not intended to assert that any person or ethnic community is any better or less than another. They are not intended to denigrate nor condemn any people for actions that were not always viewed as being constructive. For I believe that "Everything works together for the good of them that love the Lord and are the called according to his purpose." I am daily reminded that there are psychological scars that I will forever have to live with. There are emotional viruses that erupt from time to time that fade away. I will never deny them. I simply use them to propel me to be a greater American and encourage others to do the same. For we are inextricably connected to each other.

Carter G. Woodson perhaps made historical discoveries similar to the many facts that my daughter recently made concerning "black entrepreneurs." His excitement resulted in the formation of the Association for the Study of Negro Life and History in 1915. The formation of this group ultimately resulted in the celebration of Negro History Week during the month of February. Negro History Week was renamed Black History Month in the sixties and continues as such today.

THE QUEST FOR KNOWLEDGE

The words of Pastor Peay clearly reflect the sentiments of this author. Each of us needs to develop a burning for learning. We learn to enhance our abilities and our usefulness to humanity. We learn so that we do not ignorantly doom ourselves by repeating the sins of previous generations. We learn so that our relationship with God and our neighbors will improve. Our heritage is all about the lessons learned and implemented by our ancestors. It is a direct result of their hunger and thirst to maximize their abilities, resources and opportunities so that life could be better for themselves and subsequent generations. It is imperative that their legacy continues to be captured and shared with the present and future generations for posterity.

There are three factors that must be examined if one is to truly appreciate the history of Baptists affiliated with the Missionary Baptist State Convention of Missouri. The first factor is our African and Middle Passage heritage. The second factor is our American heritage. The third factor is our ability to make brick without straw.

OUR AFRICAN AND MIDDLE PASSAGE HERITAGE

It is unfortunate that our connection with the continent of Africa is often forgotten. I suppose that it is difficult to identify with that which is unknown emotionally and experientially. However, one cannot function authentically if he or she has any area of disconnects in their lives. It is a joy to note the work of men such as Dr. Charles Copher, John L. Johnson, John G. Jackson, Drs. John Hope Franklin, Lerone Bennett and others. These writers have done a tremendous job bridging the gap between our past and present experiences. Their research has destroyed a number of myths that have been perpetuated throughout the four-hundred-plus years' sojourn of our people in what is now called the United States of America.

It has been conclusively proven that life originated on the continent of Africa and moved beyond her borders over time. Dr. Lerone Bennett provides the following information that came from his research in *Before the Mayflower* (p. 4).

> Olduvia Gorge: A series of astonishing discoveries in this Tanzanian canyon suggest that the most important and fascinating developments in human history occurred in Africa. Discoveries by Dr. L. S. B. Leakey and other archeologists indicate that the human race was born in Africa. A growing body of research from this and other African sites indicates further that toolmaking began in Africa and that this seminal invention spread to Europe and Asia.

> The Nile Valley: Important finds in the Sudan and the Nile Valley prove that people of a Negroid type were influential contributors to that cradle of civilization—ancient Egypt. Discoveries at excavations near Khartoum in the Sudan and at El Badari on the Nile indicate that Stone Age Negroes laid the foundation for much of the civilization of the Nile Valley and manufactured pottery before pottery was made in the world's earliest known city.

Dr. John G. Jackson in *Introduction to African Civilization* presents extensive research that has resulted in new revelations concerning the development of African cultures from the northernmost point to the westernmost point.

St. Claire Drake suggests in *The Redemption of Africa and Black Religion* that the exploits of Ethiopia were known throughout the civilized world. He quotes Homer, Lucian and Herodotus' comments about the superior virtues of the Ethiopians and of them being the people among whom the gods vacationed (page 58).

The Central kingdoms included Zimbabwe, Monomotapa, Kitwara, Kongo and Zhand. Western kingdoms included Ghana, Songhay, Mali and Kanem-Bornu. These kingdoms controlled enormous territories across the continent even into India and Asia.

Dr. Lerone Bennett wrote in *Before the Mayflower* (p. 33) that:

> The letters and diaries of traders show that down to the eighteenth century, they had no conception of Africans as racial pariahs. On the contrary, many of these traders said Africans were their equals and superior to many of their countrymen back home. Africans were of substantially the same mind. They did not consider themselves inferior to Europeans. If anything, they considered themselves superior to the odd-looking men with pale skins.
>
> We are told that the King of Dahomey seldom shook hands with white men and that when he did, it was a very uncommon mark of royal condescension. A French trader complained in 1660 that the Fanti were so proud and haughty that a European trader there must stand bare to them.

This preliminary information has been shared to remind the reader that we have a noble past that is filled with blessings as well as curses for which we can be grateful. We have an unusual past that can be celebrated and appreciated. We are the sons and daughters of a people with a noble heritage. I remember my first trip to the continent. I was filled with so much joy and awe as I looked at the massive terrain that was unfolding before me. Something cried out within, "That's home!" I don't know where, but that is home, thank God.

Dr. C. Eric Lincoln in cooperation with Dr. Lawrence H. Mamiya suggests in *The Black Church in the African American Experience* that, "A good way to understand a people is to study their religion. Their religion is addressed to that most sacred schedule of values around which the expression and the meaning of life tend to coalesce" (p. 30).

Hence, our concern here is not so much an accounting of the historicity of African people. It would require much more time and space than we are presently willing to invest in. We are simply convinced that the faith of those Africans significantly influenced the faith development of the saints affiliated with the Missionary Baptist State Convention of Missouri. We desire to share some spiritual antecedents that perhaps helped facilitate the faith transition of Africans who inhabited the lands that became known as Missouri.

The Old and New Testaments also attest to the prominence of the sons of Ham in the life and history of the sons of Shem and Japheth. John L. Johnson in *The Black Biblical Heritage* (p.19) states:

> Ham the patriarch was not cursed dark but created (born) dark. He is considered the paternal ancestor of Ethiopia, Egypt, Libya, Carthage, and many African tribes, Northern and Southern Arabia, Crete, Cyprus, Asia Minor (Hittite)... A portion of Israel and the black Americans. These progenies are called Hamites, and many ruled for centuries with great power over other known civilizations. Rawlison says that the descendants of Ham acted as pioneers and led the world in various new fields of art, science and literature including alphabetic writings, astronomy, architecture, historical chronology, plastic art, sculpture, agriculture, navigation and textile industry.

Moreover, the Old and New Testaments are replete with the names of people of African ancestry who participated in God's covenant relationship with Israel. As we thumb through the Scriptures, we can discover faithful and unfaithful descendants of Ham.

We can find stories of successes and failures. Names such as Nimrod (Genesis 10:8-10), Ishmael (Genesis 28), Rameses II (Numbers 33:3), Abimelech (1 Samuel 26:6-7), Rahab (Joshua 2:1), Hadad (1 Kings 11:14-22), Simon of Cyrene (Matthew 27:32), Simon the Canaanite (Luke 6:12-16) and the Ethiopian Eunuch (Acts 7:23-39) are individuals of African ancestry.

Dr. John M'Biti, a noted African theologian and philosopher, has stated that Africans are notoriously religious. They were primarily polytheistic; that is, serving many gods. They had a tremendous respect for life and all of the component parts that enrich the quality of life. They maintained an uncanny awareness that they were accountable to their god for their actions. They took advantage of every opportunity afforded them to worship their god(s).

Dr. M'Biti wrote in *African Religions and Philosophy* that:

> Christianity and Islam are deeply rooted in the history of our continent.... Christianity in Africa is so old that it can rightly be described as an indigenous, traditional and African religion. Long before the start of Islam in the 7th Century,

> Christianity was well established all over North Africa, Egypt, parts of the Sudan and Ethiopia. It was a dynamic form of Christianity producing great scholars like Tertullian, Origen, Clement of Alexandria and Augustine. African Christianity made great contributions to Christendom through scholarship, participation in church councils, defense of the faith, translation and preservation of the Scripture, martyrdom, the famous Catechetical School, Liturgy and even heresies and controversies (p. 300).

Dr. Lerone Bennett wrote in *Before the Mayflower*:

> Of whatever tongue, of whatever color, Africans were a deeply religious people. For a long time their religion was written off as a form of animism. We know now that it was a great deal more complicated...Religion, to the African, was life. Every event was charged with religious significance, and the climax of life was death. The African attitude toward death, anthropologists say, survived the Atlantic crossing and took root in the soil of black American life. Another religious root, spirit possession, thrives, they say, in the shouting and ecstasy complex of some black American churches (pp. 15-16).

The African's folklore and traditions, by the providence of God, influenced the development of Judaism, Christianity and Islam. Hence, it is not coincidental that they would quickly adapt to the teaching of Judaism, Christianity or Islam. It is not coincidental that they would "Africanize" these belief systems and use them in ways that would be meaningful for themselves and others with whom they interacted. We are told in the book of Exodus how Moses was directed by Jethro, a Midianite priest (Exodus 18), to utilize the family organizational structure of the Hebrew people to minimize his work load.

We are further told in the Bible about how Egypt and Ethiopia were at times allies of the southern and northern kingdoms of Israel. Moses, the lawgiver, and many of the Jewish leaders married people of African origin before and after they entered Palestine.

It is also interesting to note that on the Day of Pentecost, there were representatives from Egypt, Nubia and probably Ethiopia. We say probably Ethiopia because of the Eunuch who was evangelized by Phillip on his way back to Ethiopia. He was converted from Judaism to the Christian faith. It is believed that these individuals were converted and returned home and began to share the Gospel that they heard with their fellow countrymen.

Dr. Jackson writes in *Introduction to African Civilization* that:

> Many aspects of the present-day Christian church were developed in Africa during the formative years of Christianity...From the north, the church continued to spread southward and eastward. Ethiopia received Christianity at an especially

early date. Part of tradition suggests that St. Matthew, who wrote one of the gospels, preached in Ethiopia (p. 15).

One might deduce that prior to the arrival of Islamic and European Christian colonialism that the Christian message was exchanged as African kingdoms conquered and enslaved each other. The impact in all probability was not on the scale that it was in any other place. Yet, there had to be something special about the spiritual psyche of a people who, for whatever reason, embraced and "africanized" the evangelistic messages of these contending faiths.

OUR AMERICAN HERITAGE

Dr. Jackson wrote in *Introduction to African Civilization that:*
> It is a fact that the first Spanish and Portuguese explorers found colonies of black men on the eastern coast of South and Central America, and in Yucatan and Nicaragua. Father Roman, one of the earliest Catholic missionaries to arrive in the New World, records that a tribe of black men came from the South and landed in Haiti, and they were armed with darts of guanin (an alloy of gold, silver and copper) and were called the Black Guaninis (p. 233).

Moreover, Dr. Lerone Bennett wrote in *Before the Mayflower* that:
> The most important events were the European discovery of America and the opening of the New World. It is a point of paradoxical interest that descendants of the first black captives—black Christians born in Spain and Portugal—were with the first European explorers and settlers. Black explorers-servants, slave and free men, accompanied Spanish and Portuguese explorers in their expeditions in North and South America (p. 34).

Dr. Bennett clearly points out that Africans came to what is now known as the United States as explorers, servants, free men and slaves. We will note all three categories later when we look at our Missouri heritage. However, we would like to look briefly at two factors that significantly influenced our development as a people and a State Convention. The first is the Middle Passage, and the second is the experience of enslavement on the continent and other places. The Middle Passage was perhaps one of the most inhuman experiences that a people could have. Thousands of Africans were crammed into small quarters. They had no privacy and were provided with minimum provisions for survival. The transmission of disease was an everyday experience because of the overcrowded condition of the ship. One can say emphatically that only the strong survived. The weak died at sea or on the island that served as a transition point in the voyage from Africa to America.

However, those who were strong physically, emotionally, intellectually and spiritually landed in the Caribbean and ultimately in the United States. It will be noted later that the majority of Africans arriving in Missouri initially came from French-controlled Haiti and Spanish-controlled St. Dominque. These are individuals that we can be proud of. They were able to survive the Middle Passage, adjust to a new culture, learn a new language and develop survival skills that made it possible for us to be where we are today. The bottom line is that the Africans who came to America were not just plain ordinary people. They were special people capable of accomplishing whatever task and challenge set before them.

Slavery was not a new experience that had just developed in North America. All cultures at one time or another allowed some form of slavery. This practice was exercised on the continent of Africa for centuries. An African Pharaoh was responsible for the enslavement of the children of Shem in Goshen, Egypt.

Arabs invaded the continent during the time when the Sahara desert began to consume so much of the land and the great Eastern and Interior kingdoms were in decline and enslaved large numbers of Africans. Kings of several of the powerful Western and Eastern kingdoms were responsible for the enslavement of people from Central Africa and Western Africa who were transported to America by the millions.

All Africans arriving in Missouri were not slaves. Some arrived here as indentured servants. Some even owned slaves themselves.

Kremer and Holland wrote in *Missouri Black Heritage* that:
> Black Americans first came to the territory we know now as Missouri early in the eighteenth century. Brought against their will by Frenchmen who enslaved them for profit, blacks were seen as the solution to a severe labor shortage encountered by Europeans everywhere in the New World...Des Ursin soon put to work in the mines five black slaves, presumably brought from the French-controlled island of Haiti. In 1720, Phillippee Francois Renault was sent from France to direct lead-mining operations. He, too, brought with him a few slaves... There were 26 freed Africans in St. Geneive and 38 in St. Louis around 1791 (p. 18).

These individuals were brought to Missouri to work in mines harvesting precious metals and minerals. It was noted that better than forty percent of the population of St. Genevieve, the first European community in Missouri, were Africans. Slavery had become a mainstay of the French colonial Missouri. The French sought to enforce the *A Code Noir* or Black Code. Kremer and Holland wrote in *Missouri Black Heritage*:
> The code clearly defined black slaves as property that could be bought and sold, but it also recognized that slaves were human beings with certain rights. The code, for example, required masters to provide adequate care for their slaves and

prohibited the breaking up of families through sales. The code also provided slaves with the right to sue their masters if they thought any of their rights were being transgressed.... Slaves were allowed to purchase their freedom. The *Code Noir* forbade masters to work their slaves on Sundays or holidays (p. 10).

Many of the Africans brought to Missouri were probably baptized and exposed to the Christian faith in Spain and France as free people or Haiti and St. Dominque as slaves. It was customary for slaves to be baptized and be introduced to the Christian faith. That is why many of them worshiped with their slave masters or had services of their own with an European overseer. The original African freedmen and European slave masters made provisions for their slaves to purchase their freedom. That was a common practice with the French and Spanish. Slaves were allowed to work extra hours to earn enough funds to purchase their freedom. Many of them worked conscientiously and in crafty manners to that end.

The number of slaves increased significantly in Missouri following the purchase of the Louisiana Territory by the United States. Kremer and Holland wrote in *Missouri Black Heritage* that:

> The United States purchased the Louisiana Territory in 1803. There were perhaps 1,320 people of African descent at that time. The population began to swell as people began to arrive from Kentucky, Tennessee and Virginia. Many of these people came to this area with their slaves. The majority of Missouri slaves were located in the Mississippi and Missouri River Valleys. St. Louis, of course, led the way. The commander of the Missouri territory, Captain Amos Stoddard, reported that there were 667 slaves in the district of St. Louis in 1804 and 740 by 1810. Other areas with high concentrations of slaves in those early days of the territory included St. Charles, St. Genevieve, and Cape Girardeau (p. 20).

> Slavery in America was perhaps one of the most horrifying experiences in the annals of history. Our people were separated from their homeland and families. No persons speaking the same language were allowed to serve together.

> There was no viable family unit allowed to exist. Every conceivable effort was made to deny the Africans an opportunity to continue traditions that were shared by their families and community. The night certainly must have seemed long and dark for them. The number of slaves in Missouri was over 10,000 by 1820. The African-American population, slave and freedmen fluctuated between 14.4% to 9.7% of the total population between 1820 and 1860. The population percentage reached a high point in 1830 at 17.8% of the population. There was a large concentration in Clay, Cole, Boone, St. Louis, New Madrid, Lafayette, Marion, Macon, Jackson, Callaway, Crawford, Cooper, Howard, Pike, Saline, Lewis and St. Charles counties to name a few.

Bricks Without Straw

This concept was taken from what the people of God experienced in Egypt. We use this concept in a twofold manner. We first speak concerning the demands made upon the slaves by the masters to produce whatever product they were selling. We also use this concept to talk about the ability of the slaves to take a little of nothing and do amazing things with it. We speak especially of the viable unauthorized communities and structures that developed among them. This is especially true for the formation of churches.

The days following the purchase of Missouri by the United States, as mentioned earlier, resulted in an influx of people from states where slavery was harsher than Missouri. Rebellions in many of the Southern states caused slave owners to become alarmed about the possibilities of similar actions occurring in the territory. Therefore, life for African Americans in Missouri was very difficult at times. Slave owners made minimum provisions for their slaves. The *A Code Noir* was completely unenforceable. The slaves were forced to work from sunup to sundown every day. There was little regard for Sunday. Slave owners responded rapidly and brutally to acts of rebellion. It became increasingly difficult for slaves to earn enough money to purchase their freedom. Freedmen were no longer allowed to enter Missouri following the territory's admission to the Union for fear that they would instigate or encourage rebellions.

Yet, the Africans successfully made bricks without straw. The slaves proved to be both resilient and resourceful. They refused to allow the hostility and brutality perpetrated against them to debilitate them. They were able to translate the Gospel message that was shared with them by the master's preacher into concepts that were meaningful for them.

There were also slaves who would serve as the local spiritual leader. They provided the spiritual and emotional force that made it possible for their fellow slaves to make bricks without straw. They dared to believe that freedom would be a reality for them. They perhaps echoed my favorite line from the poem "Invictus": "Our heads may be bloodied, but they are unbowed." They had an abiding faith that the Lord would make a way somehow and that freedom would become their reality. Kremer and Holland stated in *Missouri Black Heritage* that:

> The Missouri slave was not the docile, happy Sambo that many masters and historians once claimed he was. All of the available evidence suggests that black slaves hated their servile role in the white man's world and they were quite

creative in their protest against the way of life imposed upon them. They were numerous, both non-violent and violent (p. 44).

There are some chilling stories told in the book mentioned above concerning acts of violence perpetrated by slaves against their masters, families and property. These acts of violence simply resulted in counter actions by the slave owners that became more severe.

The conclusion of the Civil War brought great excitement and anticipation to the land. The Africans in Missouri dared to pursue their impossible dreams.

Freedom did indeed come to Missouri on January 11, 1865 with a Proclamation issued by Governor Thomas C. Fletcher. Eleven to twelve months later slavery was abolished in the United States by the Thirteenth Amendment.

This act resulted in many of the slaves leaving their small towns and moving to St. Louis, Jefferson City, Columbia, Cape Girardeau, Popular Bluff, Springfield and Kansas City. They moved with an undying determination to offer their offspring a better life than the one they had experienced. Assistance was provided to them by the churches that had developed and by freedmen living across the state. Most of these people were located in the larger cities.

To paraphrase Joseph's statement in Genesis 50:20, what our European brothers meant for evil, God meant for good. Neither Missouri nor America would be what they are today had God not planted the men and women from the continent of Africa in this land. The miracle of this drama is not that the Africans survived, but that they thrived. They were able to take the little that was given to them and allow it to become much in the Master's hand. They overcame barriers of language and culture to establish a firm foundation upon which subsequent generations could build. They took a little bit of nothing and allowed God to multiply it. God multiplied their little in a manner that resulted in the development of a people and institutions that have positively impacted the history of our local, state, national and international communities. They chose to look at things that never were and asked why not make this a reality.

A Concluding Word

We have been influenced tremendously by our African and Middle Passage heritage. We have also been greatly influenced by our American heritage. Our people could be extinct or relegated to a reservation somewhere in obscurity. We could have impacted the history of this great state, nation and world in counterproductive and destructive ways. However, none of that happened. We have been a greater blessing to humanity than a curse. The Africans who made it to these shores were resourceful, resilient, rebellious, resolute, recalcitrant, reconstituted, repugnant and religious. They dared to dream the impossible dream.

My friends, what the greedy African and European traders meant for evil, God meant for good. God conceived the Missionary Baptist State Convention of Missouri prior to the arrival of our forefathers to this territory now known as Missouri. He even allowed us to refocus our energies in the crucible of the horrendous experience of slavery so that we might be able to create unique spiritual bricks that would significantly impact the lives of generations to come.

We can sing boldly with Fanny J. Crosby and Phoebe P. Knapp.

> Blessed assurance, Jesus is mine! O what a foretaste of glory divine!
> Heir of salvation, purchase of God, Born of His Spirit, washed in His blood.
>
> Perfect submission, perfect delight, Visions of rapture now burst on my sight.
> Angels descending, bring from above Echoes of mercy, whispers of love.
>
> Perfect submission, all is at rest, I in my Savior am happy and blest;
> Watching and waiting, looking above, Filled with His goodness, lost in His love.
>
> This is my story, this is my song, Praising my Savior all the day long;
> This is my story, this is my song, Praising my Savior all the day long.

Yes, we have a story to tell. It is a story about great people, churches, district associations and a great convention—The Missionary Baptist State Convention of Missouri—providing innovative and prophetic ministry within our local communities, the State of Missouri, our National Baptist Convention, U. S. A. Inc., and the world at large. Yes, we continue to "Make Bricks Without Straw." We can echo the words of Kenneth Morris in the song "We've Come a Long Way." The writer asserts:

> We've come a long way, Lord, A mighty long way,
> We've come a long way, Lord, A mighty long way,
> We've borne our burdens in the heat of the day,
> But we know that the Lord has made the way,
> We've come a long way, Lord, A mighty long way.

We can also echo the words of Albert A. Goodson when he penned:
> We've come this far by faith
> Leaning on the Lord;
> Trusting in His Holy Word,
> He's never failed me yet,
> Oh can't turn around,
> We've come this far by faith.
>
> Just the other day I heard a man say
> He didn't believe in God's Word.
> I can truly say the Lord has made a way,
> And He's never failed me yet.
>
> Don't be discouraged when troubles
> Get in your life.
> For He will bear your burdens,
> And move all misery and strife.

Chapter 2

Our People

Women Mission Union Encampment at Western Bible College, Kansas City

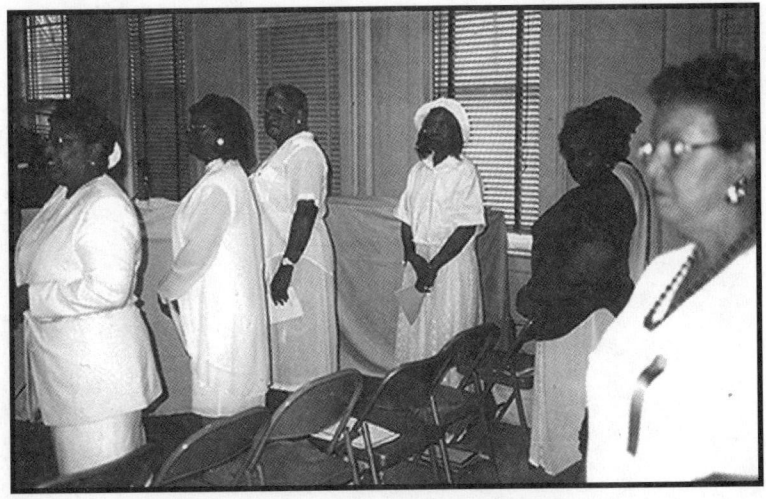

President Rutny Sanders and Women Mission Union workers at Youth Encampment

INTRODUCTION

It is interesting to note that Genesis chapters one and two provide us with a view of the creation of man and woman from the Jehovistic (J) and Priestly (P) interpretation traditions. One presents man and woman being created simultaneously, and the other presents them as being created separately. The order is inconsequential. The important fact is that God chose people to inhabit and exercise stewardship of His majestic creation. He chose people to enter into a loving covenant relationship with Him that is personal and real. He created them in His image and likeness. The editors of the *Interpreter's Bible* Volume 1 suggest that:

> In view of the fact, however, that in Hebrew thought the body was a part of the whole man and was necessary to his complete being, and that it was furthermore the outward manifestation of the reality of which it was a part. The representation that man was made in the image of God meant much more than that man looked like God or like the divine beings which formed his retinue, the image included likeness to them in spiritual powers—the power of thought, the power of communication, the power of self-transcendence. No doubt these concepts remained to some extent inarticulate in the author's mind; nevertheless they were there. He was trying to state in concrete terms— the only terms with which he, being a Semite, was familiar—what could only be stated, however inadequately, in abstract terms.

Moreover, David asked God on one occasion, when he was dealing with his folly and that of his people the question, "What is man, that thou are mindful of him? and the son of man, that thou visiteth him?" (Psalm 8:4). I would like to suggest three reasons in response to David's inquiry.

First of all, we are finite creatures. We are indeed fashioned in the image and likeness of God. We have the marks of divinity and creaturehood within our being. We are an indivisible unity and interact socially through our physical, emotional and intellectual capacities. We have the ability to dream, create and transcend. We also have been given responsibility for participating as fully as possible in the development and maintenance of God's creation. That includes humanity, our environment and created beings. In other words, "We have been made a little lower than the angels" and given primary responsibility for the care of God's creation as stewards.

Secondly, we are goal-centered social beings. We use our total being as a subordinate function for the accomplishment of our selected life goals. Our lives can be characterized as a dynamic striving for self-realization and actualization. We have the potential for socially constructive and destructive behavior. Therefore, we conduct ourselves in socially constructive ways when we recognize and accept our dependence upon God. We behave destructively when we lean to our own understanding and dismiss the importance of God.

Finally, we are a free willed open system. We are not the masters of our own destiny. We are impacted by and impact upon our environment and the people we interact with. We more often than not gravitate toward those things we feel will preserve our self-esteem, provide us with security and give us a place in the world.

Moreover, we become discouraged and alienate ourselves from ourselves, our neighbors, our environment and God when those things that we consider vital for our existence are denied. This alienation and the subsequent tension we experience between our creaturehood and the image of God provide us with opportunities to sin.

St. Augustine has suggested that "anything created from nothing and not sustained by its Creator will ultimately return to a state of nothingness." That perhaps is a basis for God's concern for humanity's welfare. He created us to interact with Himself, His creation and to function within the context of community with opportunities to live spiritually accountable lives. (Please note that the author believes that all of life is sacred and is controlled by the sovereign power of God.) I am convinced that God places a high premium on the lives of all people. He is no respecter of persons. We are told to love Him with our total personality, and our neighbors as ourselves. He wants us to lift Christ up. We must also lift each other up.

One of my favorite songs is "Up with People." The writer states in that song:

> Up, up with people. You meet them wherever you go.
> Up, up with people, they're the best kind of folks to know.
> If more people were for people, all people everywhere,
> There'd be a lot less people to worry about and a lot more people to care.

Another song that I heard at a Southern Baptist function called "Mission 70" was

> Do you really care?
> Do you know how to share?
> With people everywhere.
> Do you really care?
> Will you take the dare?
> Spread good tidings everywhere.
> The cross of Christ to bear.
> Do you really care?

> I look around in the place that I live.
> I see people with so much to give.
> Yet there are those who are dying to know,
> Just that somebody cares. Do you really care?

During the seventies, songs like "People Make the World Go Round" and "Ordinary People" became popular. They highlighted the emerging notions concerning the importance of respecting the dignity and worth of all people.

I would like to suggest to you that there were extraordinary and ordinary people in the membership of the Missionary Baptist State Convention of Missouri today and yesterday who dared to care for people of every ethnicity and social status.

We will look at a few of these individuals who have made small and great contributions to the ministry of the Missionary Baptist State Convention of Missouri through their local churches and district associations. There is not a document that can contain all of the names of past and present saints who have impacted the work of our Lord as Baptists.

We have simply recorded the information that was forwarded to us. Surprisingly, many of the ladies who have made significant contributions to their churches and the state were reluctant to provide information for us. So this document is somewhat slanted toward the men who responded to our inquiries. We have arranged the personalities with the intent to (1) Salute the first Baptist Preacher of African ancestry, Pastor John Berry Meachum. (2) List some names of individuals who made significant contributions to the development of the Convention. (3) Highlight the men and women who have led our state convention and auxiliaries since 1970. (4) Highlight Missourians who have served in their local churches/communities, national and international ministry arena.

Pastor John Berry Meachum was born May 3, 1789 to Tom and Patsy Granger of Goochland County, Virginia on Paul Meachum's plantation. John and his mother were separated from his father, a Baptist minister, when their owner decided to move his slaves to North Carolina. They later moved to Hardin County, Kentucky.

Pastor Meachum worked untiringly in the salt petre caves, a component of gun powder, of Kentucky until he earned enough money to gain freedom for himself and his family members in 1812. Meachum's first concern after securing the release of his family in Kentucky was to return to Virginia and secure the freedom of his father whom he had not seen in years.

Elva Kuykendal Norm wrote concerning the reunion of father and son in *Biography of a Church*.

The old man sang with joy that Sunday morning when he learned he was free. With tears of gratitude trickling down his cheeks, he embraced the son who had freed him. "You have given me freedom," he said. Now let me give you a new life in Christ. Within the month, young John Berry Meachum became a Christian and was baptized by Elder Purinto into the fellowship of the Baptist Church. Then packing their belongings in a knapsack, the father and son set out on a 700-mile walk to Kentucky for the joyous reunion of the parents, who had been separated for so long... Shortly thereafter, their old master, then more than 100 years old, offered to free his 75 slaves if John Berry Meachum would take them to free territory for their liberation (p. 23).

Pastor Meachum accomplished that task with very little difficulty. He returned to Kentucky with his father and discovered that his wife Myra had been taken to St. Louis with her owner. He had barely enough money to cover his transportation cost. However, he did not allow that to be a major factor in his quest. He had developed a number of skills over his life span to include carpentry. He found employment in St. Louis and later purchased Myra's freedom. He continued his entrepreneur activities by purchasing slaves, teaching them trades and allowing them to purchase their freedom. At one time, he owned as many as 25 slaves.

The classes were taught aboard the ship he owned in the Mississippi River. He had classrooms and a library there for him. He was threatened on several occasions. However, he simply told those who sought to close the school that the school was in federal waters. He is said to have owned a farm in Alton, Illinois, river front property, two ships and two houses. Meachum's commitment to improving the lot of his people spoke volumes about how God was working with and through him in all that he endeavored to do.

Pastor Meachum was the first Baptist of African ancestry to minister west of the Mississippi River. His commitment to God and love for people launched him on a journey that contributed immensely toward the organization of the Western Colored Baptist Convention on March 11, 1853. The Missionary Baptist State Convention of Missouri can proudly trace its origin through this historical body.

Mrs. Hazel K. Howard, of the First African Baptist Church of St. Louis, wrote in the March 21, 1992 Bulletin commemorating the "Rededication of the Monument at John Berry Meachum's Gravesite" that:

> As a fixture in St. Louis and an exhorter of Baptist faith and doctrine in private home meetings, Meachum was solicited by James Welch and John Peck to organize the church that stands today as the First Baptist Church in the City of St. Louis. Meachum's unanimous election as its first pastor guided the 300 members into its first brick edifice on Fourth and Almond Street...His fame spread nationwide when he equipped one of his ferry boats with a library, chairs and its

own English scholar as a Freedom School to sail unhampered in Federal waters on the Mississippi River. Meachum died in the place he loved, his pulpit, after taking his text from the tenth chapter of John, and yielded up the ghost freely. He is now buried in Bellefontaine Cemetery.

Pastor James Monroe Booker, D.D. was born in Cumberland County, Virginia in 1863 to Randal and Inda Booker. He was the oldest of seven children. There were six boys and one girl. He accepted the Lord at an early age in 1886. He was baptized at the Mt. Zion Baptist Church in Hardy, Mississippi. He served the Lord and his church faithfully in a number of capacities. He later moved to Memphis, Tennessee and joined the Salem Baptist Church in 1887. Shortly thereafter, he was licensed to preach and was ordained two years later.

Pastor Booker pastored the Mt. Zion Baptist, St. Luke Baptist, New Salem and Bloomfield Baptist and the Salem Baptist Church in Memphis from 1889 until 1906. He was called to Pleasant Green Baptist Church in Kansas City, Missouri in 1906. He remained with that congregation until 1929. He then pastored the New Era Baptist Church in Kansas City until his death in 1959. The Pleasant Green Baptist Church chronicles many of his contributions to the spiritual enrichment of the citizens residing in Kansas City and the state of Missouri.

He played a significant role in the organization of the New Era District in Kansas City, Missouri, serving as treasurer and president. He was one of the moving forces in the organization of the State Sunday School Convention. He served that body also as president and treasurer. He is the great uncle of Mrs. Ann Pittman, the oldest member of our convention. This article is in honor of her.

Sister Auvelia H. Arnold was born October 13, 1935 to the household of Benjamin and Auvelia Arnold in Kirkwood, Missouri. She graduated from Sumner High School in St. Louis, Missouri and received her Bachelor of Arts degree from Harris & Stowe Teachers College in St. Louis. She taught in the St. Louis School System for thirty-three years before retiring June 1993.

She joined the Unity Missionary Baptist Church in December of 1945 and was baptized January 6, 1946. She was active in Sunday School, Baptist Training Union, Red Circle (called Girls' Auxiliary, GA's) and Y.W.A. She has been very active in her church, community, District Association, State and National Conventions.

She has served her church in the capacities of Sunday school teacher, Sunday school superintendent, Young Women's Auxiliary counselor. She presently serves as Church Clerk, Bulletin and Publishing Chairperson, and Young People's Director.

Auvelia has served on the city of Kirkwood Human Rights Committee for several years. She also is a member of Unit 10 and treasurer of St. Louis Metro Church Women United. She has served the Berean Missionary Baptist District Association as Young Women Auxiliary counselor, Young People's Associate Director and Director, Corresponding Secretary of the Christian Education Congress, and chairperson or member of various committees. Presently, she serves as the Women's Missionary Union President and is the association's treasurer. Additionally, she is a Board member of the Berean House Christian Care Center and serves on the association's publication committee. She serves as a member of the Scholarship Committee and Business Manager for Western Baptist Bible College—St. Louis Campus for the Missionary Baptist State Convention of Missouri. She also has served as Young Women's Auxiliary counselor, Associate Young People's director, prepares reports, Kit envelopes, and registration cards. She has served as Young People's director since 1984.

She also serves on the national level. She is a member of the Directors' Department, Newspaper (Talk It Out!) writer, and the Western Region Youth Conference Committee. Our State Convention hosted the first and fifth regional conferences.

Dr. Ronald Bobo is God's gift to Wallace and Willie Mae Bobo of Detroit, Michigan. He was born April 4, 1954 in Detroit, Michigan. He was educated in the Public School System of Detroit. He entered Oakland University, Rochester, Michigan in 1973 and graduated in 1977. He later attended Southern Theological Seminary in Louisville, Kentucky. He completed his academic work in 1989 after completing both a Master's and Doctorate of Ministry degrees.

He has served in various capacities in church life throughout his life. He has positions such as choir director, teacher and Bible College instructor. Pastor Bobo has been active in pastoral ministry continuously since 1978. He was called to serve as pastor of the West Side Missionary Baptist Church in St. Louis, Missouri in 1986.

He has a burning passion for mission work. He continues to serve as the Foreign Mission National Representative for the Missionary Baptist State Convention of Missouri to the National Baptist Convention, U.S.A., Inc. He has also served as President of the Youth Department of the Baptist World Alliance. He has preached and taught the Gospel in Africa, Asia, South and North America, Europe, the Caribbean,

India, Tiawan, Vancouver, Canada, Mexico City, Mexico, and Berlin, Germany. He organized the Royal Priesthood Ministries, Inc., an international outreach ministry, in March of 1997. This ministry includes teaching, preaching, ministry in song, the development of leaders, evangelists, church structure and organization, just to name a few. He is married to the former Darlene Anita Daniels and has three sons, Charles, Ronald, Jr. and Michael.

Dr. Jimmie Lee Brown was born December 28, 1947 in rural Mississippi to Johnnie Lee (deceased) and Annie P. Brown. He has two brothers, Eugene and Jerry, and a sister, Dorothy. He received his elementary and secondary education in the Mississippi School System. He has also attended a number of schools.

He received the Th.B. and Th.M. from Andersonville Baptist Seminary. He graduated from the National Baptist Congress of Christian Education Advanced 4-year program in 1995.

Pastor Brown acknowledged his call to the ministry in the Bethlehem Missionary Baptist Church in 1967. He was called to his beloved St. Luke Memorial Missionary Baptist Church in 1976.

He is a Board member of the Missionary Baptist State Convention of Missouri, Berean District Association, Western Baptist Bible College, National Baptist Congress of Christian Education, Covenant Blue Community Development Corporation, Berean House Christian Care Center.

Pastor Brown is also Chairman of the Board for Grand/Finney Community Development Corporation. He currently serves as President of our Congress of Christian Education. He was appointed Second Vice President of the National Baptist Convention Congress of Christian Education in 1999.

He married his beloved Dyann on April 6. 1968. To this union was born Berdina, Shontell, Jeanette, Dyanna, LaMonda and Christina.

Sister Johnnie Howard Franklin Brown, Ph.D. is the daughter of the late Reverend and Mrs. John B. Howard. Rev. Brown pastored the Fairfax Baptist Church for 48 years. Mrs. Brown is a world evangelist and concert singer. She has been associated with the National Baptist Convention, U.S.A., Inc. for 40 years. Serving under six (6) presidents as National Music director, she is Director Emeritus, but continues to work in the music department and as a board member of the convention.

She has been working in the service of the Lord for many years. God has opened so many doors for her to carry His Word in song and praise. It has truly been amazing.

Her first services were held at the old Coliseum in St. Louis, Missouri during the National Baptist Convention's Annual Meeting. She was invited by the convention chairman to sing. She sang, "Does anybody here know my Jesus?" She was selected to sing in a white robe and blue cap. Her singing career was launched at that time.

She has sung from coast to coast in the continental USA and throughout Europe. She studied for a period of time in Rome. She is especially pleased to be assisted by her daughter, Mary Louise Franklin, Ph.D.

She continues to exercise her musical talents believing that she can do all things through Christ who gives her strength.

Dr. William H. Claiborne came to Missouri in July 1946 as the Director of Christian Education for Central Baptist Church in St. Louis, Missouri under the pastorate of the late Dr. Thomas E. Huntley. He is a native of Johnson City, Tennessee. He became acquainted with the convention, which later became the State Congress. He became Director of the Youth Fellowship during the presidency of Brother William S. Brookfield. He later served seven years as Dean of the Congress of Christian Education prior to being appointed to his present position by former Convention President Pastor I. H. Henderson.

He has served in that position providing the State Convention with a liaison to the National Convention to monitor the accreditation of schools, seminars and institutes held by churches, districts and congresses. He has been active in the Antioch District Association. He worked for several years as an instructor in the Leadership School, Youth Director and Dean of the Congress of Christian Education. He is an avid supporter of the Western Baptist Bible College since coming to Missouri. He served as Chairman of the Board of Trustees for three terms and later as Secretary. He also served as an instructor and Director of the St. Louis Extension school during the tenure of the late Dr. William D. Singleton.

Pastor Manuel Dillingham, D.Min. was born in Black Mountain, North Carolina to Mr. and Mrs. John Hamilton on April 16, 1951. He was baptized in the AME Zion Church at an early age. He completed his secondary education at the Charles D. Owens High School in Swannanoah, North Carolina. He accepted his call to the preaching ministry in 1969.

Pastor Dillingham is a graduate of Livingston College, Hood Theological Seminary and Pittsburg Theological Seminary.

His first pastorate was the Shiloh Baptist Church in Mocksville, North Carolina. He has also pastored Ebenezer Baptist Church in Wilmington, North Carolina; Mt. Ararat Baptist Church in Pittsburg, Pennsylvania; Canaan Baptist Church in Philadelphia, Pennsylvania and currently the Friendship Baptist Church in Kansas City, Missouri.

His honors include being selected Who's Who Among Outstanding Men in America; Adjunct Professor of Black Church Administration at the Lutheran and Eastern Seminaries in Philadelphia, Kansas City Globe Influential African American Leaders; and former President of the Kansas City Ministers' Coalition.

He has served as a member of the Philadelphia Fair Housing Commission, Progressive National Baptist Convention, North Carolina State Baptist Convention, Lott Carey Foreign Mission Convention and American/National Baptist Convention Board of Directors. He is currently the president of Western Baptist Bible College in Kansas City, Missouri with campuses in Missouri and Kansas.

Pastor Willie J. Ellis, Jr., D.D. was born July 14, 1937 in Clarksdale, Mississippi to Willie J. Ellis, Sr. and Modia Lee Ellis, as the eldest of four children. He is a product of the St. Louis Public School System. He received his ministerial license on July 6, 1960 and was ordained April 22, 1962.

He became pastor of the New Northside Missionary Baptist Church in St. Louis and has remained in this position for the past 35 years. Through his leadership, New Northside Missionary Baptist Church has grown from a membership of a few faithful to an active membership of over 1,500.

Through the years, Reverend Ellis has received numerous accolades for his involvement in the community. He served as Chairman of the Task Force that helped resolve the teachers' strike in 1982. He received the Outstanding Contributor for the Humanity and Welfare of the Community to improve Human Relations Civil Rights Award in July of 1983. The Mayor of Compton, California presented him with a citation for his commitment in civic and community work in July 1985. He chaired the Ministers' Task Force to win approval of a tax increase to improve, renovate, remodel and repair schools in the city of St. Louis. He was honored with proclamations from Governor Mel Carnahan and the Honorable Freeman R. Bosley, Mayor of St. Louis declaring June 3, 1994 as "Reverend Dr. Willie J. Ellis, Jr. Day." He was recently appointed a member of the Public Defender Commission in the State of Missouri.

Reverend Ellis is known throughout St. Louis, the state and nation for his civic leadership and community work. Many have described him as "a man with a vision." His belief in the institution of family and being a father caused him to envision the construction of a child development center. His vision of the child development center was based upon the belief that parents needed a credible community child development center that would eliminate transporting their children to an unfamiliar environment. The New Northside Child Development Center became a reality during the month of November in 1990. The center provides children from ages 2-5 with a Christian, educational and family atmosphere.

Reverend Ellis is sensitive to the needs of our youth and senior citizens. Members of his congregation were introduced to the "Jesus First" program, a multi-million dollar program for the development of the New Northside Baptist Church Family Life Center-Ellis Complex. This complex will house facilities such as a sports complex for youth, ongoing activities for senior citizens of the community, a chapel, school and banquet center. It is his belief that the church must take a stand on the unpopular as well as the popular issues of the day and commit to providing a safe, spiritual and healthy economic base for our community.

Being committed to improving the total community requires total commitment. Reverend Ellis is hopeful that through his works, he can encourage others to "dare to make a difference."

He is married to the former Beverly Elaine Coleman. He is the proud father of two daughters; Pamela Ellis Spencer and Rolanda Ellis Kisart.

Pastor Haymond Fortenberry was born on June 20, 1929 in New Hebron, Mississippi to Tinnie and Leffie Fortenberry. He is the youngest of six (6) children. He served the Lord in a variety of capacities in the church. He has been pastoring, teaching and preaching for over thirty-seven years.

He graduated from Lanier High School and attended Jackson State University, Harris Stowe State Teachers College, Missouri Baptist College, St. Louis Christian College and Christian International University of St. Louis. He has an honorary doctorate degree from Western Bible College.

Pastor Fortenberry served in the U.S. Army for two years. He spent the majority of his time in the Republic of South Korea. He has served two churches over the past thirty-seven years. He served the New Tower Grove Baptist Church for five (5) years. He has served the Fairfax Baptist Church in St. Louis for thirty-two years.

He served as President of the Baptist Pastors Conference for over ten (10) years. He served as First Vice President of our state convention during the tenure of Drs. McKinley Dukes and Sammie Jones. He helped initiate a radio ministry on KIRL that has lasted for twenty (20) years. He helped organize the Clergy Coalition and served on the Advisory Committee responsible for helping to make regional hospitals a reality. He has served this Convention faithfully for over forty years.

Pastor Harry Givens was born February 13, 1926. He was the only boy and second child given as God's gift to Howard and Lula Givens of Lebanon, Missouri. He was educated in the Lebanon School System and attended Lincoln University. He became a member of Wood Street Baptist Church under the pastorate of Reverend A. B. Morgan in 1940. He was ordained as a deacon on April 10, 1955 at the Wood Street Missionary Baptist Church by Pastor W. C. K Wright. He accepted his call to the preaching ministry in June 1970 and was licensed on July 19, 1970 by Pastor James Arnett. He was called to pastor Wood Street Missionary Baptist Church during the month of May in 1971. He was called to Unity Missionary Baptist Church in Joplin, Missouri during the month of June in 1974. He assumed leadership of the church in August of the same year.

He served the Southwest District Association as Auditor for two years and as Moderator from 1973 until his retirement in 1996. He currently is the District's Moderator Emeritus. He worked in the State Convention as statistician and treasurer. He served in the latter position for ten (10) years. He taught Stewardship for six years. He also served as recording secretary. Pastor Givens has received special recognition from the Missionary Baptist State Convention and the Congress of Christian Education. He has also served as president of the Lebanon Kiwanis and the Joplin Branch of the NAACP. Additionally, he has chaired the Community Housing Resource Board in Joplin for eight years, and the Laclede County Heart Association Financial Campaign.

Pastor Givens owned and operated a janitorial service for twenty-five years in Lebanon.

Brother Dan Griffin was born on December 3, 1924 in Hattiesburg, Mississippi to Dan and Grace Griffin. He is one of six children born into this union. He worked various jobs until he enlisted in the Army. He served on active duty from June 1943 until January 1946. He saw duty in Africa, Italy and Southern France during World War II.

He moved to St. Louis in 1946 following his discharge from the Army. He was employed by the Army Record Center on Goodfellow Air Force Base. He remained with them until 1962.

He also attended St. Louis University and received a B.A. degree in Business Administration and Accounting in 1952. He worked for the Internal Revenue Service from 1962 until his retirement in 1980. He also has worked for the City of St. Louis as Auditor in the Comptroller's Office from 1980 through 1990.

Dan has been a member of the Mt. Bethel Baptist Church in St. Louis since 1960. He served as president of the Laymen for twenty-eight years. He started with the Laymen of the Missionary Baptist State Convention of Missouri in 1973. He has served ably as recording and financial secretary during that time. He has also served as recording secretary in the Berean Association since 1985.

Pastor Otis Landon Hawes was born April 1, 1936 to the union of Reverend Otis Landon, Sr. and Minnie Hawes in Broadwater, Missouri. He received his elementary and secondary education in the Popular Bluff School System. He has matriculated at Southern Baptist College, Walnut Ridge, Arkansas, Three Rivers College, Midwestern Baptist Theological Seminary and also completed a series of Seminary Extension courses from Southern Baptist College located in Jackson, Mississippi.

Pastor Hawes has worked in a variety of ministries in the church including being a deacon. He was licensed and ordained for the pastoral/preaching ministry in 1963. He has pastored four churches during his ministerial career.

He presently pastors the Bethesda Baptist Church, a congregation that he founded in 1995. Pastor Hawes' ministry includes serving as the association's missionary for Friendship District (32 churches) from 1963 to 1965; Director of Southeast Missouri Baptist Fellowship from 1975 to 1983 and as an Associated Dean of the Missionary Baptist State Convention of Missouri Congress of Christian Education for eight years. He also was the Editor for the Convention's Newsletter.

Sister Viola Howard was born in Little Rock, Arkansas August 11, 1920 to Mrs. Etta Boyd and Leslie P. White. She received her education in Kansas City School System. She has attended Penn Valley Junior College and Midwestern Seminary.

She worked for the Kansas City School District for over twenty years. She presently provides tutoring services in a reading program sponsored by the YMCA called Seniors for School.

She married Mr. Sellers W. Howard in July of 1946. They were married for over forty-seven years, and are the proud parents of Dwight Howard and Diane Howard Dixon. They also have two grandchildren.

Mrs. Howard joined Friendship Baptist Church in 1931. She has served as Director of Music and Choir Director for over thirty-seven years. She has also worked with the youth choir for twenty-seven years. She has participated in Christian education ministry and served as a Deaconess for the past four years.

She has served as Director of the New Era District Choir for over twenty-nine years. In that capacity, she has directed the Vesper Hour Service Concert.

She has been Director of Music for the Congress of Christian Education since 1989. She also served as an assistant Directress to Mrs. Annie Moore for years. She has taught Church Music in the Congress for over fifteen years

She teaches music at Western Bible College. She has also been a song leader at the National and Southern Baptist Conference at Windemere. One of her favorite songs is "I've Been to Calvary" by Bill Gathers.

Dr. Daniel Hughes was the thirteenth child of fourteen children born to John and Luvenia Hughes on November 25, 1926 in St. Louis, Missouri. He accepted Christ at the age of seven, and was baptized at Antioch Baptist Church during the pastorate of the late Dr. Perry in St. Louis, Missouri. He graduated from J. Milton Turner Grade School in Kirkwood, Missouri. He graduated from Douglas High School in Webster Groves, Missouri.

He served three years in the U.S. Navy during World War II and was awarded the Victory Medal prior to his being honorably discharged.

Dr. Hughes finished the college of Mortuary Science. He served as a funeral director and licensed embalmer with the Ellis Funeral Home and the A. L. Beal Undertaking Company. During this time, he united in holy matrimony with Ora Enochs of St. Louis on August 28, 1949. This union was blessed for forty years. They are the proud parents of Hazel, Terry and Denise.

Dr. Hughes continued his educational pilgrimage by receiving a B.A. degree from Harris Teachers College; and a B.D. degree from American Baptist Seminary, Nashville, Tennessee. He also received a M.A. degree from Webster College, Webster Groves, Missouri; and engaged in further studies at St. Louis University. He taught in the St. Louis School System for several years. He accepted his call to the ministry during the pastorate of Dr. Leon P. O'Hara.

He has pastored the Mt. Zion Baptist Church and Eastern Star Baptist Church. Each of these ministries prospered under his dynamic leadership.

Dr. Hughes was very involved in ministry and social issues on the local, state and national levels. He was actively involved in the St. Louis Branch of the NAACP and Urban League. He served as one of St. Louis' Mayors Ambassadors; as Second Vice Moderator and Moderator of the Berean Baptist District Association from 1976 to 1986.

He also served as President of the Missionary Baptist State Convention of Missouri Congress of Christian Education from 1973 to 1990; as Coordinator of the Pastors' Division and Board Member for the National Baptist Convention, U.S.A., Inc., S.S. and B.T.U Congress of Christian Education; as associate member Trustee Board of American Baptist Seminary, Nashville, Tennessee and Western Baptist Bible College, Kansas City, Missouri; as a Trustee on the Webster College Alumni Association Board; the Board of Welfare, City of St. Louis; and the Board of Arts and Letters.

He was able to travel to Europe and South America. He especially enjoyed his travel through the Scandinavian countries as he served as an instructor in a Master Degree program that offered six hours to participating students.

Pastor Donald Hunter is a native of St. Louis and was educated in the area's public school system. He has attended Western Bible College and Concordia Theological Seminary.

He was called into the ministry in September 1960 and was ordained on January 17, 1961. He came to New Sunny Mount Baptist Church on September 23, 1977, with a membership of approximately two hundred (200) members. Today, the church has a membership of over two thousand (2,000) members.

Pastor Hunter was the founder of the Continuing Education Program for Black Churchmen while employed at Concordia Theological Seminary. He received further theological training through this program. He is a lecturer for the Pastors' class for the Berean District Association, member of the Mid-City Optimist Club, and a member of the St. Louis Clergy Coalition.

He was appointed Chairman of the St. Louis Housing Resources Commission in 1991. This agency is responsible for the allocation and disbursement of hundreds of thousands of dollars to agencies involved in assisting the homeless.

He is married to Mrs. Arthurine Mason-Hunter. They have six daughters and ten grandchildren.

Mrs. Marguerite Jones was born February 8, 1919 (deceased on January 16, 1998) in Parsons, Kansas to the union of Edmond and Katherine May Jones. She received her education in the Kansas City School System, graduating as Valedictorian of the graduating class of 1935. She continued her education at Western University in Kansas. She united with Friendship Baptist Church in 1941 under the pastorate of the late Reverend S. E. Doyle. Sister Jones was a loyal and faithful worker in the church as church secretary, in Sunday school, Clubs and Christian Education.

She also was actively involved in the work of the New Era District Association, State Congress and the National Baptist Convention, U.S.A., Inc. She worked with the Classification Committee and Finance Department of the Women's Convention. She was a life member of the National Congress of Christian Education's Administrative Workshop and Jernegin Lectures.

Deacon Thaddeus Jones was born May 13, 1953 in Kansas City, Missouri to Mr. Victor and Mrs. Irene Jones. He is one of five children born to this union. He attended the Kansas City Public Schools and graduated from William Jewell College.

He is a member of the Second Baptist Church in Independence, Missouri, pastored by Samuel Nero. He has served in a number of leadership positions to include Director of Vacation Bible School, Youth Sunday school instructor, Director of Nurture for Baptist Churches, Street Ministry Coordinator, Sunday School Superintendent, Secretary and Chairman of the Deacons' Ministry.

He is very active in Laymen work at every level of the ministry. He is the President of the New Era District Laymen and Vice President-at-Large for the State Laymen. He also actively serves in several capacities on the national level. He is the Publisher and Editor of the *National Laymen's Newsletter,* the Coordinator for the Walter Cade Southern Regional Workshop, and Director of the National Laymen's Movement Promotional Materials.

He has extensive experience in all areas and aspects of general accounting and general corporate administration. He has served as Assistant Controller, Cost Accounting and Data Processing Manager for Kansas City Structural Steel Company, Corporate Controller for Murphy Industries, Treasurer, Chief Financial Officer for Kuhlman Diecasting Company and Vice President of Finance and Technology with the Midwest Regional Credit Union.

Thaddeus is an alumni liaison for the Black Student Association for William Jewell College. He is the Chairman of Western Bible College Board of Directors and served as Interim President from 1994 until 1997. He is married to Sandra and they have two children.

Pastor E. C. Keeble hails from Lilbourn, Missouri. He was born February 7, 1934. He attended Public School in Popular Bluff, Missouri. He also attended the American Baptist Seminary in Nashville, Tennessee. He married Barbara Smith. To this union was born ten children.

He was the first African American to be employed by the Veterans Administration Hospital in Popular Bluff. He worked there for forty-two years until his retirement. During that time, he organized and led the AFGE #22 Local Union as president for ten years. He was an EEO Counselor at the hospital for eight years. He was also in the Alcohol and Drug Abuse program as a counselor.

Pastor Keeble is active in the social and political life of Moulden and Popular Bluff. He is a City Councilman and Mayor Pro Tem of Moulden. He also served as Vice President of the city's Utility Board for six years. He actively interacts with school and city officials in Popular Bluff where he pastors. His church, Pleasant Hill, participates in a cooperative program with the Popular Bluff School utilizing the old black school for outreach activities for the youth of the community.

He has served the congregations of Morning Star, Macedonia, Zion Groove, Good Hope and the Pleasant Hill Missionary Baptist Churches during a twenty-four year ministry span. He has served as Moderator of the Southeastern Missouri Baptist Friendship District Association. He also served as Recording Secretary of the Missionary Baptist State Convention of Missouri for twenty years.

Sister Ollie Lofton was born in Dixie, Arkansas to Rayfield and Cleo Bush. She was educated in the Blytheville, Arkansas School District. She accepted Christ as her Savior and was baptized at the New Mount Zion Missionary Baptist Church in Blytheville during the pastorate of F. A. Parker at age 10. She has faithfully served Christ and His church since that day as a Sunday school secretary and teacher, recording financial secretary, Women Missionary Union President and Youth Director. She has served as President of the Ministers' Wives and Widows Auxiliary of our convention for the past seven years.

She graduated from Tennessee State University receiving a Bachelor of Arts in Elementary Education, and Arkansas State University receiving a Masters of Arts in Special Education. She has also received certification to work as an Educational and Psychological Tester as well as certification in school administration.

Mrs. Lofton has served the Blytheville School District with distinction as a classroom teacher, supervisor for Special Education and Educational and Psychological Tester.

Her affiliations include membership in the Arkansas and National Association of Federated Women; Founder and board member of the Mississippi County Special Workshop for Handicapped Adults, board member for the Mississippi County Red Cross, Mississippi County Black Culture Committee, Mississippi County Arts Council, and Focus Incorporated.

She has received numerous awards and recognition from community and county agencies. She is married to Pastor Emanuel Lofton. They have three children, Michael, Rosalind Lofton Durant and William D. Lofton.

Pastor Raymond Mallory was born in Marion County Missouri, November 27, 1940. He was educated in the Palmyra School System and graduated from High School in 1958.

He attended Western Baptist Bible College, William Jewell College, Liberty, Lincoln University and the University of Missouri, Kansas City. He earned a Bachelor of Education degree with emphasis in Psychology and Christian Education.

Pastor Mallory served as President of the NAACP for six years in Hannibal. He served with the Missouri Branch of the NAACP. He has served as Vice President-at-Large of the Missionary Baptist State Convention under two presidents for over ten years. He has faithfully served as a member of Western Bible College. He pastored the Ruby Street Baptist Church of Macon and the Second Baptist Church of Shelbina for over forty years. He is socially and politically active, having served on a number of committees in Northern Missouri.

Sister Betty Jean Martin was born in Joplin, Missouri February 23, 1930 to Mr. and Mrs. Rufus Pyles. She received her elementary and secondary education in the Joplin School System. She attended Philander Smith College in Little Rock, Arkansas following her graduation.

Sister Martin accepted Christ as her personal Savior in 1939 and was baptized during the ministry of Pastor J. T. Smith. She later served as a Sunday school teacher and Baptist Training Union secretary. Sister Martin moved her membership to the Second Baptist Church in Neosho, Missouri in 1962.

She has served as Teacher for the Women's Department and Sunday school; President of the Women's Missionary Society; Assistant Superintendent of the Sunday school; and Vacation Bible School Adult Leader. Sister Martin has taught a class on the Women's Missionary Union in the Southwest District Congress of Christian Education. Additionally, she served as Vice President of the Women's Missionary Union from 1968-1973. She accepted the presidency of that Auxiliary in 1973 and continues to ably lead the women of Southwest District Association.

She has also worked as a Saleslady for Kassab's Women Ready-to-Wear since 1953. She feels that her calling is to the Ministry of helps and encouragement.

Pastor William Z. Matthews was born in Hardenman County, Tennessee on December 27, 1929. He was raised by his grandparents. He accepted Christ as his personal Savior in 1939 at the Green Grove Baptist Church. He attended elementary school in Boliver, Tennessee, and completed his education in the school system of St. Louis after he moved there in 1941.

He has an Associate of Arts degree from Missouri Baptist College. He has also received an honorary doctorate degree from Western Bible College in 1998.

He entered the U.S. Army in 1948 and served in the Far East during the Korean Conflict. He returned to the United States in 1952 after five years of military duty. He was honorably discharged.

He united with the St. Memorial Baptist Church in 1955 during the pastorate of J. L. House. He served as a deacon and held many other positions in the church as well as the Berean District. He served as president of the Laymen's movement for six years. He also served as Vice Moderator and President of the Berean Congress of Christian Education. He presently is the president of the Missionary Baptist Ministers Union of St. Louis and Vicinity.

He accepted his call to the preaching ministry in 1978 during the pastorate of J. L. Brown. He was called to pastor the Mt. Zion Baptist Church of St. Charles, Missouri in November of 1981. The church has recently completed a major building program with the completion of their new sanctuary. He is married to Jean, and they have three sons and two daughters.

Sister Wesley Mae McDowell was born September 22, 1908 in St. Louis, Missouri. She was the oldest of ten children born to Wesley Eli and Mary Lee Haskins. She accepted Christ as her Savior on April 1, 1919 during the pastorate of J. T. Carter, Sr. at the Fifth Baptist Church in St. Louis. She became a member of Calvary Baptist Church in 1941 and served on the Ushers Board and Health Unit, Trustee Board and wherever she was needed.

She has been very active in the Missionary Baptist State Convention. She served as president of the Ushers' Auxiliary for fifteen years during the presidencies of Dr. John Richardson and I. H. Henderson, Jr. She was also the First Vice President for the National Baptist Convention Ushers' Auxiliary for fifteen years

Pastor John Modest Miles was born May 15, 1945 in Magnolia, Arkansas. He became actively involved in Christian ministry at an early age. He began preaching at the age of eighteen. Pastor Miles graduated from the New Hope High School in Mount Holly, Arkansas.

In 1963, He completed his undergraduate work at Arkansas Baptist College in Little Rock and his graduate work at the Ouachita Baptist University in Arkadelphia, Arkansas. He has done additional studies at Philander Smith College in Little Rock, Arkansas, Highland Park College in Detroit, Michigan, Midwestern Baptist Seminary and was awarded a Doctor of Divinity degree from Central Mississippi College in Kosciusko, Mississippi.

Pastor Miles has been involved in every aspect of community life in Detroit, Michigan, Little Rock, Arkansas and Kansas City, Missouri. He was a public school teacher and instructor for Arkansas Baptist College in Little Rock for several years. He has also pastored True Faith Missionary Baptist Church in Detroit, Michigan, Liberty Hills Missionary Baptist Church in Little Rock, Arkansas, Mount Sinai Missionary Baptist Church in Little Rock and the Morning Star Baptist Church in Kansas City, Missouri.

He has served in a variety of capacities in the District Association, State Congress and Convention and the National Convention such as Moderator of the New Era District Association; an instructor for the Missionary Baptist Convention of Missouri Congress of Christian Education; Second Vice President of the Missionary Baptist State Convention; National Baptist Convention, USA, Inc. Governmental Affairs Liaison and General Chairman for the 1998 National Baptist Convention, USA, Inc. Host Committee.

He was given the honor of speaking for Governor William Jefferson Clinton during his 1979 Inaugural Ceremony in Little Rock, Arkansas.

He is a member of the Presidential Task Force "Americans for Change" The National Baptist Congress of Christian Education General Assembly in Milwaukee, Wisconsin and the National Baptist Convention Laymen's Department in 1989, 90 and 94. He has also been honored as one of the One Hundred Most Influential African Americans in Greater Kansas City for five consecutive years, commencing in 1993. Pastor Miles is married to Jeanette Richards Miles. Their children are Gerald, Janet and Derrick.

Pastor Samuel W. Nero is the fourth of six children born to the union of Pastor Henry Russell and Daisy Fortson Nero on January 15, 1941 in Bristow, Oklahoma. His family moved to Kansas City, Missouri very early in his life. He received his public education in the Kansas City, Kansas Public School System. He also has attended Park College and Western Baptist Bible College.

He accepted Christ at the age of five while attending the New Jerusalem Missionary Baptist Church where his father pastored. He acknowledged his call to ministry February 12, 1967 while attending the Bethesda Baptist Church in Kansas City, Kansas during the pastorate of Pastor O. L. Brown. He has been bi-vocational throughout most of his ministry. He worked for the U.S. Postal Service for over thirty years. During that time, he pastored two churches. He has pastored the historic Second Baptist Church in Independence, Missouri since 1987.

Pastor Nero serves as one of three pastor advisors of the National Baptist Laymen's Movement, an auxiliary of the National Baptist Convention USA, Inc. He is a prayer partner with Mr. Jerry Gash of Los Angeles, California, the newly elected National Laymen's President. He serves as the New Era District Association Laymen Pastoral Coordinator. He is Third Vice President of the Missionary Baptist State Congress of Christian Education. He is married to Mrs. Edna Boswell and they have two children, Samuel, Jr. and Leonna. He has been blessed to travel to Italy, Germany, Jordan, Egypt and Israel.

Pastor Ronald Bradnax Packnett was born July 2, 1951 to Nicholas and Mamie Packnett. He earned a Bachelor of Science degree in Accounting and Economics from Illinois State University. He also earned a Master of Divinity degree from Yale University.

Pastor Packnett was called to the Central Baptist Church, the second oldest African American church in St. Louis in 1985. Under his leadership, Central celebrated its 150th Anniversary. During his eleven years at Central, the ministry continued its tradition of evangelism and outreach. Pastor Packnett led the congregation in the establishment of a Crisis Intervention Center. The center provided food for almost 150 homeless men weekly and provides groceries, clothing and a variety of other social services to more than forty families. Central provides hundreds of food baskets to needy families at Thanksgiving and Christmas. Toys are also distributed during the Christmas Season.

Pastor Packnett was actively involved in the community, working diligently to make St. Louis a better place to live in. He participated in the Urban League, the

Black Leadership Roundtable, the Dialogue Group on Civic Progress, the Monsanto YMCA, the Million Man March, St. Louis Public Schools Mentoring Program, the Success by Six Initiative of the United Way and the St. Louis Clergy Coalition. He also hosted a radio program called "The Lighthouse" on KATZ Radio.

Pastor Packnett was also active in the Antioch Association, Missionary Baptist State Convention of Missouri and the National Baptist Convention, USA, Inc. He was on the executive boards of the state and national conventions.

He departed this life Tuesday, December 17, 1996. He was married to Gwendolyn and they have a daughter Brittany, and a son Ronald.

Pastor Oliver K. Patterson serves as a Vice President of the Missionary Baptist State Convention of Missouri for Special Projects and Director of the Department of Evangelism. He was born December 23, 1943 in Fort Worth, Texas. He surrendered to the Lord at the age of eight at the Fourth Street Baptist Church, where the Reverend J. H. Singleton was pastor. He received his Bachelor of Science degree in 1966 from the University of Texas at Arlington, Texas in Mathematics and Physics. He received his Master of Arts degree in 1986 from Eden Theological Seminary in Biblical Studies. Pastor Patterson was a member of the Mount Olive Baptist Church in Forth Worth, Texas, prior to moving to St. Louis in 1973. There he served for six years as Sunday school teacher, and Director of the Youth Department. He also has served as Director of the State Youth Convention of Texas for six years. In August of 1972, Pastor Patterson surrendered to the ministry and was licensed to preach by the late Reverend J. L. Dawson.

He moved to St. Louis in April of 1973 for employment with McDonnell Douglas Automation Company. He was a consultant in Data Processing. He became a member of the Greater Mount Carmel Baptist Church, where the Reverend Earl E. Nance, Sr. was pastor. In September 1973, Pastor Patterson was ordained by Reverend Nance. At the Greater Mount Carmel Baptist Church, Pastor Patterson created and served as instructor for the young people's class in the Baptist Training Union. Pastor Patterson has served as an instructor for Eden Theological Seminary, Missouri Baptist College and has provided Pastoral Counseling for Washington University. He has also served twelve years as an instructor for the Congress of Christian Education of Missouri. He teaches the Holy Spirit Class. He served for two years as the Dean of the Congress of Christian Education, and a writer for the National Baptist Sunday School Publishing Board.

He has served as Chairman for the African Aids Trust Fund, Inc., Planning Committee for Continuing Education for Eden Theological Seminary and the Committee for the Medically Underserved for the Arthritis Foundation, Eastern Missouri Chapter. Currently, he is a member of the Board of Directors for the Arthritis Foundation, Eastern Missouri, the National Diversity Committee for the Arthritis Foundation, Executive Board for the Berean Christian Care Center, National Program Director for Christ Alive, the National Baptist Convention's Evangelism Crusade.

He currently serves as Director of Evangelism, Third Vice President of the State Convention and Assistant Director for the Ministers' Division of the Congress of Christian Education of Missouri. Pastor Patterson has received numerous awards for contributions to civic activities that include the Alpha Kappa Alpha Sorority, Inc., Salute to Black Men Award for Excellence in Religion 1990, an Award of Appreciation for Drug Enforcement Administration of the United States Department of Justice 1993, the 1994 Eastern Missouri Chapter Arthritis Foundation Volunteer of the Year, 1996 Nation Volunteer Citation of the Year, 1997 Leadership Chapter Award Eastern Missouri Arthritis Foundation. He married the former Miss Lois Jean Mosley in 1968. To this union two sons and a daughter were born. Both sons have surrendered to the ministry of Jesus Christ.

Dr. I. C. Peay is a native of Mississippi. He was born June 3, 1910 in Stone County to Will and Hattie Peay. He received his primary and secondary education in the state school system. He graduated from Jones County High School, Laurel, Mississippi. He received his B.A. degree from the College Department of Mississippi Baptist Seminary. He later received his B.Th., MT.C, M.Th. and Th.D. degrees from Mississippi Seminary, Jackson, Mississippi. He was awarded a Doctorate of Law degree by Missouri Baptist College. He also received a Doctorate of Humane Letters from the National Theological College and Seminary in Baltimore, Maryland.

Pastor Peay accepted his call to the preaching ministry in 1934 at the Pleasant Grove Baptist Church in Hattiesburg, Mississippi. He was ordained in 1936 to accept the pastorate of Antioch Baptist Church in Brooklyn, Mississippi. He has pastored New Bethel, Mt Zion, and Mt. Vernon Missionary Baptist Churches in Hattiesburg; the Good Hope Missionary Baptist Church in Ellisville; and the Friendship Missionary Baptist Church, Laurel. Each of these churches was located in the State of Mississippi. His last pastorate before retirement was with the Galilee Baptist Church in St. Louis, Missouri.

He has had a very distinguished career. He has served as secretary for the Shiloh District Association; President of Second Sweet Pilgrim Sunday School and B.T.U. Congress of Mississippi; Vice Moderator of the Berean District Association; Second Vice President; and Managing Editor of the Missionary Baptist State Convention of Missouri's *Messenger*.

He has also served as President of the Ministers and Laymen's Association for Equal Opportunity; President of Missionary Baptist Ministers' Union of Greater St. Louis; Board of Directors of the National Baptist Convention, USA, Inc.; and on the Finance Committee of the National Baptist Convention of America for six years.

Pastor Peay was a lecturer and writer. He has taught classes in Homiletics and Greek Etymology. He annually wrote a variety of literature for his Christian Education Ministry in the churches that he served. Additionally, he has written, *I Have A Question, God Has the Answer; Faith That Counts; The Attributes of God;* and *The Pastor Speaks*.

Sister Ann Pittman was born January 14, 1908 on a tenant farm midway between Coffeyville and Tillatoba, Mississippi in Yalobusha County. She was the second child (and daughter) born to Oray Booker and General Washington. She attended Normal School in Grenada, Mississippi and taught in the rural school district of Leflore County. It was during this time that she met and married Mr. Eddie Pittman in November of 1927. They moved to St. Louis in 1928.

She has been an active member of the Central Baptist Church since 1931 serving on the Ushers Board, Missions Ministry, Singles Ministry and the Deaconess Board. She has been active in many fraternal organizations through the years, including the Prince Hall Order of the Eastern Star, two appending houses, the PTA and Mothers' Club of the schools attended by her two daughters, Edda and Andrea (who along with her husband have preceded her in death).

She earned an Associate of Arts degree from Douglas College of St. Louis University. This school had the distinction of being the only non-teaching provider of higher education for Blacks in St. Louis at that time. She also has the distinction of being the oldest graduate from the Metropolitan College of St. Louis University.

Mrs. Pittman is a researcher, lecturer, musician and author. She has traced her genealogy back to 1779. She is a collateral descendant of Pastor James Monroe Booker, who founded the Missouri State Sunday School and Baptist Training Union Congress. She has published "Little Touches of Soul" and "Hand me de Bounty Down."

She is now ninety-one years old. She lives independently, drives her own automobile, handles her finances and is learning to use the computer to speed up the process of compiling her wealth of folklore knowledge which she intends to share with the community. Mrs. Pittman is the oldest active member of our convention. We included information presented to her on her great uncle, Pastor Monroe Booker, in recognition of this fact.

Sister Ruthy Sanders is President of the Missionary Baptist State Convention of Missouri Women's Mission Union. She has served in this capacity since 1996. She is one of six children born to Fred and Mattie Roberts (both deceased) in Eufaula, Oklahoma. Her sisters, Wilder Moore and Quanita Polk preceded her in death, her brother Samuel and sister Hortense Coverton. Mrs. Sanders attended the public schools of Eufaula.

She has always been active in the church, committed to caring for people. She attended both the Baptist and African Methodist Episcopal churches where her membership was during her formative years. She moved to Kansas City, Kansas in 1948 and united with the Antioch Missionary Baptist Church in 1952. She attended the Central Baptist Seminary where she received a diploma after three years. She then moved to the Missouri side of Kansas City in 1959 and united with the Progressive Missionary Baptist Church in 1960. She has served with the Sunday school, Baptist Training Union, Women Missionary Union, Youth Ministry and Finance Ministry.

Sister Sanders has served with the Women Missionary Union on the state level since 1962. During that time, she has served as Promotional Chairperson for four years and Vice President for thirteen years. Sister Sanders was married to Mr. Arburn Sanders for forty-two years. They are the proud parents of Cleophus Sanders and Aldine Tolliver. She has four grandchildren and five great-grandchildren.

Reverend Corneleus S. Scott was born in Camden, Arkansas on March 25, 1909 to the household of Cornelius S. Scott and Elizabeth Reed Scott. He was self-educated. He accepted Jesus as his Savior at the St. John Baptist Church in Wheeler Spring, Arkansas in 1916. He was called to the preaching ministry in January 17, 1933 at the Springhill Baptist Church in Wheeling Spring, Arkansas. He served in the pastoral ministry for fifty-four years. He pastored the Star Light Missionary Baptist Church in Derlark, Arkansas and New Light Missionary Baptist Church outside of Arkadelphia, Arkansas prior to moving to Kansas City, Missouri in 1946.

He worked with Dr. Daniel A. Holmes at the Paseo Baptist Church in Kansas City until a call was extended to him from the Shiloh Baptist Church in Warrensburg, Missouri. He has also pastored the Mt. Olive Baptist Church in Marion, Kansas; the Second Baptist Church in Independence, Missouri and the Eastside Baptist Church in Kansas City, Missouri.

He served as the New Era District Moderator from 1953 until 1958. He also wrote a book entitled *"History of New Era District"* in 1981. He has been very active in the spiritual and civic life of the cities where he pastored. He has been married to his wife Willie Mae for fifty years. They have five children.

Reverend Dr. Willam Albert Scott, Sr. was born June 16, 1905 in Fort Scott, Kansas to James Henry and Ella Simpson Scott. He was born into a God-fearing and loving home. He completed his secondary education in Garnett, Kansas. That training was followed with attendance at Ottawa University, Central Baptist Seminary, Washington University in St. Louis, Kansas University and later the Chaplain School at Harvard University and Carlise Barracks.

Pastor Scott commenced his ministerial journey at the Second Baptist Church of Garnett Baptist Church in 1924. He was ordained at the Bethany Chapel Church of Ottawa, Kansas in 1926.

He served as a Military Chaplain during World War II and several pastorates. His pastorates included Southern Union Baptist Church of St. Louis, Calvary Baptist of Fulton, Pleasant Green Baptist Church of Kansas City, Second Baptist of Independence, First Baptist of Lawrence, Kansas, Second Baptist of Garnett, Kansas and Newstead Avenue Baptist of St. Louis.

Pastor Scott became a participant, strong supporter and renowned leader in the efforts of the National Baptist Convention, and its many local, state and national affiliates during his seventy-three years of ministry. He served as Vice President of Americans United for Separation of Church and State (Metropolitan St. Louis Chapter), and liason for the National Baptist Convention with the Southern Baptist Convention.

Dr. David Oliver Shipley, Sr. is a native of Tipton, Missouri. His parents are Galveston and Frances Shipley (deceased). He was educated in the Tipton School System prior to his attending college. He accepted his call to the preaching ministry in 1947. He has served time in the Navy and has been relentless in his educational pursuit. He has received a B.A degree from Baker University with a concentration in

Literature and Sociology. He received a Bachelor and Master degree from Central Theological Seminary focusing on Christian Education. He received a Doctorate of Ministry degree with a focus in Marriage and Family Counseling from Eastern Baptist Theological Seminary in St. Davids, Pennsylvania and an honorary doctorate degree from Western Bible College in the 80s.

Pastor Shipley was the first African American to serve as a chaplain for the Kansas City, Missouri Police Department and secretary for the YMCA. He also served as historian of the Missionary Baptist State Convention during the presidency of Dr. I. H. Henderson. He served as a pastor for over 47 years. He served pastorates in Kansas, Arkansas, Texas and Missouri. His last pastorate was with the Second Baptist Church in Kansas City, Missouri where he served for 16 years until his retirement December 28, 1997. He is called a "pastor's pastor."

He is a great teacher and counselor. His pastoral care ministry has been noted in a professional social work textbook published by the University of Kansas. He has also shared those gifts in service to the Missouri School of Religion, Columbia, Missouri; Western Baptist Bible College, Kansas City, Missouri and the Central Theological Seminary, Kansas City, Kansas. Through his leadership, Second Baptist became part of the Teaching Church program offered by Central Baptist Theological Seminary.

He is an accomplished author. He has written for Billy Graham and prepared several booklets, pamphlets, articles and books. He has written *"Neither Black Nor White," "The New Way,"* and *"Black Baptists in Missouri."* He was married to Alberta and to their union was born four sons: David, Jr., Darrell, Douglas and Donald. Dr. Shipley united in marriage with the former Erma Jean Rencher at the Second Baptist Church, October 12, 1977.

Dr. William M. Singleton was born to George and Elizabeth Singleton in Horry County, South Carolina. He was the oldest of five children. He attended Whittemore Training School where he received his High School diploma. He later received the A.B. degree from Virginia Union and graduated from the Howard University School of Divinity in Washington, D.C. He continued his educational pursuit by obtaining a Master's degree from Drew University in Madison, New Jersey. He taught at Butler College in Tyler, Texas following the completion of his work at Drew University. Dr. Singleton moved to Kansas City, Missouri in 1952 and began his career with Western Baptist Bible College.

He began his service at Western Baptist Bible College as a field representative and instructor. He became president of the college in 1964. He continued in that capacity until his retirement in 1994 from Western Baptist Bible College.

Dr. Singleton pastored the Second Baptist Church in Miami, Missouri and Ward Memorial Baptist Church in Sedalia, Missouri. Dr. Singleton was an active participant in the early Civil Rights movement. He has been honored by the Alumni Associations of Virginia Union University and Howard University. He was also recognized by the *Kansas City Star* as one of Kansas City's 100 Most Influential African Americans and one of the area's Top 50 Gospel Preachers. He submitted an article that is included in the Kansas City Globe's publication *"Preach the Word."*

Dr. Singleton married the former Florence Revels. They are the proud parents of William Jr., Elizabeth and Margaret.

Sister Sallie Titus was born in Gees Bend, Alabama to the late Alfred and Minerva Kennedy. She is one of twelve children. She attended grade school in Gees Bend and high school in Millers Ferry, Alabama. She also attended Wilcox County Training School. She joined the Pleasant Grove Baptist Church, and was very active in the church's ministries. She especially enjoyed Sunday school and the Baptist Training Union. Upon graduating from high school, she married the late Master Sergeant Frank Titus. Five children were born into this union. They traveled extensively as a family during her husband's military career before finally settling in St. Louis. Sister Titus furthered her education by taking courses in cities where her husband was stationed. She attended Tillotson College, Texas; University of Missouri-St. Louis; Forest Park Community College, St. Louis; and Ruth Payne Flowers School of Cosmetology, St. Louis. She also took courses in the local, state, and National Congress of Christian Education.

She presently is an active member of the West Side Missionary Baptist Church in St. Louis, where her pastor is the Reverend Dr. Ronald L. Bobo, Sr. She serves as Hospitality Chairperson for the bereaved families at West Side, President of Church in Community/District, and Vice President of the Ushers Board. She attends Sunday school, prayer meetings and special events.

She has served as Vice President and Treasurer of the Berean District Ushers and Nurses' Auxiliary. She chaired the Missouri Ushers and Nurses host committee for the National Congress of Christian Education when it convened in St. Louis at the

Trans World Dome in 1996. She is also past chairperson of the Building Fund for the Baptist World Center in Nashville, Tennessee.

Sister Titus has received many awards, certificates and plaques for her dedicated services. She now serves as President of the Missionary Baptist State Convention of Missouri and National Baptist Convention, USA, Inc. Ushers and Nurses' Auxiliary. She was appointed to the latter position in 1997.

She is also a licensed Cosmetologist. She was Past President of Associated Hairdressers and Cosmetologists of Missouri, Past Basileus of Alpha Chapter of Theta Nu Sigma National Sorority, member of National Beauty Culturist League, Inc., and Treasurer of United Beauticians.

Brother Everett T. Walker was born in Memphis, Tennessee. He attended public schools there. He received a Bachelor of Arts degree from LeMoyne Owen College in 1939. Through the favoritism of Mr. Edgar Davis, he worked as a carpenter until his call to the Air Force. He achieved the rank of Staff Sergeant.

He moved to St. Louis following the war and reunited with his lovely wife whom he had just married weeks before his call to the Air Force. He and two other blacks were the first blacks to receive a Master's degree from St. Louis University. Following his receiving the Master of Education degree, he began teaching in the St. Louis Public Schools. He taught Social Studies. He later became a counselor and an Administrative Assistant during the thirty-five years that he was with the school system.

He currently holds a lifetime certificate in teaching Social Studies, Counseling and Guidance, and in Administration. Brother Everett was also a part-time real estate salesman at P. C. Robinson Realtors. Presently, he works with Brown & Kortkamp Realtors.

He is a member of Central Baptist Church in St. Louis. His responsibilities there have included General Superintendent of the Church School for many years. He is presently Superintendent Emeritus. He was former Dean and President of the Missouri State Congress of Christian Education and the Antioch District Congress of Christian Education. He served as the Director General of the Antioch District Association. He presently serves as Treasurer of the State Congress of Christian Education. He has held that position for over twenty-one years serving for many years as the General Chairman of the Registration and Finance Committee of the National Baptist Congress of Christian Education.

He is the recipient of many awards and honors. His most notable award was an Honorary Doctor of Humanities degree presented by Arkansas Baptist College and Western Baptist College where he serves on the Trustee Boards.

He married Mildred Parran, and to this union was born three children: Michael, Patricia and Stephanie. His beloved Mildred departed this life March 29, 1974.

Pastor Alfred White is President of the Missionary Baptist State Convention of Missouri Laymen. He is one of four children, three boys and a girl, born to Fate and Vernell White. He was educated in the Kansas City School System. He received his G.E.D. while in the Job Corp. He spent many years incarcerated because of drug addiction. However, while laying helplessly in an emergency room, he had a fresh encounter with God that changed the course of his life. He surrendered his life and problem to God.

Today, he is a successful businessman attending Calvary Bible College with a focus on pastoral studies, and an avid evangelist serving nationally and internationally for the Lord.

Minister White is a member of the Mt. Sinai Baptist Church where he serves as Christian Education Director, Sunday School Superintendent, and the Pastor's Administrative Assistant. He is also chairman of the National Baptist Laymen's Evangelism & Prison Ministry, instructor for the State and National Congress in Evangelism. He acknowledged his ministry calling in May of 1997. He preached his first sermon on June 29 of the same year. He subsequently was ordained March 15, 1998. His favorite verse is "I can do all things through Christ which strengthens me." He is married to Sheila, and they have a son and a daughter.

Pastor Fate White, Jr. received his basic education in the Eagletown and Broken Bow, Oklahoma School System. He has done additional studies with the Moody Bible Institute, Calvary Institute, Western Bible College, Defenders and Central Theological Seminaries. He received a Doctorate of Ministry degree from the University of Central America.

He has been pastor of the Mount Sinai Missionary Baptist Church for over twenty years. He pastored two other churches prior to this pastorate. He has over 30 years of service in the ministry. He is the Vice President-at-Large of the Missionary Baptist State Convention. He has served as Moderator of the Midwest District Association; Corresponding Secretary of the Kansas City Baptist Ministers' Union and founding board member of the "One Church One

Child Board of Directors," an agency for the adoption of special needs children in Kansas and Missouri.

Additionally, he has served the Body of Christ as a Sunday school teacher and Superintendent; Congress Instructor, Dean, and President of the Midwest District Association; and Vice President-at-Large for the Missionary Baptist State Convention of Missouri. Pastor White is a "People and Preacher's" pastor who attributes his accomplishments to humility, love for people, and obedience to God. The Lord has blessed Pastor White to see the completion of the construction vision that was given to him. Mt. Sinai is now in a new worship, fellowship and Christian facility. The church building was completed in 1991 and the multi-purpose facility was completed in 1997.

He was given the Community Award for 40 Years of Leadership to Family Members & Community; and the Ad Hoc Group Against Crime Religious Leader Award. He also has received an Appreciation Award/Boys & Girls Club of America; Katherine B. Richardson Computer Magnet School Service Award; 100 Most Influential African Americans in Kansas City.

He was named to the Top 50 Gospel Preachers; Laymen & Mission Auxiliary Awards at the State and National Level. Pastor White has been married to Mrs. Vernell Blackshere White for 49 years, and they are the proud parents of three sons and a daughter who are also involved in ministries under his leadership.

Sister Vivian O. Woods was born to the union of John Henry and Effie M. Price Yargough in Okmulgee, Oklahoma on February 1, 1909. She accepted Christ at an early age and worked continuously in a variety of capacities for the Lord. She received her early education in the Okmulgee Public School System. She received her teaching certificate and a B.A. degree from Langston University in Oklahoma. She taught in the Public Schools of Barstow, Rot Sill and Native American Reservations in Oklahoma. She continued her educational pursuit at Summers College and Harris-Stowe Teachers College in St. Louis, Missouri. She united with the Second Baptist Church in Monroe City, Missouri in 1943 and served her church until she became unable. She served as President of the North Missouri Baptist Women Missionary Union from August 1951 to 1956. She began the first Youth Encampment in 1954 in the Washington Elementary School, and in 1955, the Reserve Camp for the Bethel

Baptist Association. This work was continued for 41 years. She also served as church treasurer for 25 years and taught for 22 years. Dr. Woods was elected as President of the Women's Missionary and Education Union in 1967 and served in that capacity for 28 years.

She was a strong supporter of the State Youth Encampment conducted at Western Bible College. She was also a strong supporter of the said school. She served 40 years as a trustee.

Dr. Woods was busy in state work, but could not forget her district or hometown. She served as President of the Monroe City Washington School PTA for 14 years. She was a charter member of the Monroe City Nutrition Center Board and served 10 years. She was a member of the Hannibal branch of the NAACP serving as an Executive Board and Membership Committe member.

Chapter 3

Our Churches

Musick Baptist Church, Maryland Heights

First Baptist Church

Eighth and Center Streets Baptist Church, Hannibal

Introduction

The word "church" has its genesis in the Greek term *ekklesia*. We are told that "ek" out and "Kaleo" to call have been used to express a variety of ideas. The term can apply to any called out assembly or congregation. Israel was viewed as an "ekklesia" as they departed from Egypt. Some have viewed it as a building, a denomination, an aggregate of all ecclesiastical fellowships professing faith in Christ; a single group of individuals; and the entire body of those who are saved by their relation to God. Some have viewed the church as an organization and others see it as a living organism. It is both visible as well as invisible. It is both local and international. It is the body of Christ, and yet His bride. It is both a present and eternal reality. It was spoken into existence during Jesus' dialogue with His disciples in the region of Capernaum when Peter confessed that Jesus was the Christ. Jesus at that time told Peter that His church would be founded upon the faith profession that He is indeed the Son of God. He promised that the very gates of hell would not prevail against it. That invisible church of Christ became a visible reality on the Day of Pentecost. It grew rapidly, transforming lives and cultures in the name of the Lord.

We happen to be a Baptist appendage of the body of Christ. L. G. Jordan in the *Busy Pastor's Guide* suggests the following:

> Baptist churches must be cut by the pattern of New Testament churches, as set forth in the Scriptures, in principles and polity, in doctrinal character and life. The Great Commission is the program and purpose—the task and the creed of Baptist churches. Definition: A Baptist church is a company of regenerate persons, immersed on profession of faith in Christ; united in a covenant for worship, instruction, observance of Christian ordinances, and for such service as the gospel requires; recognizing and accepting Christ as their supreme Lord and Lawgiver, and taking His Word as their only and sufficient rule of faith and practice in all matters of conscience and religion. Since they are saved by faith in Christ and baptized in His name, they are governed by His law, observing His ordinances and walking in fellowship with Him (see 1 Corinthians 1:1; Acts 2.41-43; Philemon 27; 1 Corinthians 11:2).

The Following is an historical report submitted by the Reverend Ronald B. Packnett during the 106th Annual Session of our State Convention held on October 14, 1994 at the Hopewell Baptist Church in St. Louis, Missouri.

> The African American church is the oldest and most salient institution to be found in the African American community! As such, it is one of the most powerful and influential institutions affecting the ethos of African American life. Moreover, the African American church has generally been acknowledged to be

the center of African American life and community, and yet unlike the African American family, it has received little attention from the various disciplines devoted to the study of the African American. Under the capable leadership of our chieftain, the Reverend Sammie E. Jones, the historian of the Missionary Baptist State Convention of Missouri Baptists, using scriptural, theological, historical, sociological and literary materials, the historian of the convention will document the centrality of the African American religious experience to African American culture and life. It is without exception. There is a correlative connection either directly or indirectly between the African American's religious experience and every other aspect of African American life. The influence of the African American's religious experience can never be taken for granted. If the African American is to be understood, then so must his religious experience! This understanding must serve as a presupposition to any study of the African American religious experience in the African American church!

Moreover, Dr. J. Deotis Roberts in *Roots of a Black Future: Family and Church*, says:

> Rebellion and protest as well as refuge and support have existed side by side throughout the history of the black church in this country. This was true in the slave states as well as "north of slavery." A one-sided view does not tell the whole story. It is essential, however, to put everything in historical context. The black religious experience has always been a "stride toward freedom." Blacks have had to adapt their programs to meet their freedom needs as circumstances have been altered by pressures from white oppressors. Our minds have been "stayed on freedom," but the means to obtain freedom will vary. At one time, the approach may be legal, at another time political, and again it could be economic. It is remarkable how black religious leaders, both clerical and lay, have been able to read the "signs of the times" and act through appropriate means. Black families and churches have been the main institutions participating in the freedom struggle. They have likewise been affected by the social history of black people (p. 57).

Additionally, Dr. C. Eric Lincoln wrote in *The Black Church in the African American Experience* that "The impact of the Black church on the spiritual, social, economic, educational and political interests that structured life in America, including the mainline white churches themselves, can scarcely be overlooked in any realistic appraisal of our common religious experience."

One can safely say that the black church is the cultural womb of the black community. It gave birth to the major institutions that became the lifeblood of freed and segregated community schools, mutual aid associations, housing units, and social services had their genesis with her. African American churches in Missouri have always been on the forward edge of the battlefield in the formation of vibrant African American communities. We have had our moments of glory and ignominy. Yet, we have a story to tell. A story that will be told from the borders of Kansas, Nebraska, Oklahoma, Arkansas, Tennessee, Kentucky, Illinois and Iowa. It is a story about how God raised up a people from the pits of oppression to set a standard of spiritual excellence in every segment of society in the state of Missouri. Some of these churches were birthed by white churches that most probably were functioning unofficially when the master or overseer was not around. It is amazing how so many of them sprang up so rapidly following the termination of the slavery period in Missouri. One might rightly assume that the invisible (underground) church served its purpose exceptionally well. That is to say that it continued to encouraged the people to hope against hope. It encouraged them to know that our God is an awesome God. They believed that the Lord would ultimately make a way somehow.

Hence, the invisible church and master-dominated churches burst forth into the larger society with fervency, power and the determination to facilitate opportunities and provide resources that gave hope and direction to a people that had endured a long season of despair and oppression.

The churches were able to continue the process of making bricks without straw that has made it possible for us to become the great **Missionary Baptist State Convention of Missouri!**

We will share some histories taken from Shipley's *Black Baptists in Missouri* and documents submitted by various moderators reflecting the oldest churches in their associations. Some presentations are very short. Others are fairly comprehensive. The exciting phenomenon is that the congregations truly demonstrate the notion of "making bricks without straw." They are a constant reminder of the genius and creativity of African American churchmen and churchwomen.

MUSICK BAPTIST CHURCH, MARYLAND HEIGHTS, ORGANIZED IN 1807

The first church known as the Fee Fee Baptist Church located on St. Charles Rock Road at Fee Fee Road was organized in 1807 by Mr. Thomas Musick. This was a white congregation, but Negroes worshiped with them. They also held some meetings from house to house, until some time later that year when Mr. Musick allowed them to hold their prayer meetings in his barn, where he would listen to their singing and praying. When they bowed in prayer, it wasn't for form or fashion nor was it just merely a habit, because they felt the need and care of the heavenly Father for the betterment of their conditions and especially for religious reasons. They continued in prayer services until a short time later when Mr. Musick's heart was touched and he gave them this tract of land and deeded it to our forefathers in 1811. Led by Mr. Tenor Lucas, they began clearing the land and sawing the logs for the first building. The cemetery was purchased 75 years later. Rev. Berry Mitchell was the first pastor of Musick Baptist Church. Some of the first members were: Brother Charles Catlin, Mr. and Mrs. Peter Clayborne, and Mr. and Mrs. Calbot Thomas. Reverend Mitchell's pastorate was followed by pastors Gus Brown, William Stafford, Moses Massey, and James Wright.

Rev. John Clayborne served as the sixth pastor. He was converted and baptized at this church at the age of nine. He was called to preach and later was ordained here. He was called to pastor about 1894. He served approximately 25 years, and was followed by pastors E. J. Buckner and David Chapman.

The church was without a pastor from 1922 through 1924 when there was no regularly appointed pastor, but the church was under the guidance of Rev. Banks, general missionary, and Rev. William Catlin. Rev. John Adams Shields became the ninth pastor in 1924. He served for approximately four and one-half years. Under his pastoral stay, many good things were accomplished. The church entertained the Berean District Association in 1925; built a dining room and kitchen in the back of the old church, bought pulpit chairs; and paid off the debt on the electric power machine. Rev. Shields encouraged both state and national work.

The church was without a pastor again from 1928 until 1933. The Lord sent Rev. O. J. L. Cochrell as the tenth pastor in 1933. Rev. Cochrell restored the interior of the old church. Brother Zelma Williams was the clerk and served in the position until his death in 1960.

He was followed by pastors S. T. Cook, J. N. Williams, Rev. Merriweather, J. E. Taylor, Rev. Dunn, W. Willis, and C. W. Thomas, who was serving as general missionary came to help us on our way as we had no pastor. We liked him so well that we called him to become our seventeenth pastor in May of 1959. He told us that he was going to help us build a church. So with the help of the building chairman, Brother Harry Howard, and his committee, the building began.

Help came from our friends from all over. Donations such as pews, lights, our pulpit, the piano, and cash were all given. We moved into our new church the second Sunday in May 1961. What a time we had. In July of 1961, we had "Edna Howard Day" and raised the largest amount of money ever in a one-day program—$500.

More funds were raised through the dedication and 150th Anniversary program that lasted from August through September of 1961. Money continued to be raised through the Family and Friends Night sponsored by Sister Clara Woodson. Sister Mary Alexander sponsored many dinners, and Sister Lula Howard sponsored our annual tea. Rev. Thomas served as pastor until his death in August of 1970.

Rev. J. E. Butler, the Berean District General Missionary, came to help us in the absence of a pastor. On March 28, 1971, the Rev. Robert M. Franklin was called to serve as our eighteenth pastor. Under the leadership of Rev. Franklin, several members were added to our church; by baptism, by letter, and by Christian experience. New carpeting and furniture for the pastor's study were purchased, a public address system and telephone were installed, and junior and senior choirs were organized. Rev. Franklin remained until September of 1975.

In September of 1975, Rev. Wendell B. Richardson, who was serving as the Berean District General Missionary, came to help with our services in the absence of a pastor.

In March of 1976, the Rev. Leamon Hope was called as our nineteenth pastor. Many things were accomplished under his leadership; new pews were purchased, central air conditioning was installed, the parking lot was surfaced, several deacons were ordained, several ministers were licensed and ordained, and many were united with the church by letter, by Christian experience and by baptism. Rev. Hope remained until June of 1986.

Again we were without a pastor; and Rev. Wendell B. Richardson was called to carry on our services. In December of 1986, Rev. Wendell B. Richardson was called as our twentieth pastor. With his zeal and enthusiasm, we were doing well. We added carpeting to our lower level; a cross was erected on top of the church; later, several other improvements were made to our church facility. Pastor Richardson saw the need for members to be more informed and for better communication. In May of 1987, these two needs were fulfilled with a church bulletin called *The Enlighter*. Several new members joined by Christian experience and baptism.

Musick has received publicity through the news media as an historic church. It has had the distinction of Columnist Julius Hunter writing about its history in a newspaper article, "Early Black Churches." It was published in the daily edition of the *St. Louis Post-Dispatch* on Friday, August 27, 1982. KMOV-TV, channel 4, featured Musick on "Black Profile" in recognition of Black History Month in February of 1991.

The *North County Journal* published an historical feature on our church in its May 24, 1995 edition. The *North Star Magazine* in its February 1996 issue printed an article observing Musick as an historic church.

Our church has endured and persevered in the midst of trying times. We discovered on Sunday, January 28, 1996 that our church sanctuary and facilities had been heavily damaged from a ruptured water pipe. Through faith and prayer, God blessed us to restore the beauty of His house to "worship readiness" with the installation of new carpeting, new pews and the redecoration of the interior.

Musick as a mother church has given birth to several churches. They are: First Baptist Church of Elmwood, First Baptist Church of Creve Coeur, Pilgrim Baptist Church of Richmond Heights, Macedonia Baptist Church of St. Charles, St. John's Baptist Church of St. Louis, and Second Baptist Church of Clayton.

The site of the church has never changed; however, the building has changed three times. Several times the church has been without a pastor, but the doors of the church have never closed.

Today, Musick is pressing on the upward way, gaining new heights every day. Still praying as we're onward bound, trusting the Lord will lead us on to higher ground. Musick has stood 186 successful years, with Jesus Christ as its leader. She has saved many a thousand, she has inspired many a million, and has landed many a thousand. She is the **OLD SHIP OF ZION**.

First African Baptist Church, St. Louis, Organized 1817

In the year 1817, the First African Baptist Church of St. Louis, Missouri was organized under the influence of J. M. Peck and H. E. Welch, the missionaries aforementioned coming from Virginia. The record of Reverend W. O. Lewis, historian, of the white Baptist churches is as follows concerning the Sunday school:

> On the second Sunday in March 1818, Messrs. Peck and Welch opened Sunday school for the instruction of colored children and adults. The school opened with fourteen pupils and in a little over a month, it increased to ninety. Some six or seven teachers aided the missionaries. The whole spiritual influence was soon manifested and several were converted. Although those who were slaves had not been permitted to join the First Baptist Church without the written permission of their masters, this stirred up denominational and other hostilities.

The efforts of J. M. Peck and H. E. Welch obviously created some controversy among their brethren. They received the following letter that was signed Justice on May 14, 1818.

> Gentlemen:
>
> As you have but lately arrived in this country and perhaps may not be acquainted with our laws, I would beg leave to refer you to the seventh section of

an act for the regulation of slaves and leave it to yourselves to decide whether or not you have incurred heavy penalties by your negro schools. It might also be made a question to the patriot and philanthropist whether it is more prudent or humane to give instructions to those who must be made by it more miserable or rebellious. I warn you that the sanctity of the clerical character will not hear screen offenders of the lay.

Yours truly,

Justice

Peck and Welch were not concerned about the threats. They continued to teach the Negroes to read and instruct them in the Scriptures. A part of the time was given to religious worship. Many were converted and baptized in the church. The First Baptist Church was under the supervision of the white brethren, and for ten years J. M. Peck preached to them once a month and guided them in the discipline as their pastor. In 1827, they were organized as an independent church. John Berry Meacham, a free man of color, became their pastor and had several assistants, who exhorted and instructed the people.

In 1831, the First Baptist Church joined the white Baptist association reporting a church membership of 225 members. Their first church, located at Third and Almond, was used as a meeting place for Abolitionists. A group of members asked permission to form a separate congregation in 1846. Initially, it was known as the Second African Baptist Church. Today it is known as Central Baptist Church. Reverend Meacham died about February 19,1854. Burial was at Bellefontaine cemetery on February 21,1854.

In the year 1884 or 1885, the church purchased the Third Baptist Church, Fourteenth and Clark Avenue, under the leadership of Reverend. J. R. Young. The following appeal was sent forth by Pastor Young and S. W. Marston, American Baptist District Secretary for Home Mission:

An Appeal For Help

> The First Baptist Church (colored) of St. Louis was organized in 1827 and since then has worshiped on Almond, between Fourth and Fifth Streets. This location, on account of its surroundings, had become unfit for a place of worship, and the meeting house and lot having greatly depreciated in value, the property was sold to the St. Louis Transfer Co. for $5,000, which is all it is worth. The Third Baptist Church (white), whose house of worship is located on Clark Avenue between 13th and 14th streets, sold their church property to the First Baptist

Church for $17,000, which is a great deal less than its real value. The pastor and entire membership of the colored church feel that this generous gift is of God, and that they should at once seize the opportunity of securing this property, which is centrally located, for their future place of worship. They have paid $7,000 on the property, leaving $10,000 to raise in a very short time. The members of the church are willing to make large sacrifices to do this, and even then they will need the generous aid of their white friends.

The church will thankfully receive and appreciate every gift, large or small, coming from the same. We pray for friends to help us in the purchase of the Clark Avenue Church property. Give something, give liberally.

Rev. Jas. R. Young, Pastor
3636 Laclede Avenue
S. W. Marston, District Secretary American
Baptist Home Mission Society, 16 N. Compton Avenue

Thomas R. Crawford, Church Clerk
4233 Cottage avenue
St. Louis, Mo., November 1, 1884

The church purchased the above mentioned property in 1884 or 1885 under the leadership of Pastor Young. They purchased and paid for a very excellent and beautiful building on the corner of Bell and Cardinal in 1918 during the pastorate of Reverend O. C. Maxwell. Pastor Maxwell was elected Vice President of the Sunday School and B.Y.P. Congress in 1926.

A fire destroyed the edifice in January 1940. The First Church was rebuilt on the same site and dedicated in March 1942 under the leadership of the church's twelfth shepherd, Reverend Dr. James Madison Bracy, Sr. Pastor Bracy was a practicing physician when he became pastor. The church launched the first radio broadcast sponsored by the Carafiol Furniture Company in 1950. Pastor Bracy, in collaboration with the Superintendent of the church Sunday school and director of the Baptist Training Union, decided to develop "a cultural program that would give a new approach to the religious broadcast of many of the church groups that are on the air; not that their programs are without value, but we wanted to try something different." Pastor Bracy decided to give the Antioch District Sunday School and Baptist Training Union Congress, of which he was president, the first half hour and First Baptist took the last half hour. During one broadcast, Pastor Bracy shared with his audience the following firsts:

1. First Baptist Sunday School is the oldest Protestant Sunday School west of the Mississippi River.
2. The same year the Missouri territory applied for admission into the Union, First Baptist was born.
3. The founders of the church were two missionaries sent from the east, Reverends J. Peck and Welch.
4. The church was organized out of the Sunday school. This was the first time in history that an auxiliary was older than the church.
5. The church was beginning to move its influence westward at the same time that the Monroe Doctrine circumscribed the U.S. and set it up as a world power.
6. The first nationwide movement of freeing the slaves by the purchase of their freedom began at First Baptist under the leadership of Pastor John Meacham.
7. The First Church was the western headquarters of both the colonization and abolitionist movement for forty years, led by the early pastors of the church.
8. The first schools opened for Negroes in St. Louis were held in the First Baptist Church.
9. The first Public Library in St. Louis was opened by Reverend Meacham in the First Baptist Church and on his Boat School.
10. The First Baptist Church is 133 years old and has had only thirteen pastors. The thirteenth being the present pastor—Dr. J. M. Bracy
11. The First Baptist Church has now the plans drawn and will begin the construction right away of a religious educational building at a cost of $200,000—the only one of its kind in the Middle West.

First Baptist is presently pastored by Reverend Dr. James D. Dixon, II.

(Information taken from the 133rd and 180th Anniversary Booklets, and Radio in Christian Education, prepared in 1950.)

First Baptist Church, Baldwin, Organized 1832

According to the records of St. Louis County, First Baptist Church is the oldest Baptist church west of the Mississippi River. The corner on which the church stands was once an agricultural center and slave trading post. The church was organized early in 1800, when the town of Baldwin was still a wilderness. The organizational date of 1832 was taken as the official date when Judge Higgins of Baldwin issued a decree that permitted slaves to worship on the grounds without further harassment from the vigilantes.

The first place of worship was under a grape harbor. The first two lots were purchased from John Hall in 1837, but the church was denied ownership because of rigid slave laws. However, on November 13, 1853, the members found a legal way to purchase the second two lots on which the church's first log church was built. Those lots were purchased from Frederick and Mary Shelps for the sum of $45. After reconstruction, the members built a frame building to seat 100 people on the site on which the present church stands.

The church celebrated its 127th Anniversary in 1959, which was celebrated as "A Dedication Day." A former pastor, Rev. C. O. Kelly, directed the services and declared the church site to have been a "freedom prayer ground." First Baptist Church received a letter of congratulations and encouragement from the White House to continue the efforts to build a new church and continue to serve the community spiritually. On May 21, 1961, ground was broken for a new church under the leadership of Rev. C. J. DuVall. Services began in the new edifice on the 130th Anniversary of the church on November 11, 1962.

Some of the pastors of First Baptist Church included Rev. Hurley, Rev. Morton, Rev. Critten, Rev. T. A. Patterson, Rev. Lane, Rev. Billips, Rev. Kirby, Rev. Charles T. O'Kelly, Rev. L. J. Woodward, Rev. W. Royston, Rev. Thames, Rev. Collins, Rev. S. Younger, Rev. C. J. DuVall, Rev. W. R. McCoy, Rev. Gerome Williams, Rev. George Aitch, and Rev. Lewis Works. The present pastor is Rev. George Works.

Morgan Street Baptist Church, Booneville, Organized 1844

On February 24, 1844, the church received by letter two sisters of color, namely, Nellie and Polly. No last names were given. Throughout the Civil War and the Emancipation Proclamation, notations were given concerning the admission of Negro members to the church.

In the beginning, only white male members were authorized to represent the church at association meetings, but later in the year 1847 fifty town members joined with the Baptist church at 518 Vine Street. At that time, it was known as Turner Hall. It is now Geiger's Furniture Store.

The Negro brothers and sisters were allowed to use the church two evenings a month for their services. Brother Grandison Roberts, the first pastor, was licensed to preach in May 1859.

At the close of the Civil War, the Negro brothers and sisters were given letters to form a new church. On November 10, 1865, they moved to a building at 214 Ninth Street. Two years later on December 28, 1867, this property was purchased. The deed was signed by Rev. Grandison Roberts and Deacon Richard Taylor. A frame building was erected and seventeen years later it burned to the ground. In 1874, the brick building that stands today was erected.

The name of the church was changed from Second Baptist Church to Morgan Street Baptist Church. Deacons selected were Richard Taylor, Henry Taylor, Duke Diggs and Collins Braxton. Trustees selected were Richard Taylor, Braxton Shelby and James Redd. The church grew spiritually and in stature, with the help of God and dedicated workers.

Morgan Street has had 23 ministers. They were called in the following order: Rev. Clay Barnes, Rev. Curtis Cox, Rev. A. W. Williams, Rev. I. H. Miller, Rev. Henry Botts, Rev. H. S. Curtis, Rev. H. H. Downey, Rev. J. Sterling Moore, Rev. Pryor, Rev. Ruben Williams, Rev. I. Talley, Rev. Moses Daniel Johnson, Rev. Rufus Caleb Campbell, Rev. Harvey LeVoyd Kemp, Rev. James Phillip Mosley, Rev. Roy E. Andrews, Rev. Harold Johnson, Rev. George Coleman, Rev. Craig Galbreath, Rev. Earl Jackson, Sr., Rev. Elbert Hyche, Rev. Michael C. Philips, the present pastor. The Lord led the shepherds by the wisdom and knowledge of Him through the Word.

Under the leadership of Rev. Michael C. Phillips, the Lord gave him the vision in 1993 to strive to burn our mortgage on the Fellowship Hall in eight months. On September 18, 1994 our Annual Trustee Day, we burned our mortgage. In October 1994, a mural was painted on the wall in the Fellowship Hall, theme Psalm 133:1. The Deacon Ordination Service for Brother Walter Bell was held on November 6, 1994. The Lord blessed us with a van for the handicapped with a lift for the physically impaired that may want to attend the worship services. In February 1995, two trustees were added to the Board: Sister Marnetta Vaughn and Sister Chaneta Elbert. An office was added in the back of the chapel. In 1996, a new parking lot in the back of the Fellowship Hall was added which accommodates 10 vehicles.

The Lord blessed us to accomplish the following in 1997: The WMU started a ministry of giving every baptized believer a King James Bible. The remodeling and renovation of the baptismal pool that brought about many changes within the sanctuary and chapel was competed in August 1997. The church was blessed to receive ten followers in Christ. The Lord called four of our members to rest. Rev. Michael C. Phillips resigned August 1997. He was called to Antioch Baptist Church, Youngstown, OH. The Lord has blessed us with Rev. Craft and family as our Interim Pastor.

We realize that for 132 years, the church has marched onward by faith and humble prayers. We are knowledgeable of God's Word in Revelation 2:10 "Be thou faithful unto death and I will give you a crown of life" (material received from the church historian).

CENTRAL BAPTIST CHURCH, ST. LOUIS, ORGANIZED 1846

Central Baptist Church has been known as the Second African Baptist Church and Eighth Street Baptist Church before receiving its present name. It is a child of First African Baptist Church. Second African was established on the 22nd of March 1846 under the leadership of Reverends Richard Sneether and J. R. Anderson (products of the Freedom School). Worship was started in the hall adjoining the Liberty Engine House at Third and Franklin Avenue. From the very beginning, meetings were well attended and continued to increase.

There was a deep desire by some to sever relations with the Mother Church. There was a feeling that members had moved too far North and needed a church closer than Almond Street. There was also the widening generation gap and the desire on the part of both for more personal involvement in decision making. This move was not welcomed by the Mother Church, but time heals many wounds.

On October 24, 1847, the young church was formally set apart and constituted as a regular Baptist church. The organizing council members were Reverend Mr. Nelson, who gave the address to the church and Brother Bailey of the North Church; the Reverend Dr. Lynd, who gave the right hand of fellowship, and Brother P. J. Thompson, who served as Secretary Pro Tem, from Second Church (white); and Reverend Mr. Parey from Indiana, who concluded the service with prayer.

There were twenty-three original charter members: John Phillips, J. C. Walker, W. P. Brooks, Sylvia Glasgow, Letitia Jackson, Agnes Jefferson, Fannie Hill, Corehenia Bartlet, Samuel Green, Sguire Brown, Randolph Smith, Tomsel Jackson, Emily Lee, Mary Anderson, Winnie McKinney, Jeff Camp, Tarlton Jackson, Hester Hefferson, Angeline Camp, Matilda D. Anderson, Betsey Gray and Martha Augustus. As early as 1846, these laymen had been holding prayer meetings in the homes of Brother and Sister Lewis, Sophie Scott and Scott Sexton. Finally, they secured a hall at Third and Franklin Avenue (then Cherry Street) adjoining the Liberty Engine House. Reverend Sneethen was chosen as pastor. Richard Sneethen was a man of stalwart character, a strong preacher of the gospel and an uncompromising Baptist. Reverend S. P. Anderson, who lived in New York City, thought highly of Reverend Sneethen.

He felt that he was a great man because of his honesty and uprightness. He had full charge of all the affairs of his church both temporal and spiritual and paid all bills.

His word was law along all lines and he never betrayed a trust. We must remember the times and the untutored condition of the people, most of whom were slaves.

On May 17 and 18, 1849, St. Louis was almost destroyed by fire. This event is mentioned here because the steamers were fill with Negro stewards, stewardess and waiters, and many of the stevedores handling the freight on the wharf were Negroes. Several Negro businessmen served these boats with foodstuffs. Along this or a similar line of streamers, John Berry Meachum, Pastor of First Baptist Church, sailed his steamer serving them with foodstuff (see Duncan, *History of Missouri Baptists*, page 756). Many black people so employed were members of the Second Colored Baptist Church and were worshipers at Liberty Hall. One such person, Anthony Brown, was a river steward who brought in much money to build the first place of worship on Eighth Street. He was later an honored trustee.

It should be remembered that while this conflagration was raging, the terrible epidemic of cholera was at the same time taking hundreds of lives weekly; and Negroes, bondmen and free, in their proportion suffered with the rest from fire and disease.

Reverend John R. Anderson succeeded Reverend Sneethen at Second African Church. The church grew rapidly, but with many problems. Pastor Anderson was young, energetic and sensitive to all these influences. The congregation caught his spirit as the members became involved in community issues. John Anderson cultivated an ecumenical spirit. He invited all Christian ministers to his pulpit and his house. He gave them the best of his means. He performed for them the most menial deeds, even to the polishing of their boots. He did not live to celebrate the Emancipation Proclamation with his people in 1865. He died from accidental poisoning during the summer of 1863.

Reverend J. Freeman Boulden was elected pastor after the death of Pastor Anderson. Pastor Boulden was called from Philadelphia. He was well known to Central Baptist Church from his previous pastorate at Olivet in Chicago. He served the church for two years. He was followed by the Reverend W. P. Brooks. Through his ministry, Second Baptist touched other churches of Missouri as no other church had ever done. Pastor Brooks organized churches in Warrensburg, Booneville, Chesterfield, Columbia, Louisiana, Mt. Zion, St. Louis, Tipton, Rocheport, New London, Mexico and Chambers Street, St. Louis. A crowning moment in the history of Central was the purchase of the Pilgrim Congregation, known as a Church of Chimes. The purchase price was $45,000. It was a marvelous financial transaction for Central that had known for several years of its need to relocate. They swapped land for a $15,000 discount on the purchase price.

Under the leadership of Dr. T. E. Huntley, tenth undershepard, another crowning moment in the illustrious history of our congregation occurred. The church edifice was rebuilt in 1975 following a fire that destroyed the older facility. An ultra modern facility, now valued in excess of a million dollars, was constructed. The congregation entered into the gates with thanksgiving and the courts with praise. Pastor Huntley's ministry was followed by the ministry of Reverend Cydrow Durbney. He was followed by the congregation's thirteenth undershepard, Reverend Ronald B. Packnett. Pastor Packnett provided the congregation with a solid proactive community needs-based ministry. Annually, thousands were fed and clothed. Central became one of many advocacy voices interceding on behalf of the downtrodden and outcast. (Material taken from Shipley's *History of Black Baptists in Missouri* and the *1987 Anniversary Booklet*.)

EIGHTH AND CENTER STREETS BAPTIST CHURCH, HANNIBAL, ORGANIZED 1853

The history of Eighth and Center Streets Baptist Church is a story of progress presented in pictures and written materials depicting the history of our church from the very beginning. The first written history published in booklet form was written by Edward M. January, Sr., Head of the Department of Social Sciences of Douglas High School, Hannibal, Missouri in 1930. Professor January died in Booneville, MO, November 28, 1962. The appearance of a new history probably calls for some explanation and the motive for its writing.

We as a church realize that much has happened since our first history was written and we hope to preserve the inspiration and successes of the past years and pass them on to the future generation.

The churches of Hannibal began their existence in a very humble way. Most of them rented halls; and by their spiritual and moral development, have shown steady progress. It required faith, perseverance and patience in the early years to cling to that torch of Christianity which has come down through the ages, and far more to erect and maintain a structure to serve God. At a very early date, the churches in Hannibal united frequently in union evangelistic services. The good results from them are the many beautiful edifices that can be seen in our city today. The Baptist church of which the Fifth Street Baptist Church is the successor was organized November 25, 1837, by Robert Hendren, Mary A. Hendren, Francis A. Nunn, Stuart Self, Nancy Self, James Brown and two colored women known as "Maria and Providence." The first meeting was held at the home of Stuart Self, two miles west of Hannibal. It was then known as the Zoar Church and the membership worshiped in a school house, after which it moved to Hannibal and was reorganized under the name of the Hannibal United Baptist Church. This church was located at 4th and Church Streets. Other colored members were Mr. Dealy, Mr. Gore, and Jerry Turner, colored, who was buried from this church.

It thus appears from official records that the Negro Baptists of Hannibal were organized with the white Baptists and other organizations for almost a century. The land granted for the use of the Second Baptist Church, now known as Eighth and Center Streets Baptist Church, was purchased from a man named Zachariah B. Draper and Eleanor M. Draper, his wife, for the sum of thirty-seven dollars and fifty cents ($37.50). This sale occurred April 22, 1853 in the city of Hannibal.

The trustees who bought the ground in 1853 were James Daws, Carter Braxton, George Bishop, Jerry Wade and John Hannex, all free persons of color. The property was out of lots 75 and 76.

> "It is understood and agreed by the undersigned grantors and grantees that the lot of ground herein described and sold has been purchased by voluntary contributions of colored persons, within and near the city owned by others who are friendly to the cause for the purpose of erecting thereon a church edifice or place of religious worship to be called the "The African Church"—under rules and regulations which shall be made under the direction of trustees for the several denominations as the said trustees may according to such rules and regulations permit. It is also provided and agreed that either one, or any member of such denominations, may sell out, or, become purchased from the others." On the 30th day of December, 1861, Simon Tanner of Hannibal, sold to his son, King Tanner, a piece of property for the sum of two hundred and fifty dollars in out lots 75 and 76, ten feet from the African Church. (See old deed of Simon Tanner to son, King Tanner.)
>
> On December 31, 1868, the trustees of the church, James Daws, Carter Braxton and George Bishop failed to pay an assessment of thirty dollars that was against the church property (The west 25 feet by 32 ¾ feet off lot No. 9 in out lot No. 75). This can be seen in City Ordinance No. 152. So the city Marshall advertised the same in the city paper from the 5th day of February to the date of the sale.
>
> At public venue, the property was bought by David Foster, Rafel Helm and Thomas Shropsher who were trustees, also highest bidders, for the sum of thirty dollars.

By consulting warranty deed for property dated 1839, the trustees of the Second Baptist Church, Jeremiah Turner, David Foster, Horace Taylor, John Clay, Isaiah Booker and David Walden agreed to purchase from the Methodists their share of the property, and the Methodists pulled out and organized their own church on Church Street. This was done on the 28th day of October, 1869. (Notice: This is not the date of erection of the building occupied by the A.M.E. Church in 1930.) (See author's History of Negroes in Hannibal and Marion County; abstract and title, Dec. 16, 1895.)

In September 1863, the Allen Chapel A.M.E. Church purchased the Professional Building located on the southwest corner of Sixth and Center Streets to be used as a church building. Robert Phillips, James Martin, W. W. Bryant, Allen Bohon, Milo Jackson and George Lewis, trustees of Allen Chapel A.M.E. Church of Hannibal, for the consideration of $100.00, sold their share to Frank Dealy, David Foster, David Smith, Monroe Johnson and Charles Bush, trustees of Eighth and Center Streets Baptist Church, Hannibal, Missouri.

Some date between October 8, 1880 and August 13, 1884, the name of the church was changed from the Second Baptist Church to Eighth and Center Streets Baptist Church, and so the true beginning of Eighth and Center Streets Baptist Church was on April 22, 1853, or one hundred and ten years on its present site.

It appears that Robert W. Cash or Bob Cash was the agent who bought or made certain transactions between the Second Baptist Church trustees and Eighth and Center Streets Baptist Church trustees in the years 1880-1884. Father O. H. Webb was the first pastor, organizer and founder of Eighth and Center Streets Baptist Church. He was also first moderator of the North Missouri Baptist Association organized in 1865 in Chillicothe, MO. He served as moderator for six consecutive years and was pastor of Eighth and Center Streets Baptist Church for 40 years, dating from 1893 back, that being the longest period for retaining any one pastor.

Father Webb built the church, and during the time he was not in the pulpit, he worked on a transfer wagon. He labored with the others in the construction of the church as they gave their contributions in the terms of bricks. Many of the members worked late at night with the pastor with lathes and putting on the roof. There were large congregations in those days as the church was a common meeting place. This church stood on the ground where the parsonage is now located. The date of the building of the parsonages was 1903. This union church had alternating services; the Methodists one Sunday, the Baptists and other denominations another. Some of the old members were John Hannex, Sam Kimboe and Jerry Turner, who were also charter members. The Methodists pulled out in 1869.

Mr. Byron Lakenan and Mrs. Queary of Hannibal (now deceased) stated that the old church fronted Eighth Street and that school was held in the rear. One Mr. Sam Smith lived in the basement. The members finally decided to build a larger church so they put a foundation on Eighth and Center Streets since the foundation that was laid on Eighth and Hill Streets was thought not to be the proper place for the church. A strange coincidence is the fact that the author of this first historical report tore down the ancient foundation where the church foundation once stood and built his home where the old church foundation was built. (It seems that Father Webb was with the congregation during most of the building period.) Before the new church was completed, a certain pastor by the name of Barton Hillman was called from Springfield, Illinois, but within ninety days he resigned, so the second pastor of the church was the Reverend G. H. McDaniel. This was before 1894.

(Mr. Fred Dabney was a watch-care member in 1890 and ran a printing establishment on Broadway—a Baptist paper.) This Christian gentleman, the Reverend McDaniel, had many scholarly attainments and was editor of the *Missouri Baptist Standard*. This weekly paper was the largest colored publication in the United States at that time and the only one in the state of Missouri.

Reverend McDaniel was followed by the third pastor, Rev. E. C. Cole. He preached about three years. Then the fourth pastor, Rev. W. E. Helm, was called about this time. Fifteen feet were added to the church property on the east side of the church. A man by the name of Mr. Brady covered the church and did a number of favors for the church. He was white and lived at Seventh and Center Streets. The Rev. Helm was pastor from 1896 to 1901.

The fifth pastor was the Rev. C. R. McDowell, who rendered great service while in office. The lot where the parsonage now stands was bought during his pastorate and a parsonage was built. He also paid a mortgage of one thousand dollars and the interest. He built cupolas and remodeled them, obtained stained glass windows, built concrete walks and bell towers. Rev. McDowell resigned in 1916 and was succeeded by Rev. R. A. Broyles who pastored until 1918.

The seventh pastor, Rev. E. H. McDonald, Assistant Secretary of the National Baptist Convention at the time of his pastorate, made a fine financial record while in charge. He borrowed four thousand dollars and paid it back in three years. He decorated the interior of the building and put in a steam heating furnace. An indirect lighting system was installed, also. His services were from 1919 to 1922.

Rev. Ernest S. Redd was the eighth pastor. He came to us in December 1922. Some of the many things he accomplished were improving the social rooms and church kitchen, putting roofing on the church parsonage and organizing the church into working units. Many programs of special days were observed, such as Women's Day and Men's Day. He conducted the first and only chautauqua for several seasons, bringing to Hannibal the best colored talent in literature, music and culture. One of the most successful revivals in the history of the church was when he brought the Rev. Herman Gore, the boy Evangelist, of St. Louis, Missouri to Hannibal in 1937. There were 88 converts added to the fold. During the year of 1931, Rev. Redd offered his resignation to Eighth and Center and returned to a former pastorate at Columbia, Missouri.

Rev. C. Lopez McAllister was the ninth pastor. He began his pastorate in 1932. He organized and supervised the first Vacation Bible School for colored youth of Hannibal. He resigned in 1942 to become the pastor of the Maple Street Church at Des Moines, Iowa. During the year of 1942, Rev. W. R. Payne was called to be our tenth pastor. He resigned in 1946.

Rev. C. W. Carter was our next choice for pastor. He came to us from LaGrange, Missouri. He was a graduate of Western College and was highly esteemed by his co-workers. He was moderator of the North Missouri District Association. During the last years of his pastorate, he was ill and on January 28, 1954 passed into eternal rest, leaving behind a loving wife, Mrs. Hattie Carter and family, and many sorrowful friends. Once more the church was without a pastor, however, under the faithful leadership of Deacon M. D. Powers, she carried on.

Our next choice was Rev. H. L. Johnson, Jr., a young minister in his senior year at Western College. Rev. Johnson came to us in 1954. During his pastorate, the floor of the sanctuary was refinished, a carpet and new piano were purchased, new front doors and a light over the doors were also purchased. Rev. Johnson resigned in 1959.

Rev. Lee Roy Cunningham, our present pastor, was called in August, 1959. He came to us from a pastorate at Canton, Missouri. He began his pastorate the first Sunday in September. He is the thirteenth pastor of the church and the youngest who has ever occupied our pulpit as pastor. Our pastor's wife, Sylvia, and their children are active in church activities. During his pastorate, the hail-damaged roof has been repaired, windows leaded, new pulpit furniture purchased and revivals held and a number of children have been baptized. Rev. Cunningham's fourth anniversary was observed by the church during the month of September. He has done much in establishing unity with the sister churches and in trying to create a greater desire for spiritual strength in the membership. His motto is "The Church With a Friendly Welcome."

In concluding this report, it is only proper and fitting that we list some of the prominent members of the Eighth and Center Streets Baptist Church. Their names are as follows: Doc Nelson served as treasurer for 25 years. Brother J. H. Dealy was church clerk for 22 years. Dr. O. C. Queen was secretary of the trustee board for 20 years. Brother William F. Campbell was chairman of the trustee board for over 25 years. Perry Ambers was chairman of the deacon board for many years. Others deserving mention by reason of their long years of service are:

Rev. William Powers, James Starks, Deacon Ed Washington, W. H. Dixon and Dan Gibson. Serving members from 1930-1963 are: Brother George Robert—Trustee for 45 years. Mrs. Bertha Roberts—Clerk from 1936-1944 and from 1950-until present, Deacon M. D. Powers—Superintendent of Sunday School for 36 years. Brother Fred Longmire—Deacon for many years. Mrs. Elizabeth Bell—President of Choir for 15 years. Brother Merrill Forte—Chairman of Trustees Board for 15 years. Brother William Irving—Trustee and Deacon for many years. Mrs. Daisy Brown Tinsely—Deaconess and Sunday school teacher for many years.

Pastors that have served this church are as follows: Father O. H. Webb Reverends C. H. McDaniel, E. C. Cole, W. E. Helm, C. R. McDowell, R. A. Broyles, E. H. McDonald, Ernest S. Redd, Lopez McAllister, W. R. Payne, C. W. Carter, H. L. Johnson, Jr., Lee Roy Cunningham, William Hale, Leon Lowery, Donald Sprague, Madison J. Williams. Our present pastor, Rev. Wesley J. Foster, is our eighteenth pastor. Rev. Foster has served as pastor of Eighth and Center Streets Baptist Church for 14 years. During his pastorate, Rev. Foster has stressed Sunday school attendance, consistent Bible study, Evangelism, and the effectiveness of prayer (submitted by Sis. C. D. Powell).

BRIDGETON BAPTIST CHURCH, BRIDGETON, ORGANIZED 1853

Bridgeton Baptist Church was organized in 1853 by slaves. The slaves went to the Bridgeton Plantation of Dr. William Norris by the use of the Underground Railroad. Dr. Norris was not a believer in slavery, and considered the slaves as free men. He gave them the first ground and a log cabin on his plantation for a church. The church was originally called First Baptist of Bridgeton. The church was organized by L. W. and Elmira Granderson, Herbert and Ella Word, Billy Benson, and Sam and Martha Simpson, with Rev. James Dodge as the first pastor.

The former pastors of the church were Rev. M. A. Stafford, Rev. T. L. Alexander, Rev. I. W. Green, Rev. S. L. Buans, Rev. T. H. Foster, Rev. A. D. Davis, Rev. W. W. Perry, Rev. A. M. Cheek, Rev. D. L. Bell, Rev. J. E. Boden, Rev. Ben A. Waddelington, Rev. J. Hopel, Rev. H. Channey, Rev. David Chaptman, Rev. William Freeman, Rev. James Fiddmont, Rev. Benjamin Catlin, Rev. James Ghoolsby and Rev. R. R. Watkins. The present pastor is Rev. Claude E. Shelby.

Mount Zion Baptist Church, Chillicothe, Organized 1854

The Mount Zion Baptist Church of Chillicothe, Missouri was organized by the Wood River Baptist Association of Wood River, Illinois in 1854. One of the organizers was a Rev. Dolin and these were charter members: Sarah Alex, Eliza Montgomery, Charles Johnson, Moses Lewis, Lucinda Lewis, Thomas Clark, Jane Clark, Eliza Hudson, Charles Clinkscale, Mary Clinkscale, Nancy Kiles, Milton Kiles, Mat Spears, Dave Roundtree, Fanny Roundtree, and Brother Cowhorn. The impact of these brave pioneers that established a church in 1854 before the Emancipation Proclamation could not be known by them. Their efforts were far-reaching.

As the Territorial Assemblies and National Conventions became organized, they were able to exercise greater influence and to give more valuable assistance in clarifying their purpose and mission to individual states. Nevertheless, duplication of work, jealousy among leaders, and unrest created by the attempt to draw up territorial boundaries were to be of grave concern for many years to come.

Yet, the original commitment that brought even the first organization into being never lost its glow: "The evangelization of the race, the intense eagerness to provide Christian education for the youth and the establishment of churches where blacks could worship God according to the dictates of their conscience." This commitment outweighed any emerging establishment that stood in the way of the realization of that dream. The desire to be gift-givers was never lost.

New churches were being organized rapidly throughout the nation by white missionary groups, black expositors and individual blacks who were simply voluntarily withdrawing from white churches. The demand was even more acute for a national and state organization. Eventually, the national organizational pattern was to be duplicated on the state level, but this required several decades of teaching and structuring.

It must be kept in mind that independent churches came first. Secondly, the associational groups that, on a voluntary basis, were functioning years before a state organization was formed. One of the oldest associations to be organized in Missouri was "The North Missouri Baptist District Association." It was organized at Mount Zion Baptist Church in September 1865. Some of those who attended this organizational meeting were: The Reverends B. F. Baseman, Dr. Hildreth, Barton Hillman, George Hudson, Thomas Clark, J. Cox, Preston Oliver, B. F. Marshall, and Adam Dimmitt.

At this first meeting, the Rev. O. H. Webb was elected moderator, and the Rev. Baton Hillman was elected secretary. The following year, in September 1866, the association met in Hannibal, Missouri. The Rev. O. H. Webb was reelected moderator and H. H. White was elected secretary. The first Constitution and Bylaws were established in 1872.

We must go to the North Missouri Baptist District Association Meeting, 1870, in Lexington, Missouri to see that the North Missouri Baptist District Association was divided into the Second Baptist and the North Missouri Baptist District Associations, the Missouri River making the dividing line. The Rev. O. H. Webb was moderator of North Missouri and the churches which made up Mt. Zion District were in that division. Ten years later in Columbia, Missouri, it divided again into the Eastern District and the Mt. Zion District. The first captain of this army was the Rev. H. J. Homesly. Being the oldest Afro-American church north of the Missouri River, our church is called the Mother Church of the Mt. Zion District Association.

On October 8, 1889, representatives of the different associations and churches of Missouri met with the Mt. Zion Baptist Church of Chillicothe and formed "The Baptist General Association of Missouri," now known as the Missionary Baptist State Convention of Missouri. The dominant thought in the minds of these pioneer Christian men and women was that of "Christian Education."

The constitution provided for the officers of the Convention to constitute the Board of Education and the corresponding secretary, and financial agent. On October 23rd of the same year, the Board met in Independence, and executed a lease providing for the use of the old church property for the purpose of conducting the school for a term of five years.

The institution, thus organized, commenced its work with a faculty consisting of a president and an assistant student teacher, term four (4) months, enrollment, fourteen (14), seven (7) of whom were young men engaged in the ministry. Dr. John T. Capstan, the President of the newly formed Missouri Baptist State Convention, called a meeting on January 13, 1890 at Independence and completed the organization for the school, naming it Western Baptist College, and electing Professor Wilton Boone, President.

Western Baptist College bears the distinction of being the first and the only Christian school in the Northwest founded by Negroes exclusively with the incentive of gifts of land or money.

A group of Christian women, encouraged by their pastors and other members of the Mt. Zion District Association, attended the association meeting held with the Mt. Zion Baptist Church of Chillicothe, Missouri, in September 1898. Envisioning the future and realizing a truly great work awaited them, they organized a new Christian society, The Women's Home, Foreign and Educational Convention as an auxiliary to the Mt. Zion District Missionary Association. Mrs. Mary L. Saunders was their first president, and Mrs. Addie Triggers was chosen their recording secretary pro tem. Other elective officers included Mary Morton, secretary, Amanda M. Swanson, treasurer, and Eva Marshall, a board member.

Much of the history of the church and highlights of its successes have been lost or planted in the graves with the pioneers who now are gone. The meeting places of the early organization were in the homes, schools, and an old tobacco factory on West Webster Street.

As the membership grew in the hearts and minds of the early worshipers, a burning desire was kindled for a permanent place in which to worship. In 1866 the site on which the first church stood was purchased from a man named John Graves for $1.50. The first building was a crude one. It was told by one of the pioneer women, Sister Sarah Alex, that she and other women of the church helped to hew out the logs that were used as sills in the church. Many of the older members stated that both men and women went to the woods to cut the logs which were finally dressed in crude lumber to erect the first structure. The ladies who remained at home cooked tasty meals for the workers.

The church was first forty feet long and twenty feet wide, but as the membership grew more space was needed and twenty feet was added, making it sixty feet long and twenty feet wide. During the pastorate of Rev. McMillian, the entrance was changed from the west side and a vestibule was built on the northwest corner.

During the second pastorate of Rev. Swancy, the church was raised and the basement added. The baptistery was also built at this time.

Up until the pastorate of Rev. G. D. Saunders, the ministers lived wherever they could rent a house. During his ministry, the parsonage was purchased.

During the pastorate of Rev. J. W. Harris, the church was further improved. Through the efforts of the chorus and a building fund, the walls were paneled, the ceiling changed and stained glass windows added. The church saw the need of a place in which to bury their dead and many years ago the land now known as "South Cemetery" was purchased for a burial ground.

During the five-year pastorate of Rev. I. H. Harris, the entrance to the church was again changed to its original position and the rest rooms were added.

During the two-year pastorate of Rev. J. P. Mosely, the parsonage was remodeled, new floors were laid and the exterior was covered with siding. A new floor was laid in the church and a modern heating system was installed. A Men's Chorus was organized. This group bought paint, painted the building and erected a sign at the church's entrance. The brotherhood was also revived.

Rev. Willie Louis Jefferies was pastor of the church for seven years. Further improvements were added, a new furnace was installed in the parsonage, a canopy was erected over the stoop at the entrance. The church's interior and exterior were redecorated, the Junior Choir was organized, new chairs were purchased for the choir stand and the basement, new pulpit furniture purchased, and a steam table installed in the kitchen.

During the pastorate of Rev. T. A. White, a garage was added to the parsonage property, the basement was redecorated and the church's interior paneled, choir stand changed and new lights were installed. There were also new tables purchased for the basement, a new piano purchased for the sanctuary, and changes made to the interior of the parsonage.

The Rev. W. R. Palmer served as our interim pastor. Under his leadership, a new organ was purchased.

The Rev. John R. White was the next pastor of the church. During his pastorate, the present pews and the communion table were purchased, and a new furnace and central air conditioning were installed. He also established the Mothers Board.

Continuing in the tradition of our founding fathers, the Mt. Zion District Ushers' Auxiliary was organized at the Mt. Zion Baptist Church on April 29, 1995. Those elected to office at that meeting were: Margaret White, president, Sue Richardson, secretary, LaVerna Williams, treasurer, Walter Lane III, chaplain, and board members, Wanda Crowns and Earnest Kittrell.

During the church's existence, there have been thirty-four pastors to serve during its one-hundred forty-four years of existence. The names of the pastors that have been gathered are: the Reverends Jacob Doolin, Hardin Smith, Thomas Clark, George Hudson, Barton Hillman, Daniel Sawyer, Finney West, Amos Johnson, Jackson Wright, G. D. Saunders, J. T. Thornley, McMillian, M. L. Clay, Howard, I. H. Talley, S. H. Gibson, J. W. Jones. Other pastors serving us were Miller, R. O. Johnson, J. W. Harris, W. A. Philips, I. H. Farris, O. T. Reed, T. E. Ward, J. S. Swancy (two terms), Smith, Alford, J. P. Mosley, Willie Louis Jefferies, T. A. White, W. R. Palmer, (Interim), John R. White.

The current pastor is Rev. Herbert L. Roberson. God has used him to stir the members into further action for the vision of a new edifice. God has blessed us richly as we now have the manifestation of our prayers for a new edifice. A groundbreaking ceremony was held on April 13, 1996. Steve Radcliff Construction Company has been our contractor. In the backdrop of deep snow, the first worship was held on January 12, 1997. Before us, we see a continued ministry.

It might best be stated by one of our members, Sister Eileen Price Scholls, who penned these words:

> *Lord, make us more humble, more patient, more kind,*
> *Keeping the thought of our brother in mind.*
> *Lord, may we worship through service to men,*
> *No difference how great or how low they have been.*
> *Service, that comes direct from the heart.*
> *Service with a care and a love that will blend,*
> *Service, true service until life shall end.*

We see ministry to our community as our heritage and our continued goal as we serve the Master in His vineyard (compiled by Linda L. Dodd).

FIRST BAPTIST CHURCH, CHESTERFIELD, ORGANIZED 1856

First Baptist Church was organized in 1856 on its present site of Highway 40. The church's property was given to the founding members by the slave owner, Mary Long, but did not officially become theirs until 1875. It was originally built to serve as a school and a church. The frame of the church was built by its members in 1911. The present church structure was complete in June 1975.

The church has had fifteen pastors. The last three pastors were Rev. Allen D. Dorsey, Rev. Wm. Kilgore, and Rev. Gibuson. The present pastor is Rev. Theoplois Peoples, Jr. Rev. Peoples has served First Baptist as pastor since July 1967.

MOUNT ZION MISSIONARY BAPTIST CHURCH, ST. LOUIS, ORGANIZED 1859

Despite the fact that slave laws sponsored by many slave owners in St. Louis were very rigid, a white missionary preacher—the Reverend John Mason Peck of Virginia—came to St. Louis in 1818 for the expressed purpose of educating African American slaves. Shortly after his arrival, he gathered to himself a group of slaves and started a Bible school. A direct result of his efforts was the organization in 1827 of the First African Baptist Church—the Mother Church. The first pastor of the "seed" was the very talented and industrious John Berry Meachum, a student who had been specially trained by the Reverend Peck, because of his unusual ministerial gifts.

Pastor John Meachum, whose talents and skills as a businessman had resulted in his manumission as a slave, soon began to experience difficulties in his newfound ministry to the First African Baptist Church. A controversy arose within the family. Although the cause is not clear, the question of travel distance to the church—North side versus South side—lay at the bottom of this problem. Because of the location of the "Mother Church," some of her members could not attend as regularly as they wished. Feeling the need for regular worship, these Christians began to hold prayer meeting and worship services in their immediate neighborhood in a building next to the Liberty Engine House on Cherry Street.

The result was the organization in 1846 of the Second Colored Baptist Church, now known as the Central Baptist Church of St. Louis. In 1847, this congregation was recognized as a regular Baptist church with the Reverend Richard Sneethen serving as her first pastoral shepherd.

As a circle that continues to spin, the road of history often duplicates itself. Once again, the powerful influence of prayer meetings and the undying faith of those who prayed caused history to be made. In 1859, during the pastoral leadership of the Reverend John Richard Anderson at the Second Baptist Church in the home of Mother Lucy Crawford on Chouteau Avenue near Ohio Street and Mother Hannah Cabnelle, the birth of a new Christian fellowship took place. Members of the rather new Second Colored Baptist Church (Central Baptist Church), along with other interested persons, joined together in these homes to seek through prayer spiritual guidance and direction. A fervent desire for a regular meeting facility and the establishment of a formal organization grew out of these meetings. These were the earliest and humble beginnings of the Mount Zion Missionary Baptist Church.

Some of those early (charter) members were Lucy Crawford, Alfred and Lizzie Moore, Frank Cabelle, Betty Brown, Hannah Cabelle, Henry Herring and his wife, Peter Woods, Isaiah Jones, Vince Washington, Brother Islow, Brother Huggans, I. J. Reed, Henry Jefferson, Sister Varnum, Susie Grover, Classia Hollis, Willis Martin and several others of whom we have no record.

Some of the early deacons were Brother George Cavens, George Anderson, Ephraim Finney, Isaiah Reddick—who later became the first superintendent of the Sunday church school—Willis Martin, Vincent Washington, Henry Herring and John Hall.

Indeed, ours is a noble heritage! God has richly blessed our Christian fellowship. Moreover, God has given to our religious family a very rich history and tradition. Begun in the days of slavery, the Mount Zion Missionary Baptist Church has endeavored to serve the needs of this community for more than 135 years. In 1859, we were organized as the Mount Zion Baptist Church, becoming one of the oldest African

American congregations in this city. Under the able and effective leadership of our foreparents—our mothers and our fathers—the Mount Zion Missionary Baptist Church became a strong and viable religious force within the life and history of St. Louis, Missouri and America.

Since her early, humble beginnings, Mount Zion has been a front-runner in the religious leadership of this community, especially among African Americans. She has been guided through these 135 years by the aid of the Holy Spirit and by the remarkable leadership of pastors—men of God who committed their lives and work to the glory and honor of God.

The first pastor to serve this congregation was the Reverend Wyatt Scott. The very first facility to house this congregation was provided by the gracious and generous efforts of Mother Rosie Ross—a log cabin donated by a white family who were the slaves of Sister Ross and who supported her efforts on behalf of this newly organized African American Baptist Church. The building was located East of Jefferson Avenue at Papin Street.

Subsequent to Pastor Scott's leadership, Reverend Slater assumed the pulpit. Under his pastoral leadership, the first Mission Circle and the first church choir were organized. The congregation began the purchase of the new church facility located at 2624 Papin Street. To his credit, many outstanding "firsts" were accomplished by the Mount Zion Baptist Church family. Also serving in this early period were the Reverend Burns and the Reverend J. P. Nichols.

Continuing in this outstanding tradition of pastoral leadership, the Reverend Humphrey next assumed the pastoral charge of the Mount Zion congregation. Under his leadership, a pipe organ was purchased and installed in the church facility. The church was incorporated as a religious corporation under the laws of the State of Missouri in 1889.

Next to assume the pastoral leadership was the Reverend J. W. Powell. Under his leadership, the mortgage on the church property at 2624 Papin was liquidated. Subsequent to the final mortgage payment, the congregation shared in a rather elaborate and impressive Mortgage Burning Ceremony.

Others among this group of early leaders was the Reverend G. W. Benton, under whose leadership the first piano was acquired for the church by the efforts of the Sunday church school with a special gift of seven hundred and fifty ($750) dollars to the church financial coffers. The Reverend William H. Harris was next to assume the reins of this historic church family. However, at the close of his administration, the

Mount Zion Baptist Church gave birth to its first daughter—the Calvary Missionary Baptist Church.

In 1919, the Reverend J. W. Brown accepted the call for pastoral leadership to stand as the shepherd and leader of this religious people. It was during the ministry of the Reverend J. W. Brown that the property at 2624 Papin Street was sold to the St. Louis Board of Education (the L'Overture School was erected on the site). Worship services were held temporarily in a building known as the Chouteau Hall, while efforts were underway to secure a new church facility that was completed in 1923. He served the congregation for six additional years, accomplishing many outstanding things for God, the church and the people.

In 1929, the Reverend W. Fields became the pastoral leader for this flock. Under his spiritual direction, the church made great progress in religious education. Moreover, the first study course was held at the Mount Zion Missionary Baptist Church—it was sponsored by our Sunday church school. The standardization of the Sunday church school resulted from this study.

Six years later, in 1935, the church moved into a dynamic new phase in its life, legacy and history. The Reverend Jeremiah M. Baker became the eleventh pastor of this historic church and became the first pastor to serve the congregation more than forty years—some forty-four years. During his administration, the mortgage for the old facility was liquidated and a new church facility was erected. The membership marched into the new church facility on Sunday, September 18, 1949. This joyous occasion was coupled with the laying of a new cornerstone. By 1957, with the help of God, he had eliminated all indebtedness of the church. To the Mount Zion Baptist Church family, Pastor Baker has been many things. He has been pastor, preacher, teacher, leader, counselor and spiritual advisor. Through the years, he has given appropriate advice to address appropriately each situation.

In September 1979, a whole new dimension of pastoral leadership and brilliance emerged with the calling of the Reverend Sammie Earl Jones. Building on a foundation of stability and security left by the founding fathers, the Mount Zion Missionary Baptist Church moved into a new decade with a new, young and talented spiritual giant. The Reverend Jones, a young and energetic minister, immediately caught the attention of the church's membership. His personality and charm were like a magnet drawing the young and the old to the service of Christ, the church and the kingdom of God.

From the very start of his ministry, his vision for Christ and the church was shared by the church leadership. His passion for the young provided and exciting new dimension to the Mount Zion ministries. His zeal for education and missions provided a whole new thrust and energy to the programs of the church. Before long, those members who had wandered to other congregations as "watch care souls" very quickly found their way back home. Focusing on biblical teaching, Pastor Jones has emphasized tithing as the principal method in which to support the work and ministry of the church.

Through his leadership and efforts, aided by the Holy Spirit, he has completely refinished the entire church, especially the renovation of the church basement. Under his leadership, the church has developed a Mobile Ministry with the purchase of two (2) buses. Much of these accomplishments have resulted because of the significant partnership between the Boards of Deacons, Trustees and Pastor Jones. Unlike many other congregations, these bodies share a common vision and purpose for the Mount Zion Baptist Church. That vision includes the construction of a new sanctuary, education center and gymnasium. Subsequently, this dynamic leader plans to build a family life center to address the needs of the whole man—his mind, body and soul.

In 1991, the Lord blessed Mount Zion with a building expansion program. In October 1992, Mount Zion Missionary Baptist Church marched triumphantly from 2765 LaSalle to 1444 S. Compton Avenue. Since entering our new multi-facility, new ministries have been born and again Mount Zion has become the focal point of the near south side community. With the aid of the deacons and the congregation, Mount Zion is raising the standards of Christian ethics through its 1,200 plus membership. As in the past, so with the present and the future! God has blessed us. God is blessing us. God will bless us!

SECOND BAPTIST CHURCH, JEFFERSON CITY, ORGANIZED 1859

In January 1859, Emanuel Cartwright, a minister, complying with an urgent request, came to Jefferson City to preach the funeral of Julia Brock. At that time, the colored people, who were slaves, were members of the First Baptist Church where they worshiped. Following the funeral of Julia Brock, Rev. Cartwright held a series of meetings that continued for several weeks, and under his preaching some 50 or 60 persons were converted.

In 1860, the white church members concluded that the slave Woodson was sent from St. Louis to take charge of this group. Because of the excitement of the time resulting from the agitation of slavery, the newly formed group was still not permitted to hold meetings unless some white members were present.

Growing restless under this restraint, the black congregation called a church meeting of their own and elected deacons and trustees. They held services for some time in a small frame building near the corner of Jefferson and Main Streets. Their first owned building was near the corner of Main and Monroe Streets. In 1865, this property was exchanged for the present site and christened the Second Baptist Church.

In April 1970, the building that housed the congregation since 1894 was demolished and under the pastorship of Rev. Harreld N. Nance, a contract was let to Trice Construction Company for a new structure to replace it. In September of this same year, Mrs. Estella B. Diggs, a longtime member of Second Baptist, gave to the church the Ashley Street house to be used as a parsonage. One month later, Mrs. Diggs passed away after a long and fruitful life of 98 years.

In 1972, Second Baptist Church called as its pastor Rev. David O. Shipley, Sr., who has concentrated on helping the church to remain a "community service" church. Some of the innovations made by the membership under the leadership of Rev. Shipley are: (1) The reorganization of Second Baptist into three areas referred to as the Equipping, Enabling and Outreach Ministries; (2) The special emphases which highlight the Advent Season, Prayer, Black History, and the Christian Family; and (3) New member and all-church orientation programs, climaxed by an all-day planning retreat.

Deed
Dated, April 28, 1869
Filed, July 15, 1869
Book V, page 480
Consideration: $5.00

Mark Thompson, Adam Opel, George H. Perkins, R. C. White and Adam Dierking, as Trustees of the First Baptist Church in the City of Jefferson appointed by the United Baptists of said church and the successors of Jason Harrison, P. H. Steenbergin, John Owens and Martha D. Noland, former Trustees as appears by a deed executed to them in year 1838 by J. H. Henderson and wife.

TO

Howard Barnes, Patrum Johnson, Archibald Drake and Benjamin Baunier, as trustees or another organization of the same branch of said church, in said city.

GRAND BARGAIN SELL AND CONVEY the following described lot containing a church building of brick, but reserving the bell, seats and furniture, to wit:

In lot number 720, corner of Monroe and Miller Streets.

TO HAVE AND TO HOLD the same to them and their successors in office and for covenanting as trustees as aforesaid, to warranty and to defend and protect them in the sole and free enjoyment of the same as a place of worship, from the lawful claim of all and every person or persons whatsoever.

Mark Thompson
Adam Opel
George H. Perkins
R. C. White
A. Dierking

STATE OF MISSOURI
County of Cole: Dated, May 4, 1869

Before Charles S. Wells, Justice, Cole County Court, personally came Mark Thompson, Adam Opel, George H. Perkins, R. C. White, and Adam Dierking, as trustees of the First Baptist Church in the City of Jefferson, in said county, for the United Baptist Church, and acknowledged that they executed the same and that it is their voluntary act and deed for the uses and purposes therein mentioned.

Deed
Dated, July 17, 1838
Filed, August 17, 1838
Book C, page 232
Consideration: $50.00

John Owens, P. H. Steenbergin, Reuben Garnett, Jason Harrison and Martha D. Noland

RECITES:

Whereas a church has been constituted in the City of Jefferson in the County of Cole by that denomination of Christians called and known by the name United Baptist which said church so constituted is called and known by the name of "The First Baptist Church of the United Baptist in the City of Jefferson" and whereas said church has agreed to erect a commodious brick house for a house of worship in said City; Now, there, for carrying into effect the object of said church the said party of the first part for and in consideration of the object aforesaid and for the sum of $5.00 to the said party of the first part in hand paid by the party of the second part the receipt whereof is hereby acknowledged have granted bargained and sold and by these presents do GRAND BARGAIN SELL AND CONVEY unto the said party of the second part and to their successors appointed by the church in trust church a certain lot of ground in the said city on which to erect said meeting house being:

Lot number 720 as described and known on the plat of said city, being an inlot situated in the corner of Monroe and Miller Street, near the little creek.

TO HAVE AND TO HOLD said lot with the appurtenances unto the said party of the second part and their successors in office for the sole and only use of the said United Baptist Church forever. And it is by these presents expressly understood that no changes whatever in said church shall change the intention of this deed but in case of the dissolution of the said Baptist church at the said city then the said lot and house with all its appurtenances are to belong to and owned by the United Baptist Church wherever they may be and the association in whose bounds the said house may be shall have full and entire control of the same until a church of the same faith and order shall be constituted therein and the said party of the first part do by these presents covenant with the said party of the second part for the purposes aforesaid the said premises against the claim of all and every person whomsoever forever to warranty and defend.

John H. Henderson
Martha C. Henderson

The following pastors have served us since Pastor Cartwright: Reverends Albert Nelson, Gabriel Gray, H. H. White, Atwater, Richard York, H. J. Burton, S. D. Lewis, J. S. Dorsey, John Goins, Dr. J. T. Gaston, E. L. Scruggs, L. D. Hardiman, A. Wendell Ross, C. B. Johnson, Edgar L. Reid, T. Maynard Preston, Harreld N. Nance, and David O. Shipley.

ST. FRANCIS BAPTIST TEMPLE, ST. JOSEPH, ORGANIZED 1861

During the territorial period, Missouri was called the "Catholic Land." There were about 12,000 inhabitants including Negro slaves in the territory, and no Evangelical Christian churches had been organized.

Laws had been passed by Roman Catholics that prohibited any religious services except the masses of priests of the Roman Church. The Dillon Creek Baptist Church was organized and a building erected near the Buchanan-Andrew County line earlier than 1844. This church stood on the river bluffs between St. Joseph and Amazonia on K Highway. This was the first building owned by the Baptist congregation. This small church gave up its life in the establishment of the first church organized by Baptists in St. Joseph, and was known as "an arm of the Dillon Creek Baptist Church of Christ." The membership was composed of whites with a small number of Negroes. The following are excerpts from the first record book of the First Baptist Church under the pastorate of the Rev. William Harrison Williams:

> On February 2, 1861, Brother Donald, committee chairman, visited the colored members and made the following verbal report: Order quiet; good feelings prevailed. Four candidates were recommended for baptism and were unanimous in recommending the ordination of the colored brother, a slave belonging to Brother R. W. Donald.

May 3, 1862, on motion, Adam, a colored brother, was licensed to exercise his gifts among our colored brethren and sisters.

December 5, 1863, Elder Dulin stated that the colored members of this church wished to withdraw and form an independent organization of their own. Brother Dulin then submitted the following resolutions: Resolved that a committee consisting of the pastor, deacon, treasurer and clerk of this church be appointed. A Council was convened to meet with the colored brethren and sisters on December 6, 1863, to constitute them into a church and to ordain their pastor. On motion, the above resolutions were unanimously approved.

December 6, Adam Demit was ordained a minister and the First African Baptist Church was organized. He and others were dismissed by letter from the First Baptist Church. First African Baptist Church was located on Francis Street between 10th and 11th Streets.

The church was incorporated in 1889, and the trustees were: Richard Montgomery, Rebecca Parr, Tobias Cole, Charles Williams, Henry Peterson and Gentry Carpenter. The Trustee Board became the governing body of the church, pertaining to all business affairs—real estate building, repairs, etc.

In the Fall of 1889, a new church building was erected under the pastorate of the Rev. E. L. Cohorn who served the church twenty-two and one-half years. The first pipe organ was purchased for $600 from Eshelman Music Company. Miss Lennie Montgomery was the organist, assisted by Nora Regons and Lillian Jackson Edwards.

The Rev. G. L. Prince was the third pastor called to serve the church. It was during his pastorate that Miss Lois Hartshorn became the organist, and served in this capacity more than 35 years. The Rev. Prince served the church until 1925 and was succeeded by the Rev. T. M. Bedford who served only one year.

The Rev. C. P. Morrow was called to the pastorate of Francis Street Baptist Church (formerly First African Baptist Church) and began his service on Mother's Day, 1926. Not long after his arrival, the city voted to annex the area now known as the Civic Center which included Francis Street Baptist Church.

In 1927, an agreement was signed to purchase the property of Matthew B. Fitzpatrick and wife, Helen, for the sum of $1,400. The property was located at 17th and Angelique Streets. That year the church was rebuilt and the Pastor, Rev. Morrow, preached the first sermon in the new church on Easter Sunday, April 8, 1928. It was at this time that the church was re-named Saint Francis Baptist Temple. The long and fruitful ministry of this beloved pastor came to an end at his death in 1949.

The Rev. Louis L. Sikes of Kansas City, Missouri, who had served the church during the illness of Rev. Morrow, was chosen to succeed him. The ties of this pastor and membership were warm and strong. Through his humble, kindly spirit, Rev. Sikes guided his people through a difficult period and resigned in 1951.

After a period of praying and seeking divine guidance, the congregation called as its shepherd the Rev. W. A. Sparks, a man greatly beloved by many people and widely known as a "Master Pastor." It was during his ministry that the church grew spiritually and materially. Rev. Sparks' first love was his church, and this was reflected through his love for its people—both young and old, and through his tireless efforts to strengthen its program. He built a sound financial program that is still being used today.

After eleven years of successful leadership, Rev. Sparks' health began to fail and he departed this life early Sunday morning, June 24, 1962. Advised by their beloved pastor, Dr. Sparks, the congregation asked the Rev. Norman S. Fiddmont, a young man still in seminary, to fill the pulpit during the pastor's illness. The congregation grew to love this young minister and his family, and at Dr. Sparks' death, invited him to serve as the interim pastor until such time as a call could be extended.

Being without a spiritual leader again, the members were called together under the leadership of the chairman of the board of deacons, Linn A. Hedge, for prayer and consultation. After much consideration, a call was extended to the Rev. Ernest E. Thompson of Jacksonville, Illinois, who accepted the call and began his ministry in December 1962.

It was during Rev. Thompson's pastorate that a prayer chapel was built in memory of two former pastors, Rev. C. P. Morrow and Rev. W. A. Sparks. Mrs. Sparks and Mrs. Ann Gamble (daughter of Rev. Morrow), both now deceased, were present and honored at the dedication of the Chapel.

Rev. Thompson was also responsible for the creation of a scholarship program, now named the E. E. Thompson Scholarship, whereby the senior high school student ranking highest, and a member of St. Francis, receives $100 per year toward his educational goal. The scholarship is given for four years to one student; and a new student is added each year. William A. Hedge was the first four-year recipient. Clarence F. Gray, Jr., Lenetta Banks and Howard Alton Brown are the current recipients.

The Centennial Year of the congregation, under the leadership of Rev. Thompson, brought many physical improvements and an increase in baptisms of children. Rev. Thompson resigned in August 1970. In December 1970, the congregation extended a unanimous call to the Rev. Norman S. Fiddmont who had served as interim pastor in

1962. In his acceptance speech at his Installation Service, Pastor Fiddmont spoke of his ambition to make the congregation a "Fellowship of Love." "Love" continued to be his theme during his three-year pastorate. He resigned September 15, 1974.

Immediately following the resignation of Rev. Fiddmont, Dr. Donald Cottner, a frequent speaker for the youth of the church, was invited to serve as interim pastor. He served in that capacity until the church extended him a call to become pastor. He accepted the call and began his pastorate February 9, 1975, and was installed on Easter Sunday, 1975.

SECOND BAPTIST CHURCH, INDEPENDENCE, ORGANIZED 1861

Second Baptist Church had its beginning in November of 1861, when a handful of men and women, some of whom were still in slavery, gathered in a one-room house in the 400 block of North Liberty Street. With the help of a white minister, the small group of "faithfulls" organized the church under its present name. Their first church was located at 117 East Farmer under the ministry of Rev. Clark Moore.

After Emancipation, the membership of the church grew so rapidly that plans were made to purchase a larger building. The new site was a former German church, located at 116 East White Oak. The former building was given to the State Baptist Convention of Missouri. That building served two purposes: (1) The first school house for Negroes, and (2) the establishment of the Western Baptist Seminary.

The pastors of Second Baptist have been Rev. Clark Moore, Rev. J. W. Gray, Rev. O. P. Simms, Rev. Harry Thomas, Rev. J. W. Chennoworth, Rev. James Jones, Rev. Hardin Smith, Rev. C. R. McDowell, Rev. J. W. Fitts, Rev. J. B. Winrow, Rev. J. W. Ballow, Rev. J. B. Beckham, Rev. W. D. Hill, Rev. Richard Harris, Rev. Charles H. Nicks, Rev. O. H. Oden, Rev. L. D. Revoal, Rev. W. A. Scott, Rev. James Alvin Meador, Rev. C. S. Scott, Rev. Elbert Cole, and Rev. H. D. Lewis. Rev. Nero is the current pastor.

SECOND BAPTIST CHURCH, KANSAS CITY, ORGANIZED 1863

The Second Baptist Church was organized as a mission by Reverend Clark Moore near the Missouri River at 4th Street. The mission was initially known as "Stragglers Camp." He was assisted by the Reverend Mr. Lovelace. They gave each convert the opportunity to express his choice of denominational affiliation—Baptist or Methodist. Two-thirds of the attending group decided to unite as Baptists, and one-third as Methodists. These two groups were then known and have since been known as Second Baptist and Allen Chapel A.M.E.

Reverend Clark Moore became the first pastor of the Second Baptist Church and his program was faithfully directed to the greatness of God's Kingdom. After a period of time, Reverend Moore was replaced by the Reverend Joseph Strothers of Which

Cloud, Kansas. Enthusiastic in his work and receiving the cooperation of the membership, the Reverend Joseph Strothers moved the church from its original site to a place farther south, known as Walnut Grove but later changed to Tenth and Charlotte Streets. Here, the congregation worshiped in a small frame building until the Reverend Joseph Strother resigned. A call was then extended to the Reverend Henry Robinson of Booneville, Missouri, who came as a very conscientious and constructive leader. He remained with Second Baptist for twenty-six years. The church began to grow more steadily under his leadership. The first brick unit was erected at Tenth and Charlotte Streets.

A few pioneers of this initial period were Rev. P. T. Tolliver, Sister Prudy Anderson, Brother Michael Jones, Sister Lucy Davis, Sister Sarah Anderson, Brother Joe Wiggins, Sister Nellie Payne, Brother Edward Ross, Sister Booker, Brother James Allen, the Overstreets, Hamiltons, Youngs, Harrises, Kennedys, Emersons, Turners, and Greens.

The congregation called the Reverend Samuel W. Bacote in March of 1895. He was known as an outstanding young minister from South Carolina with exceptional intellectual abilities and as an outstanding, remarkable church organizer. He accepted the call to Second Baptist Church in December of the same year. Immediately after taking over the duties as pastor, his program was outlined and progress was noted. A debt of $4,000 was paid off within a year's time, and within three (3) years, a superstructure valued at more than $100,000 was erected.

The departments of the church began in a very informal manner. Some of the personalities in charge of the beginning of music in the church were: Edward Ross, Eva Sweatman, Reatman, Rebecca Countee, and Duval and Clark. Several years later the music department was reorganized by Mrs. L. Jeanette Bacote, wife of Reverend S. W. Bacote, as an outgrowth of a choral group developed by Mrs. Velma B. Roy. Mrs. Bacote became director and organist and held this position with the Senior Choir until October 1956.

Mrs. Bacote was not only instrumental in Second Baptist becoming the first black Baptist church in Kansas City to have a robed choir, but she also was the first to present famed personalities to this community and to broadcast on the radio.

Always alert to new ideas and progressive steps, Reverend S. W. Bacote organized the first deaconess board of the church after returning from a convention. The three women appointed to this board were: Mrs. Mary E. Goins, Mrs. Ella Berry and Mrs. Susie Booker.

The church was ravaged by a fire of undetermined origins on May 15, 1926. Allen Chapel A.M.E. gladly opened their arms and offered their edifice for joint use. Later, arrangements were made at the YMCA and services were held there for approximately two years.

On October 7, 1928 Robert L. Evans, Contractor, completed the first unit of a structure built at the same location. The membership was led to this new edifice and remained there until June 15, 1941. Second Baptist holds claim to having organized the first Vacation Church or Bible School among Negro churches in 1932. The dream was fulfilled by the efforts of Mrs. Maude Gamble and her work through the Council of Churches. This was a very memorable event.

A mortgage group was organized in this period—the purpose: to help raise money to clear the mortgage on the church. This organization was later changed to the Non-Surpasser Club when the church moved to its new location at Tenth and Park Avenue. The work of this club then brought cultural entertainment to the church, under the direction of Mrs. Ida R. Jackson.

Progress and enthusiasm continued to surge, and through the personal efforts of Mr. J. A. Carpenter, a member of Central Baptist Church an appeal was made on behalf of the church and pastor to transfer their property at Tenth and Park, valued at more than $100,000, to the Second Baptist Church for the sum of $200. This appeal and transaction became a reality and on June 15, 1941 the congregation marched triumphantly into the structure at Tenth and Park Avenue. The financial transaction for that property was ably sponsored by Mrs. Lazetta Hanley who with members of her committee raised a total sum of $2,700.

By the latter part of the year 1945, Reverend Bacote had served the church fifty years and was entering into his fifty-first year of service with Second Baptist. Having given the best years of his life to the service of the Lord, he began to feel the need for retirement and to allow a younger man to step in and carry on his work.

The church and pastor made many contacts and held several interviews. After much consideration, a committee appointed by the church unanimously called the Reverend Emerson Ezekial Chappelle, who was the Pastor of the First Baptist Church in Suffolk, Virginia. Later in April 1946, Reverend Chappelle was en route to the city. His appointment was to have become effective within sixty to ninety days after arrival. He arrived on April 30, 1946 and was asked to fill the pulpit immediately on Sunday, May 2, 1946 following the unexpected passing of Dr. Samuel W. Bacote.

Pastor Chappelle initiated a "Homecoming Day," a Unified Budget supported by a "Faith Plan" that resulted in over $46,000 being place in savings. Additionally, a full-time secretary position was established, along with a voluntary recreation director. A parsonage and an expanded Christian education ministry was also established.

On April 30, 1946, David Shipley was licensed to preach by the Reverend E. E. Chappelle and was accepted as pastor of the junior church and acknowledged assistant to the pastor. Young and consecrated in his work, he became an inspiration to all associated with him. He was ordained in 1948. The spirit of this act later led to the issuing of licenses and ordination of two other young men who were ready and willing to let God use them. They were the Reverends Charles Briscoe and E. Burleson Stevenson. Recognition must also be given to Reverend William E. Singleton, who later became President of the Western Baptist Bible College. He served as the educational director of the church and assistant to the pastor.

The church continued to prosper under the leadership of Pastor Chappelle. A bus was purchased in 1956; additional property was purchased on Thirty-Ninth and Monroe in 1961; Pastor Chappelle wrote two books entitled *The Voice of God* and *Poetry, Wisdom, and Humor to Live By* in 1963. The Chappelle's donated a parcel of land in Holliday, Kansas to the church in 1964. This property was later used as a retreat area for older members and a recreational area for the youth. The entire church's indebtedness was cleared August 29, 1965. This occasion was celebrated in grand fashion.

SECOND MISSIONARY BAPTIST CHURCH, LEXINGTON, ORGANIZED 1865

The Second Baptist Church was organized on May 10, 1865 by the Rev. Robert Dodd. During his pastorate, the congregation bought a lot at the extreme end of Eighth Street, which is now the northwest corner of Eighth and Branch Streets. The membership built a frame building in which the congregation worshiped for six or seven years. Other pastors who followed Rev. Dodd were the Reverends Roberson, Jordan Williams and Hardin Smith.

It was during Rev. Smith's pastorate in 1873 that the present location at 1201 Main Street, which was once a Christian church, was purchased. The Christian church established a church on the corners of Poplar and North or Main Streets at a cost of about $4,000.

The History of Lafayette County stated that "it was sold to the Colored Baptists in 1873 or 1874." However, an abstract shows that the Christian church was sold on June 14, 1873. Other pastors who followed Rev. Smith were the Reverends Pondexter, Lane, Sims, Howard, and J. H. Holmesly.

It was under Rev. Holmesly's pastorate in 1893 that the building was remodeled to its present structural appearance. To this day, there have been several additions to the main structure. Other pastors succeeding Rev. Holmesly were Reverends Richardson, Howell, Norris, Chinn, R. W. Williams, Glenn, Henderson, Bratton, and H. C. Haynes.

Rev. Haynes served as pastor at Second Baptist Church from March 1930 to August 1957, serving faithfully for 27 years. Other pastors have been the Rev. J. B. Randolph, Rev. H. I. Thomas, Rev. Robert Dabney, Rev. Leroy Cunningham, Rev. C. E. Leach, and Rev. Gary Jones. Our current pastor, the Rev. Everett W. Hannon, Jr., has served us faithfully for the past eleven years.

SECOND MISSIONARY BAPTIST CHURCH, COLUMBIA, ORGANIZED 1866

This chronicle describes the love, blood, sweat and tears willingly given by our ancestors in the building of Second Missionary Baptist Church. While this history is not exhaustive of all contributions to the building, it represents a memorial to those who helped build Second Missionary Baptist Church. The next paragraphs unfold the leadership of Christians and the giving of tithes and offerings that brought forth Second Missionary Baptist Church on Fourth and Broadway in Columbia, Missouri.

Second Missionary Baptist Church, originally named Broadway Baptist Church, was organized in July 1866 by Father William P. Brooks and nine African Americans from Kansas City, Missouri and from First Baptist Church in Columbia (formerly Smithtown), Missouri.

Initially, and for only a short time, this first African American Baptist church was organized in the home of John Lang, Sr., a prominent African American butcher. Until 1873, worship service was in the colored, one room, school building on Third and Ash; Cummings Academy. African American Methodists and Baptists held services there on alternate Sundays.

In March 1873, under the untiring leadership of Elder Henry Williams (1872-1873), the first church building was erected at Fifth Street, approximately one-third of a block south of Broadway. The cost of the structure was $2,500.

By about 1890, the debt on the church building had been paid-in-full. The pastors' leadership up to the time the mortgage was paid-in-full included Reverends E. Wildman, Barton Hilman, Jacob Dulin, Daniel Sawyer, J. H. Homesley, Edward Stewart and Amos Johnson.

In 1884, Rev. Amos Johnson spearheaded the fundraising needed to purchase the property on Fourth and Broadway where we are currently located. The foundation as originally laid was never used. Rev. Johnson had plans for a more "commodious and modern edifice." Finally, in 1984, the foundation was enlarged and the cornerstone of the current building was laid. John Lang donated the lot and Judge John Steward lent the church $4,000 to erect the building. However, Rev. Amos Johnson, called to pastor for the second time, died before completion of the building. Rev. T. L. Smith then assumed the responsibility of leading the church to the completion of the building.

Rev. Smith oversaw the installation of golden oak pews and the decorative art glass windows, most of which were financed by members of the church in memory of friends. For more than twenty years, the small congregation struggled to pay on the debt. However, in about 1908, the Lord sent Rev. T. T. Ward (1908-1912), a financial wizard, to lead the congregation in paying off the mortgage within four years. They were so happy that they had a mortgage-burning party. HALLELUJAH!

Rev. J. Lyle Caston (1920-1924) established a fund for the erection of an annex to the church for purposes of Sunday school classes and other activities. Church members began to murmmer and believed that they could not raise adequate funds to build an annex, so they purchased a residence for the minister. The five-room cottage, located at North Fifth Street, was first occupied by Rev. W. D. Hill.

Twenty years later, Rev. Ernest S. Reed returned as the pastor for ten years and grew the membership to about 465. He led in redecorating the church's interior and improving the lighting system.

By the 1930s, under the pastoral leadership of Rev. J. Lyle Caston (1920-1923) and Rev. W. D. Hill (1923-1931), an addition to the building and the formation of plans for an annex commenced. However, in 1947 under the direction of Rev. N. P. Wilson (1945-1957), these plans were terminated to build a choir room and two rest rooms on the northeast corner of the church.

Details on renovations of the church after the 1930s are somewhat sketchy, but following is some evidence that I was able to find. Under the leadership of Rev. J. O. Bass (1960-1962), the long-awaited ground breaking ceremony for the annex occurred. Rev. D. Daniel Clater (1963-1968) witnessed the completion of the building of the church annex. Rev. Jewell D. Jones (1974-1980) worked with the congregation for the purchase of a new organ that was placed in the sanctuary, and the renovation of the pastor's study.

In September 1989, a major church renovation began under the leadership of Rev. Clanton Dawson, Jr. (1986-1994).

With the determination of Deacon Lonnie Ratliff, the pulpit area of the sanctuary, baptismal pool, choir loft, adjoining rooms and basement area were gutted to construct a new pulpit, baptismal pool, choir stand, seating area, dressing rooms (2) and an additional rest room have been added and improved. By 1995, under the leadership of Interim Pastor Rev. Devoy Hill, handicap ramps and a new air conditioner were installed, and ceiling fans and carpet were replaced in the sanctuary.

We are indebted to God for these ministers, deacons, trustees, church members and friends that contributed to the building of Second Missionary Baptist Church. God has ingratiated us with a spirit-filled beautiful red and white church home. We should continue to preserve and enhance this church home for future generations wanting to praise God. One of our missions should be to make this a spiritual sanctuary where all are welcome to praise the Almighty God. Let us be obedient to God and follow the example of our ancestors by giving our tithes and offerings so that our children and grandchildren can have a beautiful church in which to worship.

MOUNT NEBO BAPTIST CHURCH, ROCHEPORT, ORGANIZED 1866

The Mt. Nebo Baptist Church was organized in 1866 at Rocheport, Missouri by Rev. Ed Burnam. The first meeting house was in a building known as the Blue House. The windows facing the front are of stained glass, donated by Brother Nathaniel Wilhite, in honor of his mother. The building was dedicated in 1910. Modernization included the installation of electricity, carpeting, installation of a pool and an organ.

The pastors succeeding Rev. Burnam are as follows: Rev. Ruben Nelson, Rev. Robert Williams, Rev. C. C. Calhoun, Rev. A. W. Tarve, Rev. Capt. Miller, Rev. Fred Watts, Rev. Ed Wilson, Rev. Jesse Washington, Rev. Helm, Rev. O. F. Nelson, Rev. Robert Woods and Rev. Horace Hopkins, the present pastor.

LOG PROVIDENCE BAPTIST CHURCH, COLUMBIA, ORGANIZED 1866

The Log Providence Baptist Church, near Columbia, Missouri was organized in 1866, as an outgrowth of the New Salem Baptist Church (White). After the signing of the Emancipation Proclamation, the New Salem Baptist Church decided to separate from its Negro brethren.

In February 1866, George Hubbard proposed the following resolution, "Whereas we believe it to be organized as a separate body, therefore, resolved that we thereby detach them from us and enroll them on a separate church book, thus organizing them into an African church of New Salem." The resolution was accepted and the colored brothers and sisters were organized into a church of their own. The first building was built of logs on property purchased from Eli Bass in 1866.

The first membership was comprised of thirty-two members. In 1925, under the pastorate of Rev. Grant Hayes, a new frame church was built. In 1911, a four-room parsonage was built by Deacon William Pitts.

With the exodus of members from the community, the parsonage was sold because the remaining members of the community did not feel able to support a full-time pastor.

Numerous improvements have been added over the years, including a church bus, chorus robes, new pews, a piano, church furniture and office equipment.

The following is a list of the pastors of Log Providence in order of their terms of service: Reverends Ed Burnam, Robert Adkinson, Glasgow, E. H. Buekner, Tasley, W. Panky, J. W. Young, Giant Hayes, Rheuben Nelson, John Ellis, James Collins, W. Coleman, H. J. Robinson, P. H. Gilmore, C. T. Rucker, C. J. Davis, W. H. Vaughn, Frank Williams, Robert L. Parker, William A. Givens. The current pastor is Rev. David Ballinger.

First Baptist Church, Webster Groves, Organized 1866

First Baptist Church was established November 3, 1866 on Shady Avenue, with nineteen members. This church was organized before there was a public school. The white frame building bearing the name of Webster Groves School was finished in 1868. It is interesting to note that the first census revealed 225 white children enrolled and 30 Negro children. When the Negro children were separated from the white, First Baptist Church became the school for Negroes.

The growth of the church was not rapid but consistent through the years. The church had organized many auxiliaries that are still functioning today. By 1919, the building was dilapidated and no longer adequate for a strong healthy church. On October 15, 1923, the present site was purchased for the church. Due to an increase in membership, by 1952, a larger building was needed. The new sanctuary was completed on May 17, 1955. In 1956 and 1957, the church continued to grow spiritually, financially and visibly. In 1964, through the sale of Gold Seal Bonds, the church partially self-financed a second unit over Fellowship Hall. The mortgage on the church building was ceremoniously burned on March 17, 1964.

Some of the past pastors were Reverends Simon, Lott, Burton, Cartwright, Carruthers, Lyles, Langford, Thompson, Cole, Purnell, E. J. Buckner, R. E. Lee, J. L. Cohron, J. J. Blaskburn, W. D. Thompson, Jr., J. A. Hill, and Dr. Neal J. Haynes.

Calvary Baptist Church, Fulton, Organized 1866

As an outgrowth of a business conference of the First Baptist Church held on the second Saturday of 1866, the Second Baptist Church was organized. Brother Adam Renfro was the organizer and served as pastor for a number of years. For a period of time, services were held in the basement of the white Free Will Baptist Church, which was located on Fifth Street. Later, the Ironside Baptist Church on Sixth and Bluff Streets was purchased, but later torn down and a new building was erected. The ground for the new church building was given by Nores Bradford.

The founders of the church were Ben McCracken, Ben Black, Clark Shy, Robert Kibby, Henry Kibby, William Nelson, Glen Glover, Lazarus Parker, Edward Kibby, Calvin McMahan, John Kibby, Harry Bradford, Wilson Butler, Thomas Boyd, Harry Renfro and Rev. Demer Washington and their wives.

The pastors at Calvary Baptist included Rev. W. H. Young, Rev. L. W. Harris, Rev. A. W. Ross, Rev. E. Buckner, Rev. L. R. Johnson, Rev. K. C. Caston, Rev. W. S. Woolridge, Rev. R. L. Lillard, Rev. Scott, Rev. M. D. Johnson, Rev. H. F. Dean, Rev. J. B. Bates, and Rev. M. L. Piggee. The current pastor is Rev. C. D. Dawkins.

Second Baptist Church, Moberly, Organized 1867

The work of the Second Baptist Church began in the spring of 1867 in Wallace McCampell's pasture. Most meeting were held in the residences of the various members. In the spring of 1867, the church was not yet officially organized. The early organizers had no name for their church; they only knew that it was to be a Baptist church. In May 1867, Second Baptist Church was organized and an old blacksmith shop was purchased to hold meetings. The first minister of the church was Rev. Thomas Clark.

Having recognized the need for religious instruction, a church school (the Sabbath school) was organized. The people of the church wanted a permanent place for their worship; and therefore purchased two lots on West Rollins with the intention to build. Due to insufficient funds, the church was unable to build. The church later purchased a lot on Fifth Street; the site on which the church is currently located.

Under the leadership of Rev. Bates, the church split. He took most of the older members and started a new church only two blocks away from the original. That church was named the Pilgrim Rest Baptist Church.

Despite the split, Second Baptist continued to prosper. In September and October 1908, Orders of Incorporation were filed in Randolph County and certified by the state of Missouri. Some of the new improvements included the purchase of a new organ, two new furnaces, repairs were made on the church and parsonage, insurance on all church property and an increase in salary for all church employees.

Second Baptist Church, Mexico, Organized 1867

The Second Baptist Church was organized in 1867 under the leadership of Richard Ball and a few elderly men and women. Three different structures have been built on different sites. The latter structure was located at 609 E. Holt Street until March 3, 1868.

In 1951, under the pastorate of Rev. C. E. Richards (1934—August 1966), building plans for a new church were begun. The plans were completed from October 1966 to December 1969, under the pastorate of Rev. I. C. Peay, Jr. The groundbreaking ceremony was held on July 10, 1967, and the dedication service on March 3, 1968.

The present structure at Breckenridge and Union Streets is beautiful, spacious and modern with a seating capacity of 400. Mortgage Burning Day was observed on November 11, 1973. The present pastor, Rev. William Duncan, assumed his duties in June 1970.

WASHINGTON AVENUE BAPTIST CHURCH, SPRINGFIELD, ORGANIZED 1867

The Washington Avenue Baptist Church was organized in 1867, and was said to be the "Mother Church" of several different organizations in the Southwest Baptist Association. The church was originally located in a building at the southeast corner of the Public Square.

In 1872, in connection with the Cumberland Presbyterians, the members of the church erected a frame structure at the corner of Benton Avenue and Water Streets. In 1884, the church moved into a new brick building on the west side of Washington Avenue. Some of the earlier pastors of the church since 1889 were Rev. A. B. Franklin, Rev. Brown, Rev. Dorch, Rev. Bowey, Rev. Stewart, Rev. Miller, Rev. Dorsey, Rev. Holmes, Rev. Young, Rev. Petty, Rev. Curtis, Rev. Goins, Rev. Wilson, Rev. J. S. Dorsey, Rev. A. B. Simmons, Rev. M. D. Johnson, Rev. O. B. Ware, Rev. R. C. Campbell, Rev. Johnson, Rev. Pitts, and Rev. Rufus A. Walker.

During the pastorate of Rev. A. B. Simmons, from 1929 to 1938, the State Convention met here in 1932, and needed repairs were made on the church and parsonage.

During the administration of Rev. M. D. Johnson (1938-1946), considerable improvements were made, such as a dining room in the basement, a new roof and ceiling, and new hardwood floors added. The mortgage was also burned during his pastorate.

During the pastorate of Rev. O. B. Ware (1946-1950), a new parsonage was built, rest rooms added, the church organ redecorated and other needed repairs made. Rev. R. A. Walker, came to Washington Avenue Baptist Church in May 1974. The church was remodeled and a new cooling and heating system was installed. Pastor Walker was very active in the State Convention and served as Vice Moderator of the Southwest Baptist District Association.

Pastor Walker was followed by Reverends, Melvin Grimes and Rufus Kelly. Each of these pastors continued the tradition of serving faithfuly in the District as Deans of the Congress of Christian Education and the state convention. The Annex mortgage was liquidated during the pastorate of Pastor Kelly.

Pastor Kelly was succeeded by Dr. Maurice Pate. The congregation has moved into a new facility and is experiencing phenomenal growth spiritually and numerically. The former facility has been preserved as a historical site on the campus of Drury University, one block from its former location. To God be the glory for the great things He has done!

PLEASANT HILL BAPTIST CHURCH, POPLAR BLUFF, ORGANIZED 1875

In the early part of the year 1875, a group of baptized believers, under the leadership of the late Rev. J. H. Hunt, met at the home of Brother and Sister Tom Harris and organized the Pleasant Hill Baptist Church.

Between 1875 and 1975, there have been four buildings. The membership outgrew the first, the next two were destroyed by fire. The fourth, which we now worship in, was built in 1917.

There have been twenty-one ministers down through the years. They were as follows: Reverends J. H. Hunt, P. H. Parks, T. H. Rankins, W. H. Stoves, L. E. Avant, L. W. White, H. I. Hill, G. C. Chinn, A. L. Murrel, H. F. Johnson, W. M. Reeves, F. D. McKia, R. C. Hunley, F. M. Brooks, G. E. Wright, H. C. Manscol, C. R. Carrington, L. Austin, S. D. Betts, G. W. Broughton, S. Ellis, and C. Pride. There have also been three assistant ministers that have served during the years: Rev. C. Turner, Rev. Morris, and Rev. J. J. Bounds.

During the pastorate of Rev. C. Pride, a bus, parsonage, audio equipment and church steeple were purchased. The library was added, the lower level was remodeled, the Martin Luther King, Jr. Community program was observed and many souls were won.

The present pastor, Rev. Quincy Keeble, Sr., began his leadership in April of 1988. During his administration, the church has added an audio room, a baptistery, women's and men's rest rooms and finance room, eight classrooms, storage space and the Pastor's and Secretary's offices.

The choir room and the pastor's study were remodeled and the sanctuary was re-carpeted. The landscaping was also done. The kitchen was restored and cabinets installed. Various major purchases have been made or donated: organ, piano, copier, computer, microwave, television and freezer.

Several observances and programs have been organized under Rev. Keeble's leadership, namely Arts & Crafts Exhibit and Youth Essay Contest; Bessie V. Cheeks Day & Scholarship Fund; Youth of the Month Recognition; Brotherhood's Wild Game Feast and WMU's Tea and Salad Supper and Bazaar. Pleasant Hill has not only survived, but has prospered and grown both spiritually and financially. God's triumphant church has been forging forward through the years. Pleasant Hill has a rich heritage of warriors that have stood the test of time regardless of the situations.

As we reflect on both the material and spiritual accomplishments, it is apparent that God has truly blessed this congregation. As we reminisce on the number of souls baptized, marriages and the babies blessed, we realize that if it had not been for the Lord on our side, we would not be able to stand VICTORIOUSLY.

SECOND BAPTIST CHURCH, NEOSHO, ORGANIZED 1876

Court records show that a merger and incorporation was made between Second Baptist and Pleasant Hill Baptist, and was approved March 19, 1876, both churches being organized prior to this time. Those signing the petition for the incorporation were: Phillip Givens, Pastor, Stephen S. Frost (who was later called to pastor and was the first pastor of the Washington Avenue Baptist Church in Springfield, MO). We do know that around 1870 when George Washington Carver came to Neosho, Stephen Frost was his first teacher. Others signing the papers were Samuel Perry, Peter Graves, Edwin Martin, James Dale and eight others.

Pleasant Hill was originally located north of Neosho, near Pleasant Hill Cemetery. Three lots were purchased from John and Emma Shatliffin in August 1876 for the sum of $200. The lots are the present location of the church. A one-story frame structure was built by members at this site that was later destroyed. On November 10, 1896, $500.00 was borrowed from the American Baptist Home Mission Board. This money was used to build the present brick structure. J. M. Clendenon was serving as church clerk at this time. Mrs. Della White, Misses Ora and Ophelia Baker were present at the dedication of the new church building.

There has been a number of pastors since the wonderful pastoral work provided by Reverend Givens. The pastors have been Reverends Palmer, Curtis, Green, Embry, Dudley, O. D. Bond, Rice, Kin Sam Smith (who later organized the Mount Eagle Baptist Church in Springfield) Reverends Brown, L. T. Thompson, Zachariah Johnson, W. E. Burns, Platt Ransburg, Parker, M. G. Edmondson, Mack McConnell.

Other ministers were V. L. Roy Liburd, Elwood Johnson, and Titus Johnson. The following ministers served as Assistant or Interim Pastor: Reverends Leo Barbee, Charles Askew and Maurice Reaves.

Reverend Larry C. Anderson is the current pastor serving over six years. On January 4, 1996, Second Baptist was officially entered into the National Register of Historic Places. This was the first structure in the city of Neosho to be accepted as an historic site by the Keeper of the Registry. The Second Baptist structure was the fourth structure in

Newton County to be listed in the National Registry. The other three are Jolly Mill, The Ritchey Mansion in Newtonia and the George Washington Carver National Monument. Second Baptist was one of the recipients of the 1998 Neosho Heritage Awards, presented May 17, 1998, by the Neosho Historic Preservation Committee. Second Baptist's historic Victorian Gothic brick church stands tall as a center for all to worship in the community.

Ward Memorial Baptist Church, Sedalia, Organized between 1876-1878

Between 1876 and 1878, Rev. Mitchell of East St. Louis, Illinois came to Sedalia, and with the help of determined Christians organized the Morgan Street Baptist Church. The first place of worship was a small house located on East Morgan Street. As membership grew, the need for a new sanctuary was realized. The new sanctuary was built, but after a few years, it was destroyed by fire.

Rev. J. H. Downey became pastor upon the resignation of Rev. Mitchell. In 1912, Rev. T. T. Ward became pastor and began to search for a location upon which to build a new church. The present sanctuary was designed and built under the leadership of Rev. Ward. He was so beloved by the members of the church that upon his death, the church was renamed in his honor.

In 1920, Rev. A. Toss Brent became pastor of Ward Memorial Baptist Church. The new structure was completed under his pastorate, but before one service could be held, fire destroyed all but the four walls. With the diligence of the pastor and members, work was completed within a few months and the new building was ready for use.

Some of the pastors to follow Rev. Brent included: Rev. Goings, the State Missionary, Rev. Hill, Rev. B. T. McMiller, Rev. Hunter, Rev. L. D. Hardiman, Rev. J. E. Erickson and Rev. Robert L. Parker. Under the leadership of Rev. L. D. Hardiman, the mortgage on the church was paid-in-full.

Wood Street Baptist Church, Lebanon, Organized 1879

Prior to December 1879, the Wood Street Baptist Church was founded in Lebanon, as the First Baptist Church (Colored). The exact date is unknown. On January 10, 1884, the church purchased its present site from John S. Lingsweiler and his wife, Emma Lingsweiler.

In June 1953, the present sanctuary was completed under the pastorate of the late Rev. C. E. K. Wright. From May 1958 to October 1965, many additions, improvements and renovations took place under the pastorate of Rev. Grant Thomas. With Rev. Earl C. Gilbert as pastor, the church remodeled the sanctuary and installed carpet in 1968. The outside of the front of the church was remodeled in the fall of 1972 under the leadership of Rev. Harry F. Givens. The present pastor is Reverend Charles Neal.

PLEASANT GREEN BAPTIST CHURCH, KANSAS CITY, ORGANIZED 1881

The Pleasant Green Baptist Church was organized on October 10, 1881 by the Reverend John Morgan. Its first meeting was conducted in the basement of what was known as the "Kansas City Fruit Store," at the corner of 11th and Main Street. The church prospered and soon quickly outgrew its quarters.

On the first Sunday in March 1882, by permission, the congregation moved from the fruit store basement to the Second Street Courthouse and held services in one of the criminal court rooms. The congregation conducted its first Baptismal Service at 3:30 p.m. on the riverbank at the foot of Grand Avenue where twelve converts were baptized.

The congregation moved to an old frame building that stood in an alley between Forest and Tracy Avenues, fronting what was known as Belvider Street during the spring of 1886. It was here that the church became a corporation and the following persons were recorded as charter members. (It is well to note that they were all males. Women were not allowed to sign legal documents at this time.) Signatures were Aaron William, James Allen, James H. Marshall (trustee), Squire Smith, Henry Holly, Charlie Lane, Scott Barber, Lewis Franklin, James R. Allen, Abraham Brown, Edward Wheeler, Henry Combs, Isaac Smith, Tobias Murphy, Napoleon Railey, John Scroggins, Eliza Frye, Richard Harris, David Lewis, Charley Chapman, George Dennie, William Elmore, W. H. Collins, W. M. Claybrooks, James Pollard, C. H. Pendleton, H. Neal, Straughter Morgan, P. Holly, Beverly Robinson, Henry Farmer, William Kiser, Johnnie Hale, E. L. Bigly, Robert Leonard, William Ridley, Richard Oliver, J. B. Ingraham, Thomas White, William Nevien, Stephen Hingston, Simon Lee, J. Bowler, Charley Holiday, Frank Powell, Dabney Lightfoot and Milo Strong, Clerk of the Church.

The church grew numerically and spiritually, but in the summer of 1898, Reverend Morgan passed and was laid to rest in the Union Cemetery of Kansas City, Missouri.

Reverend William Alford of Kansas was called after Pastor Morgan's death. His stay was short. He was followed by Reverends Emmanuel M. Wilson and G. W. Burdette.

Reverend James Booker of Memphis, Tennessee was the next minister to receive a call from Pleasant Green. He reluctantly resigned as pastor of the Salem Baptist Church in Memphis to accept the call. This man of God came with a vision, and the first real effort of the church under his leadership was to find an attractive site. A site was purchased at 595 Tracy Avenue and plans were made to erect a building at the cost of $7,000. The pastor succeeded in getting a gift of $800 from the Carnegie Organ Fund and the church raised $800 and purchased a pipe organ for $1600 factory price. Up to this time, no other Negro church had such an organ.

During the church's ten years at 595 Tracy Avenue, the church's membership began to dwindle due to the relocation of our membership. The pastor began to consider a new location. This far-sighted trait of his proved to be just the thing that was needed. The church left the north end of town and moved to 14th and Michigan Avenue. Many members fought against the move. However, the move took place with the purchase of the Seventh Day Adventist Church for a sum of $10,000.

Pastor Booker was very active in the District and State work. He helped to organize New Era District along with Reverend S. W. Bacote and J. W. Wilson. Pleasant Green was the first Negro church to have daily Vacation Bible Schools. The Deaconess School, now known as the National Training School, conducted the first school. Pleasant Green was also the first church to conduct training schools for workers.

Reverend Booker organized the first Sunday School State Convention in Hannibal, Missouri and was its first president until the two were combined as Sunday School and B.T.U. Congress. The first Annual Session was held at Pleasant Green. Reverend Booker resigned as pastor in 1928 to accept a smaller charge.

Reverend Booker was succeeded by the Reverend J. W. Underwood from Keokuk, Iowa. He was a native of Marion, Alabama and went to school at Selma University. His education was continued at Virginia Union University in Richmond, Virginia.

The church grew during his administration. He reorganized many of the church's ministries. He taught the congregation about the importance of tithing. Southern Baptist literature was also introduced.

He led the church to relocate to 2621 Benton Blvd. and purchased the Latter Day Saints' facility that was located there for $37,000. Our stay there was short due to the growth that we were experiencing. The church purchased the First Lutheran Church at a cost of $115,000 in 1956. We marched into the building on October 1956. Pastor Underwood served the church a total of twenty-nine years. Reverend Underwood was succeeded by the Reverend W. A. Scott of Ft. Scott, Kansas in 1938. He remained with the church until he entered the military as a chaplain during World War II.

Reverend Gerald H. Schiele, a native of Frogmore, Louisiana, was called to succeed Reverend Underwood whose health had begun to fail. He had been a member of Pleasant Green since 1941. He graduated from Western Bible College and Central Theological Seminary.

Prairie Grove Baptist Church, Tipton, Organized 1888

During the period of slavery, some slaves learned to reverence God and depend on Him. For the most part, the slaves in this area were well treated, although there were some few exceptions. A few were sold south and left their families here. One was hanged in this county for killing his master. Many slaves attended church with their masters and enjoyed a degree of religious freedom.

Most of the slaves here came into this region with their owners from Virginia, the Carolinas, and Kentucky and settled in the region round Clarksburg, Vermont, Round Hill and the present day Tipton area.

After freedom, these Christian slaves assembled for worship, coming from miles around, riding in wagons, riding on horseback and some even walking. A central assembly place was a grove of trees in what is now northeast Tipton. Here they would spread their dinners, sing, pray and exhort one another. This spot later became the site of the original Prairie Grove Baptist Church.

The original site of one acre was given by Mr. William Tipton Seely, the founder of Tipton, Missouri. Some families in the founding of the church were the Howards, Shackelfords, Owens, Maupins, and a few years later, Davis, Redmon, Hunter, and Shellcrays joined.

There have been three building sites. The first was in the extreme northeast corner of Tipton, the second about 30 feet west of the present site on Howard Street. The reasons for the new locations were, first to be near the center of Negro population, and second the need for a church basement.

Two efforts have been made to provide a parsonage for our pastors, first a building was purchased in the south part of town for $450 and moved west of the church. Second, after this building became worn, it was torn down and sold. The proceeds made a portion of the purchase price of the old Harrison School building, which sold for $1,000.

During the 100 years, we have had twenty (20) pastors; namely, the Reverends Cheneworth, Diggs, Cushon, Nelson, Wiggins, Veulman, Saunders, Burton, Mudd, Ratliff, Knott, Hardiman, Halley, Pollard, Harris, Steward, Jacobs, Watts, Cooper and in 1944 our present pastor Rev. N. H. Coleman.

Three of our pastors have been moderators of the Central District Association. They were Rev. H. J. Burton, Rev. L. D. Hardiman and Rev. G. W. Watts (History compiled by Galveston Lee Roy Shipley, oldest member in church—1966; sources: History of Moniteau County, church records 1888-1891, Laura Johnson—oldest Negro woman in Tipton; and Marion Howard).

Skylight Baptist Church, Kansas City, Organized 1891

In 1891, a few members of the Pleasant Green Baptist Church withdrew from the church and met together in a storeroom on the north side of Independence Avenue and organized the Emmanuel Baptist Church. Rev. R. T. Hoffman was chosen as pastor. Early in 1893, the congregation moved to a store building at Fifth and Charlotte Streets. In 1894, Rev. Counter became the shepherd of the flock. By July 1896, the membership had prospered to such an extent that a new building was necessary to hold the congregation. A new lot was acquired at Sixth and Charlotte Streets for the construction of a new edifice. Upon the erection of the new building, the name was changed to Pilgrim Baptist Church. Rev. J. W. Hurse became the pastor, but the church split and a large percentage of the members organized the St. Stephen's Baptist Church.

In 1912, Rev. C. C. Calloway became the pastor of Pilgrim Baptist Church, under Pastor Woodland in 1929. Under his leadership, the church moved to its temporary quarters in the Brinks building at 1001 Michigan, until the new building was completed at 1003 Michigan. The name was subsequently changed to Skylight Baptist Church. In December 1957, the church moved to its present location at 1912 Linwood Blvd.

In 1972, Rev. Alton Metcalf was appointed to serve as assistant pastor, due to the illness of Pastor Wilson. On January 6, 1974, Rev. Wilson was compelled to resign, due to illness, after serving for 45 years. In June 1974, Rev. T. L. Arnick became the pastor of Skylight Baptist Church.

Galilee Baptist Church, St. Louis, Organized 1898

In June 1898, an evangelist known as Sin Killing Griffin, along with Reverend Nicholas and Reverend John Williams, organized a church in a small house at 609 S. Second Street just three blocks from the historic Mississippi River. Those present were Sisters Jane N. Buckner, Amanda Littles, Malinda Ellis and Sallie Moss. The church was named "Galilee Baptist Church" by Reverend Griffin. Reverend John Williams was the first pastor of the church. The deacons were : Brothers Wade Jones, Douglas Mills, Gable Coleman and William Littles. Other members included Sisters Sarah Anderson, Amanda Littles, Malinda Ellis and Jane N. Buckner.

For a more convenient place to worship, the church moved from its original location to 227 Plum Street. A few months later, there was a need to move to a larger place to worship. This building was located at 613 S. 6th Street. In 1900, Reverend E. G. Gosby was called to pastor the church. During his administration, the church grew to 300 in membership making it necessary to move to another location, 710 S. 6th Street.

Deacons added to the Board were Brothers White, John Gibson, Tom Bailey, Sam Mosley, Conico Tucker and Mack Tucker. Reverend Smith followed Reverend Gosby as pastor, but for a short time.

Continuous growth necessitated the church's moving again in October of 1907. We moved to 2802 Adams Street, later know as Spruce Street, to a building that was partially brick and frame. The building was built by Reverend Wright. Reverend Powell from Carondelet preached the Dedicatory Sermon. Pastor Gosby's first sermon in the facility was entitled " Beware You Don't Forget the Lord."

Reverend Malachi Owens, D.D., a product of Arkansas Baptist Church School, came to pastor Galilee from Cape Girardeau, Missouri in February of 1912. The church membership had dwindled to 46 with an indebtedness of $15,000. Having only the ground floor for worship, he and his faithful few members made many new additions to the church. A second floor auditorium, choir stand and balcony were built. Several auxiliaries were added to the church and the church's indebtedness was paid off. Pastor Owens remained with the congregation for thirty-eight years. He led the congregation into the First Church of the Nazarene on Delmar Street at the close of 1946. The actual move took place on April 16, 1947. The first annual day celebrated there was conducted by the ushers. Pastor Owens departed this life on April 9, 1952 following and extended illness.

The Reverends Earl E. Nance and Andrew Taylor served the church; the church called the Reverend Isaac Charles Peay, Sr. He accepted the call the third Wednesday night in December 1953. He delivered his first sermon as pastor on the first Sunday in January 1954.

Pastor Peay served Galilee faithfully for thirty-seven years. He was seen as a dynamic visionary who had a passion for ministry. During his tenure, a Christian education facility was built and named after him. He organized and supervised a comprehensive ministry for all age groups. He was responsible for the acquisition of property located at Pendleton and Washington for parking. A bus ministry was instituted with the purchase of two maxi buses. He organized a Race Relations Day service that brought in congregations of other ethnicities. We conducted a radio ministry utilizing the services of KATZ, WGNU and KIRL on Sunday evenings. Pastor Peay was known locally and nationally as an outstanding preacher, lecturer, writer and pastor. He retired from the active pastoral ministry on August 11, 1991. He continued to serve this congregation as Pastor Emeritus until his death in 1991.

Pastor Carlton R. Caldwell, a native of Arkansas, brought "A New Attitude" to Galilee. He started his ministry on April 12, 1992. He instituted an "Annual Day of Love for Pastor Emeritus Peay." The I. C. Peay Christian Education Building has been paid off and renovations to the sanctuary were completed in April 1998. He replaced fund raising annual days with the Church Anniversary Payment Plan (CAPP). Pastor Caldwell has had a total of 157 persons to join the Galilee family through baptism, Christian experience and restoration since coming to Galilee.

UNITY BAPTIST CHURCH, JOPLIN, ORGANIZED 1901

The Unity Baptist Church was formed in 1901 by uniting two churches that had been established in approximately 1881. One of these churches was known as the Second Baptist Church with the late Rev. H. H. Curtis as its pastor, and located at 7th and Kentucky Avenue. The other member of this union was the St. John Baptist Church that was located on East 2nd Street with the late Rev. W. S. Blake as pastor. After the unification of the two churches, the name Unity Baptist was suggested by one of the charter members, Mrs. Ida Murray. Worship services were held at the 7th Street location until a storm demolished the building.

Services were held for some time in the Jasper County Court House building until a new edifice was erected at 511 East 7th Street in 1904, as a gift of Thomas Connor. In 1939, the church was rebuilt at its present location at 615 Minnesota when 7th Street became a marked U.S. Highway.

Several ministers who served as spiritual leaders of Unity Baptist Church were Rev. Vaise, Rev. Fisher, Rev. A. J. Jones, Rev. Tuggle, Rev. J. T. Smith, Rev. Henry Pullum (interim pastor), Rev. C. W. Dawson, and Rev. M. G. Edmondson (interim pastor). The present minister, Rev. Harry Givens, came to Unity Baptist in August 1974. The church has experienced tremendous physical and spiritual growth during his 25-year pastorate. Among the accomplishments are the purchase of a parsonage, expansion and remodeling of the church facility, parking lot pavement and debt free.

MORNING STAR BAPTIST CHURCH, KANSAS CITY, ORGANIZED 1905

"New Prospect Mission" located at 19th and Cherry was organized and founded by Rev. G. H. Daniel of Memphis, Tennessee in 1905. In only five short years, the Mission grew so rapidly that larger quarters became necessary. Properties were purchased at 2309-13 Vine Street. It was during this time that a more suitable name was sought and the name "Morning Star Baptist Church" was suggested by Deacon Henry McDaniel and accepted by the congregation.

From 1910 to1922, the church continued to grow. The choir was ranked among the foremost of the city. The Sunday school and BTU were outstanding. The church accomplished much under the leadership of Rev. Daniel. He departed this life for a sweeter home on June 5, 1937.

On February 22, 1938, Rev. A. B. Simmons of Springfield, Missouri accepted the pastorate of Morning Star Baptist Church with an approximate membership of 300-350. The church continued upward in stride as God proved Himself to be "a very present help in the time of trouble."

Rev. Simmons, accompanied by the deacons and trustees, investigated the sale of property then owned by the Central Christian Church at 27th & Wabash. As the church continued to grow and prosper, a building fund was initiated.

This fund was organized by the Daughters Club who contributed the first $100.00 payment towards the initial $8,000.00 payment on a $40,000.00 purchase price in January 1945. On July 1, 1946, the Central Christian Church relinquished ownership of this location to the Morning Star Baptist Church upon receipt of payment-in-full. *THE VICTORY WAS WON!!* The Victory March from 24th & Vine to 27th & Wabash was one of high emotions and spirit-filled. This *VICTORY* was the climax of a long anticipated dream. Rev. Simmons departed this life in December 1963.

After a year of being without a Shepherd, in 1964 Rev. J. A. Wilder was extended the call. Rev. Wilder and his wife served the congregation for a brief period. We were again without a leader. God, still in control, heard their cries and sent the Rev. Hubert C. Eason and his lovely wife, Sister Annie Eason, to answer the call. In July 1965, Rev. Eason became the fourth leader of Morning Star Baptist Church.

Rev. Eason kept the faith, for he had a dream. Rev. Eason was called home before seeing his dream unfold. He departed this life for a sweeter home on August 6, 1986 after twenty-one years of dedicated and faithful service. The loss of such an obedient servant and capable leader is still felt. His lovely wife and former First Lady, Sister Annie Eason, served faithfully at the Morning Star Baptist Church. Through her presence and beautiful smile, we feel the presence of Rev. Eason, and our memories live on.

The church was once again "a sheep without a shepherd." The deacons called for a season of prayer. God again heard their humble pleas and answered in the form of Rev. John Modest Miles and his lovely wife, Sister Jeanette Miles. Pastor Miles became the fifth leader of this great church in March 1987. His motto, "I Just Want To Do God's Will" speaks for his character. As his colleagues say, "Pastor Miles hit the ground running and has never stopped." Sister Jeanette Miles has become known for "running the devil out of the church."

Our church has accomplished many things under the guidance of Pastor Miles. New properties have been purchased, church renovations are in progress, development of a community center is in progress, the Mock Cemetery is nationally known and has been featured in an HBO movie, street clean-up efforts, community awareness, street ministry, etc. The list goes on and on. Pastor and Mrs. Miles have truly been valuable assets to our church family, our community and our city.

Our accomplishments as a church family from inception in 1905 to the present are too numerous to mention. We have so many things to be *THANKFUL* for. With the help of God, we can and will continue to prosper. We must keep our heads high and seek God's help.

True Light Missionary Baptist Church, Kinloch, Organized 1940

True Light Missionary Baptist Church was organized in 1940. The name "True Light" was selected by our Founder, the late Rev. J. L. Johnson. He chose this name from a little church in the state of Mississippi. And with only a few members, True Light began.

The first services for True Light were held in the U.N.I.A. Hall and there the membership began to grow. While searching for a building place of our own, our services were united with that of the True and Righteous Church where Rev. Anderson was the pastor. Finally, three lots were found. It was a struggle to buy and purchase them. However with God's grace and our faith, we were successful. The site chosen was at 5690 Frieling, Kinloch, MO.

Rev. Johnson, with the help of members and other friends, built our first church. Soon services were held. The Lord blessed and the membership outgrew the building. Rev. Johnson decided that we should add to our building. The work was tedious and hard, but when the work was completed, the first church became the lower level and the new church became the main sanctuary.

Then that which was only a dream became reality. The corner stone of our church was laid. This was a joyful time for all—a building completed and paid for by True Light members. Another dream became a reality. In the 1960s, an Educational Building was built along with a kitchen and a pastor's study. As always, when God's work is being done, Satan has to get busy.

In 1982, due to a severe snow storm, the roof of our Educational Building was destroyed. With the help of members, friends and sister churches, the roof was rebuilt.

In 1983, Rev. J. L. Johnson suffered a stroke. At that time, he asked Rev. William Catling, a young minister in the gospel who had been working with him for a year and following his teachings and leadership, to take over the pastoral duties of True Light. The membership agreed and Rev. Catling accepted.

On Monday, April 14, 1985, Rev. J. L. Johnson died. He will always be in our hearts and will always be remembered by True Light Missionary Baptist Church of Kinloch, MO.

Rev. Catling picked up the torch from Rev. Johnson and with the True Light members carried on. However, due to the airport expansion, the church had to relocate. In February 1990, a building located at 6520 Joseph Avenue, Pagedale, MO was selected. We marched in on February 12, 1990.

In 1992, George Love was crowned Deacon George Love. Bernard Knox and Herbert Damper were ordained as deacons on May 21, 1995. Deacon Herbert Damper did as the Lord bade him to do and on June 9, 1996, he preached his first sermon. He is now Rev. Herbert Damper. Brother Aaron Catling is now on trial to become a deacon.

Through sadness, joy, tears, and laughter, God continues to shower His grace and mercy on True Light Missionary Baptist Church and we strive to continue to do the work of the Lord.

We have been "Blessed By His Blessings and Held By His Grace" for 61 years.

Chapter 4

Our Associations

Pastors Fate White, Jr. and Oliver K. Patterson
sharing with Pastor Wardell Finney at the North Missouri Baptist Association

INTRODUCTION

Information presented in this chapter is a brief overview of the reasons for and growth of cooperative ministry bodies among African American churches across the nation, and particularly in Missouri. There are associations yet active and defunct on which we do not have information. This is in no way to slight any of the great bodies that have and do exist in our great convention.

Associational organizations began to spring up across America in the northern states as more and more African American churches were organized. These groups provide support by offering a centralized organization to allow the best minds and spirits in the region to provide Christian education and activities of evangelization for the communities in which they meet. Leroy Frits in *A History of Black Baptists* states:

We have begun to realize that blacks, both slave and free, had a variety of experiences and that they managed, even under the harshest of conditions, to construct a vital cultural, religious and institutional life. Under slavery, black preachers were able to preach, although sometimes hindered, a unique gospel interpretation of the black experience and to organize separate churches. After emancipation, free blacks of the North and South were able to accelerate the organization of churches and develop a cooperative movement among the churches.

The roots of the cooperative movement among black Baptists go back into the antebellum period. In the early 1830s, the organization's consciousness of black Baptists gained momentum. A mixture of the missionary motif with a general desire for racial progress fostered development in the evolution of black denominations (p. 64).

Fritz further notes that some of the earliest associations were the Providence Baptist Association of Berlin Cross Roads, Ohio in 1834 and the Union Anti-Slavery Baptist Association in Xenia, Ohio in 1843. The associations' work in Missouri was influenced by Baptists in Western Illinois.

DEVELOPMENT OF ASSOCIATIONS IN MISSOURI

New churches were being organized all over Missouri at a phenomenal pace by European and African American missionaries. Cooperative relationships were being established in northern Missouri among churches for the purpose of promoting preaching the gospel, leadership training, Christian education and the evangelization of the race. These relationships continued to develop until a meeting was conducted in the Mt. Zion Baptist Church of Chillicothe during the month of September in 1865. The meeting resulted in the organization of the North Missouri Baptist District Association. Four years later, the Union Colored Baptist Association was organized in St. Louis independently of the North Missouri Baptist Association. Berean and Antioch came into being directly and indirectly as a result of this initiative that was probably set into motion by the leadership of the historic First Baptist Church in St. Louis.

North Missouri seemingly engulfed the entire state of Missouri and included areas in Iowa and Kansas. It functioned as one body for five years. However, it had to subdivide into three regional associations that afforded closer bonding and extended ministries. From this body emerged the Boot Hill Associations, Central, Mt. Zion and Mt. Carmel within a thirty-year period.

Each associational body was composed of a Women's Convention, Sunday School Congress, Baptist Young People Union, Deacons and Ministers' Union.

According to Dr. Shipley's reports in *The History of Black Baptists in Missouri*, these bodies operated independently of the parent bodies initially. However, that phenomenon changed "as structures and constitutions were more carefully drawn, each became a supportive arm to the other" (p. 44).

Each of these associations was represented at Second Baptist Church on October 8, 1888 for our state convention's organizational meeting.

Eight associations were represented at the State Convention conducted at the Morgan Street Baptist Church, Booneville in 1900 when an updated constitution was approved for the convention. Associations represented were Mt. Carmel, Mt. Zion, Southwest, North Missouri, Berean, Southeast and Union. The number of associations had increased to fourteen when Shipley wrote *The History of Black Baptists in Missouri*. The additional associations are Antioch, Christian Liberty, Friendship, Midwest, New Era and Pemiscot Dunklin.

I now invite you to take a closer look at the great associations that are providing ministry across our state. We will start with the oldest and proceed to the youngest.

North Missouri Baptist District Association, Organized 1865

Fellowship between sessions at North Missouri Association

The history of the North Missouri Baptist District Association forms the opening chapter or the background of all other associations in the state. The men and women in the association were busy at many tasks. They served the association in many different ways, but they all did the tasks they undertook well. They never gave up. They and other men and women made the association what it is today.

The association was organized on Tuesday before the second Lord's Day in September 1865, in Chillicothe, MO by Revs. B. F. Bateman, Dr. Hildreth, Barton Hillman, George Hudson, Thomas Clark, J. Cox, Preston Oliver, B. F. Marshall and Adam Dimmitt. At this first meeting, Rev. O. H. Webb was elected Moderator, and Rev. Barton Hillman, Secretary. The next year the association met in Hannibal, MO at which Rev. O. H. Webb was re-elected Moderator and J. J. White, Secretary.

The North Missouri Baptist District Association continued as one body for five years, but like all of the early organizations, its territory was too vast; this made organizational planning difficult. During the early years, a church was being organized every month.

At the Annual Session held at Lexington in 1870, the North Missouri Baptist District Association was divided to add two districts. They were named First and Second Districts of the North Missouri Baptist District Association with the Missouri River as the dividing line. The first district became active immediately. However, the second district did not become active until September 21, 1971 in Keokuk, Iowa.

A third division was made at the Annual Session at Cape Girardeau on November 8, 1878. This division was given the name Third District. Its territory extended east of Franklin County, Frederick Town, Charleston, Cape Girardeau, Wolfe Island, Texas Bend, Bird's Point, Big Lake and Potosi.

The District was divided again in 1888 during the Annual Session at Second Baptist Church in Lexington. The Second District of the North Missouri Baptist District Association was divided into Western and Eastern District Associations as recommended by the Association's Committee on "Division of the Association." The Eastern Division was named Central Baptist Association of Missouri and the Western became known as the Mt. Zion District Association.

The Association met in Keokuk, Iowa at the Pilgrim Rest Baptist Church in Keokuk in 1893. It was agreed that the M.K.T. Railroad should be the line of division and the churches of said line were granted letters of dismissal. From henceforth, the Mt. Carmel Association came into existence.

The Association organized the Sunday School Convention in 1889. The Women's Missionary Circle was organized in 1900. Mrs. Mary Bailey of Canton was elected as the first president. The B.Y.P.U. Convention was organized in 1917. All these departments met together, each taking a separate day during the annual session.

The Sunday School and B.Y.P.U. Conventions organized into a combined unit and became known as the North Missouri Baptist District Sunday School and Training Union Congress in 1941. They continued to meet with the parent body until 1947. During this year, they met separately from the parent body in Hannibal, Missouri at the 8th and Center Street Baptist Church. During this session, Rev. N. P. Wilson, President, was leaving the district, being called to Columbia, MO. M. D. Powers of Hannibal, MO was elected president for the ensuing year.

North Missouri Baptist District Association is indeed the cradle of all Missionary Baptists' education and evangelism in the state of Missouri. She is responsible for the organization and sustenance of five associations that gave birth to other associations in the state. Her influence extended to every corner of our great state. The wonder of it all is that the association is still alive and striving in an area where the African American population has dwindled significantly.

The following ministers served as moderators: Rev. O. H. Webb, Rev. W. W. Steward, Rev. D. S. Sawyer, Rev. Amos Johnson, Rev. Wm. P. Brooks, Rev. T. L. Smith, Rev. B. Hillman, Rev. O. P. Syms, Rev. G. H. McDaniels, Rev. Mark Thompson, Rev. E. D. Green, Rev. C. R. McDowell, Rev. B. P. Gayles, Rev. J. H. Homesly, Rev. J. S. Moore, Rev. J. W. L. Underwood, Rev. A. T. Allen, Rev. C. B. Johnson, Rev. St. Mark Jones, Rev. C. W. Carter, Rev. T. R. Sayles, and Rev. W. M. Holmes. The present moderator is Rev. John Mims.

(Compiled by M. D. Powers, Historian. *Source of information: Collection of old minutes of Mrs. Genetta Smith.*)

GREATER UNION BAPTIST DISTRICT ASSOCIATION, ORGANIZED 1869

The Union Colored Baptist Association was organized as an independent District Association in St. Louis four years after the organization of the North Missouri Baptist District Association. This association had as its primary goal the promotion of the kingdom of God by preaching the Gospel of His Son, and other laudable means. It was made clear that the association would not interfere with the internal business of the churches connected with it.

It is most likely a product of the Old African Baptist Church in St. Louis. The churches south of the Missouri River located in the eastern section of the state were its primary constituency.

Driving forces in the organization of this body were Rev. Emmanuel Cartwright, C. C. Calhone, J. A. Buckner, T. Jefferson, J. W. Powell, C. Rollins of St. Louis; I. Motion, M. G. Masey of St. Louis County; A. Roberson, W. M. Roberson and G. Fishback of Kirkwood; and C. Green and J.W. Crowder of

St. Charles. There were other ministers from Booneville, Jefferson City, Rocheport and Pleasant Hill.

A controversy arose at the associational meeting conducted at First Baptist Church in Chesterfield in 1877.

The following is copied from the minutes of August 20, 1872.

> Moderator Rev. E. Cartwright, First Baptist Church, St. Louis, Missouri; Corresponding Secretary Rev. J. R. McClannahan, St. Louis, Missouri; Treasurer A. Drake, Jefferson City, Missouri; Executive Board Members: Howard Barnes, Benjamin Banner, Archy Drake, Rev. John Lane (Jefferson City); Rev. E. Cartwright, Rev. J. R. McClannahan (St. Louis); G. Freeman (Pleasant Hill); J. M. Winchester (Webster Groves); M. Miller (Warrensburg); G. Brannon; Professor Boone; Rev. R. T. Lucas (Allenton); Rev. Stafford (Manchester); Rev. A. Holland (Berger Station); N. McLand (Boone County).
>
> Annual Members: Mary Montgomery, Anna Vinng Jackson, Jane Davis, Sally Harris, Healy, Isaac Handy, H. Delaware, M. A. Serriggs.
>
> According to the 4th Annual Session of the Union Association minutes dated August 20, 1872, the Association was held at the Pleasant Hill Baptist Church, Pleasant Hill, Missouri. The Union Association was organized in 1868, which would make it the oldest of the St. Louis area associations.
>
> Excerpts taken from the history of Central Baptist Church under the pastorate of Rev. S. P. Anderson, a minister who returned to St. Louis from labors in Kentucky. He had been traveling as a (sort of) missionary to the churches in Missouri and returned to the 8th Street Church with its pulpit vacant and was called as pastor.
>
> The scope of the work expanded and it included parts of the city and county. The Berean Association was organized in 1878 at Chesterfield, Missouri (about 25 miles west of St. Louis) in the First Baptist Church of Chesterfield.
>
> Rev. Anderson was the leading spirit in this movement and they made him the first moderator. He tells how the brethren slept on the floor of the church on top of straw with blankets over them. The lady delegates were entertained, of course, in the homes of the members. Their night on the floor was said to be joyful and peaceful; and why not? They were pioneers in a great movement for God.

BEREAN MISSIONARY BAPTIST DISTRICT ASSOCIATION, ORGANIZED 1878

The District was organized in 1878 following the withdrawal from Union District during an associational meeting at the First Baptist Church of Chesterfield, Missouri. Rev. S. P. Anderson was appointed or selected as the first moderator because he was "the leading spirit" in this movement. He was pastor of the Central Baptist Church of

St. Louis. The first meeting found the brethren sleeping on the floor with straw under them and blankets on top. The lady delegates were entertained in the homes in the area.

Berean's greatest interest was in the Home Mission and Foreign Mission work to the extent of giving assistance to one of our young ministers to spread the Gospel on the Dark Continent, Africa. It was evident in the foreign mission field by co-sponsoring the sending of the Rev. L. N. Cheek to preach the Gospel in Africa. In later years, Rev. J. C. Caston and his wife Ella Mae served in the same field, doing mission work in Africa.

Berean has continued to foster the work in Home and Foreign Mission. Today six percent of our assessment income is designated to each concern, that is six percent to foreign mission and six percent to home mission.

In the field of Christian education, Berean is a staunch supporter of Western Baptist Bible College in Kansas City, Missouri.

Twenty-five percent of its assessment goes to Western. The Association also gives three percent of its assessment to American Baptist College of American Baptist Theological Seminary in Nashville, Tennessee.

A scholarship fund was begun under the moderatorship of Rev. J. E. Fiddmont. Originally it was set up to help anyone wanting to attend Western Baptist Bible College, but it has since been changed from this stipulation.

At its inception, the Ministers' Wives Committee was appointed to generate money for the fund. It was named the *J. E. Fiddmont Scholarship Fund* of Berean Missionary Baptist District Association.

In 1970, under Rev. R. T. Davis, the Publication Committee was formed and appointed. Brother E. R. Smith stated that it was necessary for the District to do its own printing of yearbooks and programs. He also said arrangements could be made whereby printing could be done for individual churches for special programs. The church would have to bear the expense for materials and labor. A few churches, very few, availed themselves of this opportunity. An off-set printing press, typewriters, a folding machine, and other equipment were purchased for this purpose. Since the initial purchases, a copy machine, and three up-to-date typewriters have been added. The folding machine has since worn out and the repair of it was quite expensive, so the committee felt that it would be better to put the money in a new one (this has not been done yet). For the past several years, all folding has been done manually. Members of the original committee were the late E. R. Smith, Pearline McKell, Dorothy Lee Morrow, and Auvelia H. Arnold.

During the years 1973-1974, the district took the Gospel to the people outside of the four walls and sponsored street evangelistic services. This started under Moderator R. T. Davis. Vice Moderator E. E. Johnson was appointed chairman of the mission. Services were held weekly during the spring and summer months. We started with one location and later expanded to two locations, carrying on simultaneously. Moderator Davis passed in 1974 while attending the National Baptist Congress in Detroit, Michigan. The evangelistic services continued under Moderator Johnson for four years and another year under Moderator Daniel W. Hughes. A portable public address system was purchased to aid in this ministry.

In 1977, the Missionary Baptist Ministers of Greater St. Louis honored pastors who had served 30-plus years with one congregation. Pastors Benny L. Catlin (First Baptist of Valley Park), Roosevelt Brown (Mercy Seat Baptist), L. C. Richmond (Mount Esther Baptist), W. L. Rhodes (Clayton Baptist) of Berean were among the honorees. Rev. Isaac C. Peay, pastor of Galilee Baptist was the president of the organization at that time.

In 1978, we observed the centennial celebration of the association. We convened with the First Baptist Church of Maplewood of which the Rev. Victor Williams was pastor. Rev. Melvin L. Smotherson, pastor of the Washington Tabernacle Baptist Church, serves as the general chairman. Brother Earley D. Johnson was serving as moderator. The theme for the special occasion was "We've Come This Far by Faith"; Scripture—Romans 1:17 and Hebrews 10:38. A souvenir program was compiled with a history of the association and all auxiliaries. Past officers as nearly as could be ascertained were included. It also included the history of any member church that submitted it to the committee.

The Grand Centennial Program was held Sunday, July 16, 1978, at the Washington Tabernacle Baptist Church. Greetings were brought by the Honorable James F. Conway, Mayor of the City of St. Louis, Ms. Ina Boone, Director of Region IV of NAACP, and Mr. Charles Wilson, President of A. L. Beal Undertakers. The speaker of the hour was Dr. R. B. Lyles, President, General Missionary Baptist State Convention of Illinois and Moderator of New Salem Baptist District Association.

Under moderator Daniel W. Hughes, the 1979-1980 fiscal year, the constitution of the association was rewritten and adopted. A five-year wait was place on the moderator and presidents of auxiliaries. The constitution was revised under moderator Clarence J. DuVall (1981-1982) and amendments have been added under moderator Jimmy L. Brown (see Constitution).

In 1983, under the moderatorship of Rev. C. J. DuVall, the Women's Missionary Union and Congress of Christian Education Auxiliaries combined their efforts to have one week of study instead of two weeks at different times during the year. The effort was overwhelmingly successful. Now, the School of Mission and Leadership Training meets under the umbrella of the association. The week has gone from approximately 300 in attendance to 700-plus and the issuance of up to 500-plus course cards for those attending four and five nights, and is accredited by our National Board of Christian Education. Our lecturers have been from national, state, and local levels.

The first school was held with the West Side Baptist Church, Rev. Moses Javis, Pastor. The second one was held at the New Sunny Mount Baptist Church, Rev. Donald Hunter, Pastor. All others sessions have been at West Side Baptist Church, Rev. Ronald L. Bobo, Pastor.

Moderator Jimmy L. Brown stated in his first annual message that he had a vision and the faith that Berean would be given a building. This would allow the district to purchase a building for a nominal amount in order to do more of the Lord's work—administering to the physical needs of the less fortunate that would lead to satisfying their spiritual needs. After all, this is what the organization is about—winning souls for Jesus Christ.

His vision came to fruition in October of 1987. The building known as Cass House, run by the Catholics, was given to the Association (a sum of one $1.00) in exchange for the deed to the property. It is now known as Berean House Christian Care Center, located at 1859 Cass Avenue, St. Louis. It consists of two large buildings on a number of acres. It is used as a temporary shelter for women and children and provides overnight shelter for men. The evening meal is served daily ranging anywhere from 35 in warm months to 150-plus in cool and cold months. The meals are served by members from the churches of the Association. The churches have taken on the responsibility for cleaning, painting, and furnishing the rooms and offices. Worship services are to be held on Sunday mornings. Ministers of our churches will conduct the services. A clothes closet is also in place. Cass House serves as headquarters for the association and eventually our equipment will be housed there. Each auxiliary will have access to office space.

The House receives sixteen percent of our assessment income (this includes six percent which formerly was sent to the Home Mission Board). We rely on the generosity of our churches and individual members to make this endeavor a part of their budget.

Auxiliaries of this association are as follows: (1) The Women's Missionary Union that was organized in 1894. (2) The Young People's Department of the WMU that was organized in 1921. (3) The Congress of Christian Education (formerly the Sunday School Convention and the Baptist Training Union Convention, also known as the Sunday School and Baptist Training Union Congress that was organized in 1943. (4) The Ushers and Health Units organized in 1945. (5) The Laymen's Union was organized in 1951 (this was formerly known as the Brotherhood).

The Berean House Ministry

Food supplies being stored by volunteers

The Berean Missionary Baptist District Association, under the leadership of Pastor Jimmy L. Brown, Moderator, operates to form a more perfect fellowship and association between the Baptist churches of St. Louis and vicinity, and supports Christian Education and Home and Foreign Missions.

On October 17, 1987, the Berean Missionary Baptist District Association acquired Cass House, at 1849 Cass Avenue, St. Louis, Missouri. The name of the emergency shelter and soup kitchen was changed to Berean House Christian Care Center.

The facility at 1849 Cass Avenue was completed and occupied by the James L. Clemens, Jr. family in 1860. This unique building has cast iron columns and window trim. It is pure American architecture of the 1850-1880 period. Cast iron became a favored building material in the area as a result of the 1849 fire on the St. Louis riverfront.

The Sisters of St. Joseph of Carondelet purchased the building for a convent in June 1885. In 1949, the Vincentian Brothers Foreign Missionary Society purchased the property for use as its headquarters. The facility was operated by the Catholic Workers Community as an emergency shelter and soup kitchen.

In October 1987, the Berean Missionary Baptist District Association acquired the facility from the Vincentian Brothers for use as an emergency shelter and soup kitchen.

The Berean District is comprised of 67 member churches, ranging in size from in excess of 2,000 members to those with fewer than 150 members. The Berean District is headed by a moderator who functions as its Chief Executive Officer. Rev. Jimmy L. Brown, Pastor of St. Luke's Memorial Baptist Church is Moderator of the Berean Missionary Baptist District Association.

The Berean House Christian Care Center (BHCCC) opened its doors as a soup kitchen on November 9, 1987, following a Grand Opening Rally on November 7, 1987.

The operation of Berean House is the direct responsibility of the Berean House Christian Care Center Development Committee. The Committee is responsible for the management, funding and overall operation of Berean House.

The emergency shelter was scheduled to open in September 1988, but due to extremely inclement weather conditions, was opened on January 6, 1988, and had housed over 18,000 persons as of December 31, 1989.

Since November 1987, the Berean House Christian Care Center, a not-for-profit organization, has served as a shelter for homeless men, women and children.

MT. ZION BAPTIST ASSOCIATION OF MISSOURI, ORGANIZED 1880

The Mount Zion District traces it roots back to the Second District North Missouri Baptist Association, including Kansas. Second District was later divided into the Eastern and Western Districts because of the enormous territory it covered. Reverend J. H. Homesley was elected first moderator at the Associational meeting conducted in Columbia. He served as moderator for only a year. He was followed by Pastors Amos

Johnson, J. W. Muse, M. L. Clay, John Goins, J. S. Swancy, L. W. Harris, H. J. Herring, L. R. Johnson, J. W. Gordon, T. R. Sayles, C. O. Banks, and A. J. Clayton.

The Association sought to promote the preaching of the Gospel and the evangelization of the race. The following standing resolutions speak volumes about the Association's priorities.

Adopted at Carrollton, September, 1886

Resolved, That whereas many of our churches are at this time suffering from priestcraft, in the form ministerial imposition, Therefore be it

Resolved, That it is the sense of this Association that no minister is justified in staying with a church to the detriment of that church and community, and ministers called of God ought not to destroy, but build up the cause of Christ. Further be it

Resolved, That any minister who remains with a church and causes trouble in the same should be censured by the Association and published as unworthy.... Further, be it

Resolved, That this Association discourage the use of all narcotics such as opium, chloroform, arsenic, laudanum and tobacco, as well as alcohol, and that the brethren use every honorable means to obliterate its use among God-fearing people in their reach.

Adopted at Plattsburg, 1887

Resolve, that the Association will not recommend any minister of other Associations to our churches as pastors, without rigid examination by the Ministerial and Deacons' Union and the official Board of this Association, on all points regarding church government as well as biblical qualifications....

Resolved, That we recommend that pastors repeatedly instruct their churches as to the recommendations of the Association.

Adopted at Bookfield, September 1892

We, your committee on resolutions, beg leave to submit the following report:

Whereas, The Mt. Zion Baptist Association has in the past eleven years succeeded remarkably well, though she has had many difficulties to encounter, but through God, she has surmounted them all. But while God has so wonderfully blessed us and given us every reason to be encouraged, we feel that we ought not to become negligent, but always be on the alert, for the adversary walketh through the earth seeking whom he may devour. Therefore, we recommend that this Association do everything it can to foster the great work of the Master.

Second, We recommend that the ministers of this Association use every means to secure the attendance of students at the Theological University at Macon City.

The Women's Home, Foreign and Education Convention as an auxiliary to the Mt. Zion District Missionary Association was organized at the Mt. Zion Baptist Church of Cillicothe in 1898. The first president of this organization was Mrs. Mary L. Saunders, and Mrs. Addie Triggers was chosen as their recording secretary pro tem.

Other officers elected were Mrs. Mary Morton, secretary, Mrs. Amanda M. Swanson, treasurer and Mrs. Eva Marshall, a board member.

The Ushers organized April 29, 1995 at the Mt. Zion Baptist Church. Officers elected at that meeting were Mrs. Margaret Whaite, president, Sue Richardson, secretary, LaVerna Williams, treasurer, Walter Lane III, chaplain and Wanda Crowns and Earnest Kittrell, board members. The current Moderator is Pastor Dodds.

SOUTHWEST DISTRICT ASSOCIATION, ORGANIZED 1887

Moderators Hodges and Smith with President Anderson

The Southwest Baptist District Association of Missouri had its genesis during the spring of 1887 at the Washington Avenue Baptist Church in Springfield, Missouri during the pastoral administration of Reverend A. B. Franklin. The association was organized to provide opportunities for cooperative ministries in the area of Christian education, evangelism and fellowship. The association's organizational structure was very simple and efficient.

It was a modification of that which was implemented by other associations. The officers were Moderator, Vice Moderator, Recording Secretary, Treasurer, Auditor and auxiliary officers.

It also organized separate Ministers and Deacons' wives auxiliaries that same year.

The Women's Mission Union was organized in 1887 and registered with the state convention in 1906. The Sunday School and Baptist Training Union Congress was organized in 1942. The Laymen's Movement was organized in 1950.

A Music and Usher Auxiliary was added in the 1960s. The need for combining the Association and Sunday School and BTU Congress was first discussed during the annual session conducted at Second Baptist Church in Neosho on August 15, 1977. During a meeting at the Mt. Eagle Baptist Church in Springfield on November 12, 1977, it was determined that the first combined session would be conducted at Washington Avenue Baptist Church that was then pastored by Reverend Rufus Walker.

The geographical area covered by the association was vast. There were churches in West Plains, Carthage, Neosho, Springfield, Lebanon and Joplin. These churches bordered Northwest Arkansas, Eastern Oklahoma and Kansas. There were fourteen churches in the association at its zenith. Presently, there are eight due to the migration of people from the southwest to other communities within and beyond the state. The remaining churches are Washington Avenue, Greater Metropolitan and Mt. Olive in Springfield; Shiloh and Unity in Joplin; Second Baptist in Neosho; Wood Street in Lebanon; and Greater Community in St. Roberts.

Pastor Harry Givens became moderator in 1974 and served faithfully for twenty-three years. Seven of those years he served as treasurer of the state convention. During his tenure, the association increased its giving to Western Baptist Bible College, established a scholarship fund to aid young people aspiring to attend college and facilitated comradery among the pastors and churches that was awesome. He was instrumental in encouraging both clergy and laymen in the association to participate actively in the state convention.

The association has hosted state board meetings and congresses in Springfield. We have been consistently represented faithfully at state and national meetings by our leadership.

Pastor Givens was elected moderator Emeritus following his retirement in 1997. He was succeeded by the Reverend Jerry Hodges, pastor of the Shiloh Missionary Baptist Church.

Central Baptist District Association, Organized, 1888

Central Baptist Association of Missouri was originally known as the Eastern Division of the North Missouri Baptist District Association. It was formally recognized during the Eighteenth Annual Session of the Second District Baptist Association of North Missouri convening in Lexington on the 15th of September 1888. Rev. William P. Brooks was selected the first moderator and the Rev. A Greed was elected assistant moderator. Other officers elected were Rev. O. T. Redd, recording secretary, Rev. B. H. McDaniel, corresponding secretary, Rev. J. T. Edwards, treasurer and W. H. Howard, M.D. and G. D. Saunders completed the executive positions. The object of the Association was to promote preaching of the Gospel in the southern portion of Missouri, and the thorough evangelization of the race.

The first constitution was drafted in 1896. That constitution was orchestrated under the leadership of Moderator Wm. P. Brooks.

There were three major resolutions that were included according to Dr. Shipley. The leaders were concerned about providing departing members with letters of dismissal to minimize their displacement as they traveled.

They were concerned about not recognizing any ministers who were known to disturb the harmony and peace of churches. They chose to use Hitchcock's Church Directory and Crowell's Church Manual for providing instructions to church members.

It is reported that the Sunday School Convention was organized in 1885 and was followed by the Baptist Young People's Union. They were consolidated and reorganized as Sunday School and Training Union Congress at Second Baptist Church, Lexington in June 1942 during the tenure of Moderator L. D. Hardiman. The first annual session of the congress was held with the Morgan Street Baptist Church in Booneville.

The Foreign Mission and Educational Auxiliary was organized during the month of August 1892 at the Second Baptist Church in Independence. The Reverend J. S. Dorsey was moderator. There were nine women in attendance. Mrs. Maggie Byas of Bunceton was elected president. The auxiliary has contributed to the erection of a dormitory for girls at Western Bible College when it was in Macon, and to mission work in Africa. They have sponsored institutes, parades, scholarships, sewing circles, etc.

They organized the Young People's Auxiliary in 1927. Mrs. O. F. Nelson was the supervisor and Miss Edith Mayberry of Lexington was the first president.

Presidents of the Women's Auxiliary with the longest tenure were Mrs. Emma Smith, Rocheport and Mrs. Pearl Haynes with twenty years, Mrs. Estella Diggs of Jefferson City with fifteen years, and Mrs. Mary Goins of Jefferson City with twelve years.

The moderator's address provides some insight into the early life of the association.

> Bishop H. J. Burton made the following statement in one of his annual addresses:
>
> I have traveled over the Central District Association and visited twenty-three churches, and would have made it around, but as Reverend A. Green of Bunceton could not attend to his church, being sick, I have been preaching at Bunceton during this summer. The spiritual attitude of our association was never better than now. While it is true that the people are not so spasmodic as in years gone by, they are entering the churches from reasonable and logical preaching. The church in South Dedalia, Rev. M. A. Eilouth, pastor; New Palestine, Reverend J. A. Wright, pastor; Odessa Church, Reverend W. M. Miner, pastor; Lexington Church, Reverend J. H. Holmesly, pastor; Jefferson City Church, Reverend J. S. Dorsey, pastor; Second Baptist Church, Miami, Reverend H. J. Burton, pastor. The above churches are all doing a noble work for the Lord, and may they do it well.

> Moderator J. Goins wrote in 1904:
>
> Our education work should receive our special consideration. The watchword of every Baptist of Missouri should be success for our college at Macon that is our school and we should see to it that success comes to it.

Our mission work should claim the attention of every Baptist in the state. The commission that our Lord gave to His disciples was to go into all of the world, etc. We desire to see a great revival of religion in all of our churches. We believe the harvest is ripe, but the laborers are few. We most cordially invite this association to take an active part in our State Mission work the coming years, and that special interest be shown toward our District Mission work.

Moderators serving this association have been Reverends William F. Brooks, J. S. Dorsey, M. J. Burton, John Goin, G. W. Watts, E. L. Scruggs, M. D. Johnson, L. D. Hardiman, C. B. Johnson, J. E. Erickson, J. P. Mosley, Ogden Lacy, David O. Shipley, Leroy Cunningham, C. L. McDavid, Earl Jackson, and Leroy E. Gilmore, Sr. The current moderator is Reverend Everrett Hannon, Jr., pastor of the historic Second Baptist Church, Lexington.

Mt. Carmel Baptist District Association, Organized 1893

The Mt. Carmel District Baptist Association had its beginning in the North Missouri District Baptist Association that was the parent for several district offsprings. After five years of existence, the North District Baptist Association divided into the North Missouri District Baptist Association and the Second District Baptist Association in September 1870. The North Missouri District Baptist Association operated unitedly for twelve (12) years. At Keokuk, Iowa, August 1893 it divided again. The Mt. Carmel District Baptist Association was the offspring of this division. Rev. D. S. Sawyer was elected as moderator for the remaining North Missouri District Baptist Association and Rev. Harris, secretary.

The Mt. Carmel District Baptist Association began its existence with hope and expectancy. The first moderator is not known by this writer. However, Dr. J. T. Caston was elected the second moderator while pastoring Calvary Baptist Church, Fulton, Missouri. The third moderator was Rev. E. S. Redd. Rev. W. H. Young became the fourth moderator while pastoring Calvary Baptist Church, Fulton, Missouri. The fifth moderator was Rev. J. B. Weaver who pastored Second Baptist Church, Mexico, Missouri. Rev. W. F. Bailey, of Clarksville, Missouri became the sixth moderator in 1934. Two years later (1936), the Mt. Carmel District Baptist Association decided to use the services again of a deliberate leader, Rev. E. R. Redd. Rev. Redd held this position eight years before leaving the state for California.

In 1944, Rev. C. E. Richards, pastor of Second Baptist Church, Mexico, Missouri was elected moderator. This dynamic leader served for twenty-two (22) years before he left to live with Jesus Christ (1965). Rev. William Givens, pastor of Log Providence Missionary Baptist Church, Columbia, Missouri was elected as moderator in 1966. Rev. William Givens' fruitful leadership encompassed the years from 1966 to 1970.

Rev. Maceo Piggee, pastor of the Calvary Baptist Church, Fulton, Missouri, became moderator in1970 and served until August 1978. Through Rev. Piggee's effective administration, Mt. Carmel District Baptist Association has received state and national recognition.

Rev. Harold Butler, organizer and pastor of the Progressive Missionary Baptist Church, became moderator after the District Association meeting held in August 1978.

The moderators of the Mt. Carmel District Association are listed again for ease of reference: 1st unknown, 1893-unknown; 2nd Dr. J. T. Caston dates unknown; 3rd Rev. E. S. Redd dates unknown; 4th Rev. W. H. Young dates unknown; 5th Rev. G. B. Weaver 1923-1934; 6th Rev. W. F. Bailey1934-1936; 7th Rev. E. S. Redd 1936-1944; 8th Rev. C. E. Richards1944-1966; 9th Rev. Wm. A. Givens 1966-1970; 10th Rev. Maceo Piggee 1970-1978; 11th Rev. Harold Butler 1997, Rev. Carlton Caldwell, and Rev. David Ballenger. The current moderator is Reverend Charlie Wright of White Rose Missionary Baptist Church of Bowling Green.

New Era District Association, Organized 1905

The New Era District Association was organized in Kansas City, Missouri in 1905. The association emerged from the MO-KS Association. This association was composed of churches and pastors from Kansas and Missouri. It is believed that a Reverend Strickland, pastor of Progressive Missionary Baptist Church, Reverend James Monroe Booker, Pleasant Green Baptist Church along with Reverends S. W. Bacote and F. W. Wilson were instrumental in organizing the New Era Missionary Baptist District Association.

The first moderator is believed to have been Reverend James Monroe Booker, pastor of the Pleasant Green Baptist Church. He served in that capacity until his death in 1917. The association's administrative and spiritual structures were instituted during this developmental period. The District's Sunday School and Baptist Young People's Union Conventions were formed.

Reverend Booker was followed by the Reverend George Henry Daniel, pastor of Morning Star Baptist Church. Pastor Daniel served the New Prospect Mission, later renamed Morning Star Baptist Church for thirty-two years. He served the association for twenty years as moderator. He continued in the tradition of his predecessor. The work of the association grew as additional auxiliaries were organized.

Pastor Ronald E. Holland was called to pastor the True Vine Baptist Church in 1933. He was viewed as a hard worker. He led the work of the association in an "interesting and successful manner." His term was shortened due to health problems.

Dr. Connie See Stamps was called to pastor the Highland Baptist Church in 1936. He served for a short period of time during the forties.

Dr. W. A. Sparks was called to pastor the Progressive Baptist Church from Fort Worth, Texas in 1942. He was elected to the office of moderator in the middle 40s. He launched a vigorous program that provided a number of improvements to the association. He worked diligently to encourage all ministers' wives to support the District's Ministers' Wives Division. This effort resulted in the work of this department to "succeed in an unparalleled manner."

Dr. I. H. Henderson, pastor of Friendship Baptist Church, became the association's sixth moderator in July of 1948. Pastor Henderson reinforced the need for ministers' wives to function with the parent body. He also was very interested in the association supporting the Western Baptist Seminary, now known as the Western Baptist Bible College. He led the district workers to join with him in full cooperation with other district associations throughout the state of Missouri in supporting the school.

Pastor Matthew Frazier, Jr., pastor of St. James Baptist Church, became the seventh moderator in July of 1952. He was not able to serve long due to health problems.

Pastor Cornealious Socrates Scott, Sr., pastor of Second Baptist in Independence, became the eighth moderator in July 1954. During his administration, association auxiliaries were challenged to become more accountable in their utilization and reporting of contributions to the parent body. The association also had to face head-on the association's ushers and choirs freelancing with other unions with the Greater Kansas City Area. Moderator Scott proposed the organization of three new departments within the association.

The departments were Choirs, Ushers and Brotherhood (Laymen). Moderator Scott concluded his tenure following the association's Golden Jubilee Anniversary celebration. Finally, the association adopted two administrative aids developed by this administration. They are papers entitled "A Model For Associational Spending" and "An Association Organized."

Pastor Rubin Fields, pastor of Corinthian Baptist Church, served as the ninth moderator. "He served in a very unique fashion from July 1958 to 1964."

Pastor W. H. White of the Emmanuel Baptist Church became the tenth moderator. He characterized his tenure as a time of church construction and raising funds to support the work of Western Bible College. He resigned the office of moderator during the April Board meeting in 1964. His un-expired term was served by Vice Moderator Andrew Monroe Hudson, Sr.

Pastor Hudson, the eleventh moderator, was the shepherd of the Progressive Baptist Church. He had served as Executive Secretary during the administration of Pastor C. S. Scott. He envisioned the need for a campsite for youth to be purchased. The association sponsored a number of events until they were able to pay the funds required to transfer the land from its original owners to the board of trustees of the association.

Pastor Claude H. High became the twelfth moderator. Subsequent moderators have been Dr. Mckinley Dukes and Dr. John M. Miles (Historical sketch provided by Pastor C. S. Scott in *History of the New Era Association*.)

Antioch District Association, Organized in 1906

The Antioch District Missionary Baptist Association of Metropolitan St. Louis was organized in 1906 in the historic First Baptist Church of St. Louis during the pastorate of Rev. H. H. Harris.

The objectives of the association were fourfold. There was (1) The desire to spread the Gospel of Christ and advance the interest of His Kingdom; (2) Provide a home for the aged and superannuated ministers of the gospel; (3) Supply vacant churches with ministers when requested; and (4) Provided Christian educational opportunities designed for the ministerial skill of its constituents. They clearly chose to avoid judiciary or disciplinary action with the exception of dropping names from the roll as prescribed in the constitution.

The association developed an organizational structure that reflected that of the other associations and the state body. Each of the auxiliaries developed over time and has become very active in ministries conducted at the local, associational, state and national levels. Of note is the Skills Shop and quarterly institutes conducted during the year.

The officers of the association are moderator, two assistant moderators, recording secretary, corresponding secretary, treasurer, missionary and an executive board. Each officer is elected annually at the regular annual meeting of the association unless removed for cause.

Rev. Emanuel Cartwright was the leading spirit and moderator of this body as long as he was able to attend its meetings. Other moderators included Pastors W. Stafford, E. Burnham, G. Brown, H. J. Burton, and Virgil Perry.

Moderators who have served the association are: Reverends David Johnson, G. W. Clemons, W. H. Harris, Dunavent; J. M. Baker, W. L. Johnson, W. D. Thompson, V. H. Wells, Neal J. Haynes, Sammie Jones, and Earl Miller.

FRIENDSHIP CONSOLIDATED BAPTIST ASSOCIATION OF SOUTHEAST MISSOURI, ORGANIZED 1954

The Friendship Consolidated Baptist Association of Southeast Missouri is an offspring of the Third District Association of Southeast Missouri. We have the following information gathered from their Constitution and Bylaws.

Bylaws & Constitution

PREAMBLE

Whereas: It is the sense of the Third District Baptist Association of Southeast and the Springhill Baptist Association of Southeast Missouri, as represented hitherto, and engaged in Missionary and Educational work of Baptist churches; and whereas seeing and agreeing that where there is unity there is strength, these organizations and their auxiliaries should and did unite in a meeting duly called and appointed by the moderators of the aforenamed organizations on the 31st day of December 1954, at the Mt. Carmel Baptist Church in the City of Caruthersville, Missouri. The said organizations did unite and agree upon certain fundamental principles and organic rules, which as amended from time to time are as follows:

RESOLUTIONS

We the Pastors, Ministers, Messengers and Officials of the Associations above mentioned, desiring to more effectively carry on the work of the kingdom; do hereby ordain and establish this constitution whose provisions shall be: First, that all properties and documents of these organizations shall become the property of the consolidated body upon adoption this constitution.

Second, that all records, materials or any possessions belonging to either or both of these organizations or any auxiliary body thereto to be immediately turned over to this consolidated body by persons now holding same.

ARTICLE I

This organization shall be known and styled as the FRIENDSHIP CONSOLIDATED BAPTIST ASSOCIATION OF SOUTHEAST MISSOURI.

ARTICLE II

The object of this association shall be to encourage unity in faith and practice among Missionary Baptist Churches; to promote associational, Home and Foreign Mission among Baptist churches; To encourage and support Christian Education, to publish and/or distribute missionary Baptist literature; and to engage in any other Christian work that the association may desire.

ARTICLE III—MEMBERSHIP
THE MEMBERSHIP OF THIS ASSOCIATION shall consist of messengers from churches which participate in the support of the objectives, as set forth in its budget; each church is entitled to five messengers plus its pastor. All ministers in good and regular standing in a regular Baptist church, have signed and paid a budget, certified by that church or pastor, all pledges must be paid in full 30 days before the annual session, will have all rights and privileges as any other member, annual and life member may become members by a vote and/or rules at each meeting.

MIDWEST BAPTIST DISTRICT ASSOCIATION, ORGANIZED 1956

The Midwest District was organized at the Highland Baptist Church with the late Reverend C. L. Dixon serving as moderator. The Reverend Benjamin Norway served as first vice moderator, Reverend Gregory as congress president, Reverend M. T. Broyle as laymen president, Jessie Johnson as W.M.U. president, Reverend S. K. Bonds as treasurer, Christine Logan as ushers president, Annie Mae Martin as president of the Ministers and Deacons' Wives, and Redwood as choir president.

The district has been a big supporter of the Missionary Baptist State Convention of Missouri. Several of the association's members have served as officers and committee members. Pastor Fate White serves as Vice President-at-Large. Minister Alfred White serves as president of the state laymen. Mrs. Bertha Bifford taught several years in the Congress. Sister Vernell White serves as Pianist for the W.M.U. and Parent Body. She is also the Music Department's treasurer.

Mrs. Hortense Johnson-Jacobs served as financial secretary for the Ministers' Wives for many years. Minister Alfred White has taught in the National Laymen Division for many years.

District representatives have fared well in the State Congress of Christian Education's Junior Memory and Sword Drills. First place winners have been Patricia Tillman (Starlight), Gwendolyn Moffett (Starlight) Shelia Snow (Bethsaida), Angie Williams (Community Progressive) and Felicia Burns (Travelers Rest).

Thomas Marshall (Starlight) and Dionell Davie (Travelers Rest) have served as officers during the State Youth Encampment conducted by the state's Women's Mission Union.

Miss Kim Dorsey (Mt. Sinai) has served as one of the Junior Matron secretaries.

Leah Gray and Muriel Temple won 2nd and 3rd places in the 1992 State Congress that convened in St. Louis. The association has consistently received the trophy for the smallest district with the largest attendance at the State Congress of Christian Education. Mt. Sinai has consistently been recognized as the church with the largest delegation.

A highlight of the association was the presentation of a Doctorate degree to Past Moderator Fate White by Dr. Donald Cottner on the 2nd Sunday in May 1994. The current moderator is Reverend Olin Shurn.

Chapter 5

Our Convention

President and Mrs. Jones confer with Vice President- at-Large Fate White, Executive Secretary Kenneth Ray, Sr. and Dr. Manuel Dillingham

Introduction

We now turn our attention to the organizational structure at the state level. We have noted that churches across the country had developed covenant agreements to support each other regionally. These cooperative efforts were labeled "Association or District." Their success resulted in a desire to organize on a state and national level.

Dr. Shipley tells us in his chapter on "The Rise of Black Baptists" that conventions on the national level for African Americans initially started with the American Baptist Missionary Convention organized by Abyssinian Baptist Church in Harlem, New York in 1840. It later merged with the Western and Southern Missionary Baptist Convention to form the Consolidated American Baptist Convention. They were followed by the organization of the Baptist General Association of western states and territories in Jefferson City, Missouri in 1874. The American Baptist Foreign Mission Convention was organized in Montgomery, Alabama in 1880. The American National Baptist Convention was organized in St. Louis, MO in 1886. The National Baptist Educational Convention was organized in 1893. Finally, the merger of the last three bodies resulted in the organization of the National Baptist Convention, USA, Inc., being organized in Atlanta, Georgia in 1895 (*The History of Black Baptists in Missouri*, p. 34). One might note that Missouri provided the state for the organization of two of the seven national organizations mentioned. It perhaps, then, was not coincidental that our state convention had its genesis before the consolidation of a national body.

The national trend for state conventions was also catching hold in Missouri. Dr. Shipley in his chapter entitled "The Folding of a Dream" states:

> A group of prominent National Baptist ministers answered the call to meet at the Second Baptist Church in Sedalia on April 12, 1888 to discuss plans to better the general condition of colored Baptist churches in the state and to establish a school where the Bible might be taught. On October eighth of the same year, 1888, the organization of the state convention was completed at the Second Baptist Church of Chilicothe and was named the General Baptist Association of Missouri. The name was later changed to the Baptist State Convention and is now known as the Missionary Baptist State Convention of Missouri. Officers elected to head the new convention were (p. 52):

President	Rev. J. T. Caston
First Vice President	Rev. William J. Brown
Second Vice President	Rev. J. T. Thornley
Recording Secretary	Rev. J. S. Corsey
Treasurer	Rev. Daniel S. Sawyer

Education, missions and evangelism were constant emphases throughout the state associations. They also became the emphases when the state convention was organized. It was apparent that the founding fathers felt that minds and souls were too important to waste and lose. They moved with a great deal of intentionality to forge an organizational structure that would accomplish their ultimate goal of the betterment of the general condition of the "colored" Baptist churches in the state via the three mentioned enterprises. The founding fathers established an executive board to supervise the overall work of the convention. It consisted of the elected officers mentioned above, auxiliary presidents, moderators, presidents and three members-at-large. The board met four times annually. They established six auxiliaries. They were the WMU, Sunday School and Baptist Training Union, Laymen, Ushers and Health Unit, Ministers and Pastors Conference, Ministers' Wives and Widows Fellowship, and Music Department.

Western Bible College

The Sunday School auxiliary was organized in 1889. The Ministers and Ministers' Wives Auxiliaries were probably formed in 1889. The Women's Missionary and Educational Convention was established in 1890 in Independence. The Baptist Young People's Union Convention was organized in 1918.

The Sunday School and Baptist Young People's Union were reorganized during a meeting at the Paseo Baptist Church in Kansas City in 1942 as Missouri State Sunday

School and Baptist Training Union Congress. The laymen were organized in 1946. The Ushers and Health Unit was organized in 1952. The Music Department blossomed in 1957. During the 70s, the positions of Foreign and Home Mission representatives to the National Convention and a Department of Evangelism were added to the slate of officers.

Western Bible College has been a continuous passion of the convention's leadership and constituency. The school was organized on October 8, 1889 at the Second Baptist Church of Chilicothe. The school provided an avenue whereby the convention could educate young men and women for Christian ministry. The first president was Professor Wilton Boone. The school conducted its first five years in an old church in Independence.

The school moved to Macon and operated there until 1921. It is presently located in Kansas City. Satellite campuses were in Topeka, Kansas, St. Louis and Poplar Bluff, Missouri. The present president is Dr. Manuel Dillingham.

The new convention voted to affiliate itself with the National Baptist Convention, USA, Inc. We maintain that affiliation even to this day as a strong and vital alliance with our parent body and the world Baptist work. Missourians have served faithfully in every capacity in the national body with the exception of President of the Convention.

Our journey starts ninety years following the formal organization of the Missionary Baptist State Convention of Missouri. We start by looking back and thanking God for the seven presidents (Pastors J. T. Caston, R. C. Clopton, E. M. Cohron, H. M. Mosely, C. E. Richards, S. C. Doyle and John E. Nance) who preceded Pastors I. H. Henderson, McKinley Dukes and Sammie E. Jones.

President Henderson's Cabinet

The Henderson Presidency, 1961-83 (Years of Consolidation)

Dr. I. H. Henderson was the last son of three born to Reverend I. H. Henderson, Sr. and Mrs. Elnora Henderson. He was born in Lexington, Mississippi. He attended elementary school there and graduated from high school at Natchez College in Natchez, Mississippi.

Pastor Henderson received a Bachelor of Arts degree from Jackson College in Jackson, Mississippi. He earned a Master's of Theology degree from American Baptist Theological Seminary in Nashville, Tennessee. He continued his studies at Union Theological Seminary in New York City and Central Baptist Theological Seminary in Kansas City, Kansas. He was awarded Doctorate of Divinity and Doctorate of Humanities degrees by Natchez College and Western Baptist Bible College, respectively, for his outstanding services to humanity.

Pastor Henderson held a number of pastorates. He came to the Friendship Baptist Church in Kansas City, Missouri following a successful pastorate at the Pleasant Green Baptist Church in Nashville, Tennessee. Friendship Church experienced phenomenal progress during his pastorate. He believed strongly in Christian Education and Youth development, and strongly supported community and civic enterprises. Under his pastorate, many physical changes were brought about with the Friendship building complex.

He has served as Moderator of the New Era District Association, Associate Director General of the National Sunday School and Training Union Congress in 1968, and Assistant Secretary of the National Baptist Convention.

He was also a member of the Advisory Board of Safety Federal Savings and Loan Association, member of the Greater Kansas City Baptist and Community Hospital Association, the Metropolitan Inter-Church Agency and the Friendship Village Board of Directors.

Pastor Henderson traveled extensively representing his congregation and our state convention. He traveled to the Holy Land, London, England and Tokyo. He also participated in a Foreign Mission excursion to the Bahamas (Nassau) representing the National Baptist Convention, USA, Inc.

He received the Friendship Village Board of Directors Award for devoted leadership and distinguished services; recognition from the Greater Kansas City Baptist and Community Hospital Association for services rendered during the building of the Martin Luther King, Jr. Memorial Hospital; and a Design Award for the Municipal Arts Commission of Kansas City, Missouri for Friendship Village, Inc.

Dr. Shipley provided us with several documents which contained insights concerning the man. He provides us with a letter dated October 1961 written by Dr. Henderson prior to his assuming the presidency. The letter clearly reflects his love for the Friendship Church family and the work of the convention.

Dr. Shipley writes:

With the vision of greater service to God and to the community, he led his church to a new location in 1961. In this same year, he was elected president of the Missionary Baptist State Convention of Missouri. In this same capacity, he had brought about a unification of workers and auxiliaries for a togetherness program. He is a firm believer that God would be satisfied with his labors and a favorite song of his is "I'm Satisfied With Jesus" (*The History of Black Baptists in Missouri,* p.108).

The following letter was written to constituents of the convention upon his election as president on October 13, 1961.

"I shall not betray your trust. The confidence you have placed in me is greatly appreciated. This job is too much for one man. I need all of your support, your prayers, your good will and good wishes.

My first loyalty will be to the Friendship Baptist Church that has stood with me for seventeen years. My first loyalty from a convention standpoint will be the Missionary Baptist State Convention of Missouri. Thanks to President Richards, a man of sincerity and devotion. He has been most encouraging to me and it has been a pleasure to serve as his vice president.

I feel somewhat like Solomon when he said, 'I am but a little child, I know not how to go out or come in…. Give therefore thy servant an understanding heart…that I may discern between good and bad.'

I cannot forget my parents upon accepting this highest office that the Baptists of Missouri can bestow, their teaching and prayers will ever be with me. I must remember here the faithfulness of a good wife, her understanding, her sacrifice, love and devotion, her loneliness when I had to obey the call of God, and be away from home many times.

Now may I ask for your prayers, your understanding and your support as we move progressively forward together here in Missouri."

The focus of his vision for the state was articulated in the First Annual Address that he delivered in Sikeston on October 19, 1962 (*The History of Black Baptists in Missouri*, pp. 108-112).

Officers of the Convention, Auxiliary Presidents, Moderators, Pastors and Christian Workers: God has given us the privilege to meet once more as messengers from churches throughout the state. This time we have come to Sikeston in the southeast section of Missouri, in Scott County, on the Frisco and Missouri Pacific Railroads and U.S. Highways 60, 61 and 62. Sikeston is located in the rich delta lands of the Mississippi River and is one of the economic and cultural centers of Missouri's cotton region. Sikeston was planted by John Sikes in 1860, for whom the city was named. The humming of the cotton gins, the smell of the cotton seed oil reminds us of our boyhood days. There are some things about Sikeston that we wish we could forget. Nevertheless, there will always be a warm spot in our hearts for the good people who have invited us here and have done all in their power to make us comfortable as we have tried to do the Lord's work.

There are times that try our faith; general unrest seems to be the theme not in our land alone, but throughout the world. We are within hearing distance and catch the sound of the heavy tramping of oncoming generations that will appraise our deliberations. Therefore, we must travel the right path so that they will rise up and call us blessed. It is by the grace of God that we have come to this significant hour. We can surely join with the hymn writer in saying "Amazing Grace." I thank the God of grace for His loving care and protection and for bringing us together in this wonderful fellowship at this appointed time and place.

It was a year ago on October 13, 1961 that you made choice of a president in St. Louis, Missouri. To be sure, I recognized that the task we wish to accomplish is not easy, but great good can be done as we work together for the advancement of the Kingdom of God. As your president, I ask for your prayers and full cooperation.

That You May Know

My First visit as your president was made with the Newstead Baptist Church, St. Louis, Missouri, Rev. W. A. Scott, Pastor, on October 29, 1961. A special Board meeting was held on November 16, 1961 at Friendship Baptist Church, Kansas City, Missouri. We tried to point the direction in which we would like to go. We tried to determine what we wanted as Missouri Baptists. A call for brotherliness and Christian understanding received much attention. I feel that was due largely because of the unrest that existed in our National Convention. We agreed that when the election was over (and it was fair for our own Dr. D. A. Holmes who brought glory to himself and did a great service to our great convention) and the majority had spoken, we had no choice other than to close ranks and keep working in compliance with the wishes of the majority, which is a cardinal principle in the Missionary Baptist Church.

We agreed that there is a definite place for Western Baptist Bible College and that our continued support was needed only to a greater degree. We had and have high hopes of reaching every pastor and all laymen in the state, for if our constituency is not informed, how can they be expected to answer the call? The idea was advanced that all auxiliaries meet together in the Annual Session. You have seen some of this in operation during this session of our convention. We sincerely believe that there is no place for a number of conventions within the convention. We need our laymen, ushers and health auxiliary, singers and women's convention, and they need us, therefore, we are striving to unify our work.

On November 5, 1961, it was my privilege to serve as guest preacher at the Olivet Baptist Church, Chicago, Illinois, pastored by the beloved president of our great National Baptist Convention, Dr. J. H. Jackson, who was en route to New Delhi, India for the meeting of the World Council of Churches.

On December 5th and 6th, we journeyed to Oklahoma City to participate in a meeting of National and Sourthern Baptist Leaders. Certainly, much good is being done as we work together. Dr. Loren J. Belt, the director of work with the National Baptists here in Missouri, has endeared himself to us because of his sincerity and Christian approach to the problems facing us.

On January 3rd, we met at the Baptists Building in St. Louis for our board meeting. Vice President Wells and our St. Louis brethren made it pleasant for us. A number of pastors and workers remained for the Stewardship and Evangelistic Clinic that is always helpful and inspiring.

In the early spring, I was in attendance at the Trustee Board meeting of the American Baptist Theological Seminary. I have served for a number of years as a trustee of said school. On May 10th and 11th, I was called to Chicago where a few National Baptists and members of the executive committee of the Southern Baptist Convention met at the Hilton Hotel to study the relationship of National and Southern Baptists in regards to the American Baptist Theological Seminary. I can say some plans were set into motion that I think will be productive in the years ahead.

On May 30th and 31st, the trustees of Western Baptist Bible College and the Board of our State Convention met on the campus. From these meetings came two main points: (1) immediate plan (roof for Goins Hall and installation of heating plant). (2) Long range plan (converting Rosa B. Johnson Hall into a home for aged Baptists, you have previously heard about this plan). We pray that God will see us through.

In June (third week), the Baptists assembled in Denver, Colorado for the National Sunday School and Baptist Training Union Congress, Dr. O. Clay Maxwell, president. This truly was a great session. The Congress is always informative and inspiring.

In July, the State Congress met in St. Louis that was the conclusion of President Walker's first year. We believe the Congress to be in safe hands, however, let the officials of the Congress never depart from Bible instruction for that is one great need of Baptists today. The tragedy is that we do not have enough of God in our minds.

On September 4th through the 9th, the National Baptist Convention met in Chicago, Illinois, the theme being **The Task of the Church in the Struggle for Peace**. I was there as your representative and because of you, I was able to be in line with those who gave two hundred dollars, thereby becoming a life member. I think those who were in attendance can say with me that it was the best session we have witnessed within nine years. It seemed that everyone who preached was at his best. President Jackson spoke with authority as only he can. It seemed that after years of unrest and strife, the convention is about to move on into a wider field of service.

Among the many wonderful happenings there, I want to mention two at this time: (1) The Ten Thousand Dollar perpetual scholarship given by the convention to Roosevelt University, and (2) Rev. R. L. Collins apologized for his role in preventing the preaching of the Gospel on Sunday morning during the convention in Philadelphia, 1960.

There seemed to be signs of true repentance. The convention forgave him and restored him to fellowship. We go to Cleveland, Ohio for the next session of the convention. To all our auxiliaries goes a word of commendation for support and cooperation given and a plea for greater service. Probably the most underdeveloped phase of denominational activities among Negro Baptists is that of our Lay organizations. This is true not so much because of a lack of interest as some would have it, as it is a lack of privilege that deprives us of the presence and availability of our men who would contribute so much to the ongoing of our churches, district and statewide programs.

Another factor contributing to the non-effectiveness of our Laymen's organization is the total lack of help and encouragement from so many of our pastors. The most pressing and immediate need of the Baptist church is to harness the manpower of our churches for good and for God. May God help us to make full use of all possibilities for the advancement of the Kingdom of God.

Our Civil Rights Struggle

Man was born with a spark of freedom in his soul. Whatever the color of his skin, he cannot rest until he is free. Let it be known to all men everywhere that we hate no one and we do not wish to carry on a program of hate. Our struggle must not be based on prejudice, envy and strife, for there are many whose skin is different in color who stand with us all the way.

In the words of Dr. J. H. Jackson, "The struggle for civil rights is not a struggle for legalized friendship or an effort to get away from our own people. The Negro citizens for whom I speak are proud of themselves, satisfied with their families and love their own people. They want for themselves and their families the same good things as any other American citizen desires. They want to purchase homes where their money can buy. They want a free opportunity for all the cultural things in life and a privilege to drink deeply of the Pierian Springs of knowledge and understanding."

In the July 15, 1962 *Pittsburg Currier*, an editorial quoted Clarence Mitchell as urging Negroes to channel some of their sit-in energy into a wade-in into politics and swim to freedom with the ballot. When this is done, we can have a different kind of sit-in. It will be sitting in seats as members of the city council, the state legislature and the congress. Of course, qualifying and registering to vote is not as spectacular as the sit-ins, the wade-ins, the ride-ins which make headlines but not much else, but it gets results almost immediately when it is tried. There are hardly any Negro communities North or South where one will find over seventy-five percent of eligible Negroes registered to vote and voting; even though there is everywhere an almost unanimous cry for freedom and equality as if shouts for help were enough.

The non-whites need political power most, but use it least. We must do more than protest; we must speak with the ballot. A one-hundred percent Negro registration across the country will do more to speed the attainment of full civil rights than anything else Negroes can do and all of their energies should be directed now to getting it done. We must never give up for this is God's world.

Can We Believe Him?

Often the secrets of spiritual success are deceptively simple. No one will deny that the entrance to spiritual life is through the gateway of belief; but how prone we are to stray away from spiritual power. Sometimes we are tragically like the children of Israel, who were on the verge of entering into the blessing when they faltered because they could not bring themselves to believe God. They believed the obstacles in the Promised Land were bigger than their God, with a heart of fatherly anguish over the reluctance of His children to trust Him. God asked Moses, "How long will it be ere they believe me?" (Numbers 14:11). This is always the question we must answer, no matter how young or old one may be in the faith. This is the simple secret of victory, and yet how often we stumble and fail to lay hold of God and His promises. Regardless of circumstances, the

Lord says to us, Believe Me. One can hardly imagine greater distress and fear than that which characterized the disciples of the Lord Jesus as they gathered with Him in the Upper Room on the night He was betrayed.

The truth of His impending crucifixion had finally gripped them. Peter wanted to know where Jesus was going, so how could they know the way. Phillip demanded to see the Father. In the midst of all this turmoil and anguish, the kind that few of us are called upon to face, the answer of the Lord Jesus was an echo of the words spoken by His Father to Moses centuries before, "How long will it be until you believe me?" The role of the church then is to believe God. Four times the word "believe" occurs in John 14:10-13. Is it any wonder, then, that we assert that obedience to the simple command, "Believe" is the key to victory?

Jesus did not urge His followers to trust in techniques, strategy, public relation gimmicks, or smart business methods. This method then and now is this: Believe me! Believe me!

MORE THAN SUFFICIENT

Millions of dollars have been spent on research to find a way to convert sea water into palatable drinking water. More millions have been spent by cities to provide adequate supplies of water. States engage in expensive litigations over the rights to water from lakes and rivers. Are we who have been born of God as much concerned about the outflow of the living water that the Lord Jesus promises as our industries and governments are about their reservoirs of water for the provision of man's physical needs?

Jesus said if you drink of me, your life will be like a river of living water. There will be life, fruit, stability, prosperity, and abundance. Our lives ought to be abundant, which simply means more than sufficient.

The true Christian experience is more than sufficient to take care of sin and moral failure. Jesus Christ cleanses from sin, defeat and despair. In His death on the cross, He took the disease and debt of sin. He paid God's just penalty for our sin. The Lord Jesus died and rose again so that we need not face the just consequences for our sin. If we receive Him and put our trust in Him, we may have forgiveness and a new life free from the bondage of sin.

It is more than sufficient to take care of fear and anxiety. If we have placed our faith in Christ, this is our portion.

It is more than sufficient to take care of sorrow and sickness. There is hope in the Lord Jesus. We need not sorrow as those who have no hope.

It is more than sufficient to take care of our eternal destiny. Christ is the only way to an everlasting life of fellowship in the presence of God. Is it any wonder then that

Jesus said, "I have come that they might have life and that they might have it more abundantly"?

We need to thirst for the Lord Jesus and keep coming to drink of Him, so that our lives will be more than sufficient in victory through Christ over every circumstance of life. Let us check our water supply, let it cleanse us, enrich us, let it be as fruit in our lives and the lives of others. If this is not true, let us cleanse out the intake pipes. Perhaps some of the pipes have been clogged with rubbish, ambition, pride, grudges, and selfishness. We must take all necessary steps to start the water flowing through will power, so that our lives will be more than sufficient, truly abundant.

SPIRITUAL STAMINA

These days when we seem to take pride in counting our numbers, we must be reminded that God's people are to be measured, not counted. God is seeking quality, not quantity. But how easy it is to slip into the error of supposing that numbers are the evidence of blessing and spiritual success. No, God is calling those who will be able to stand in the conflict and endure prolonged testing, as Gideon's three hundred, "faint, yet pursuing." Stamina is defined as a reserve of vital force enabling one to endure prolonged strain. This is certainly true in the spiritual realm. We must have Spiritual Stamina. A sharp test, a sudden trial, with relief quickly following, this is one thing. To go on day after day enduring the same trial, the steady pressure, the constant strain, this is a far different thing. It is exactly this that many of God's children are called to face.

Today, the Lord Jesus is calling for followers who will serve Him not merely for a way out of their problems, but to endure hardness for His sake. I hear Paul saying, "For unto you it is given in the behalf of Christ, not only to believe on him, but also to suffer for his sake" (Philippians 1:29). You may say that this is a lonely road, an unattractive road. I would reply, it is the only road that leads to permanent blessing and joy.

An editorial in the *Tulsa Tribune* by J. L. Jones appeared sometime ago. He reviews the collapse of moral standards today. He reminds us that our puritan ancestors possessed Spiritual Stamina. He said they had horsepower. He indicts the conditions of today. He acknowledges that there are some good things. He sums up our condition with this final paragraph: "There is rot, and there is blight, and there is cutting out and filling in to be done; if we as the leaders of free men are to survive the hammer blows which quite plainly are in store for us all."

Yes, God gives Spiritual Stamina that we may stand the test, realizing that we do not have to stand alone. Where does the church of Jesus Christ stand in this? This is no day for those who are spiritually weak. We must be strong with the Spiritual Stamina that only God can give.

I hear the prophet of old saying in clear tones: "But they that wait upon the LORD shall renew their strength, they shall mount up with wings as eagles, they shall run, and not be weary, and they shall walk, and not faint" (Isaiah 40:31). The hardest of these is to walk.

> Am I a soldier of the cross? A follower of the Lamb?
> And shall I fear to own His cause,
> Or blush to speak His name?
> Must I be carried to the skies On flowery beds of ease,
> While others fought to win the prize,
> And sailed through bloody seas?
> Are there no foes for me to face? Must I not stem the flood?
> Is this vile world a friend to grace, To help me on to God?
> Sure I must fight, If I would reign; Increase my courage, Lord;
> I'll bear the toil, endure the pain, Supported by Thy word.

1977 CONVENTION HAPPENINGS

1977 marked the sixteenth year of Dr. I. H. Henderson's presidency. He continued his efforts to keep Western Bible College afloat. He consistently sought to unify the working components of the convention. He sought to record and publish the history of the convention. Dr. David O. Shipley had been given that task. He reported that the book was at the press.

Let us now look at the years of Dr. Henderson starting in 1977. The Board met at the Western Bible College in May of this year. Pastors I. C. Peay and T. E. Baker were assigned to represent the state on Foreign and Home Mission Board at the National Convention. The main issues dealt with at this meeting were the appointment of Brothers William Hobson and Donald Cottner as Executive and Managing Editors of the Convention's Message Newsletter, respectively. Plans for the 90th Annual Session for 1979 were discussed. Aid for the people in Sedalia was discussed. An update on Western was given and reports from Auxiliary leaders were presented. The Ninetieth Annual Session of the convention consumed considerable attention. President Henderson wanted to ensure that in all planning sessions Evangelism and Witnessing; Missions and Awards; Finance; and Education be emphasized. The President asked for the names of all people working on the committees to be submitted in writing; and that all work was to be completed by the Board meeting in July.

ADDITIONAL NOTES

President Henderson called for aid to the Tornado Victims in the Sedalia, Missouri area and asked for immediate help. Rev. Robert Dabney spoke relative to the Tornado disaster in Sedalia, Missouri. It is a strong feeling that old cast off clothes are not the best thing to send in situations like this. Bed linen, towels, blankets, etc. are far better in meeting the needs of the people. However, cash contributions can serve far better in meeting the needs of the people. Send contributions to President Henderson's office, 5654 Norton Street, Kansas City, MO 64130. Reverend Robert Dabney, Pastor of the Ward Memorial Baptist Church, will serve as chairman of the Sedalia Disaster Committee. Sixty days is the time allotted for completion of this request. By all means, make checks payable to the Sedalia Disaster Committee. Please do not make them payable to the convention. President Singleton spoke relative to the closing of Western this week, graduation of students and the needs of the school (all facets noted). President Henderson asked President Singleton to bring forth plans and suggestions from the Trustee Board to finance the needs of Western. The convention is presently giving the lion's share of its funds to the school according to the plan of the convention. President Singleton said this would be done (cost of the immediate needs as presented by President Singleton is estimated between $5,000 and $6,000).

Representatives from the Women's Auxiliary, Laymen, and Ushers were presented. They made the following comments. Mrs. W. O. Wood, president of the Women's Auxiliary gave inspiring and informative remarks relative to the work of the Women's Auxiliary. The names of Reverends N. L. Symington, Charles Bell and R. E. Andrews are to be a part of the program for the annual session.

Brother Lyman Parks, president of the Laymen's Auxiliary gave very glowing remarks on the work of the laymen and will have a very interesting and informative program for the annual session. Brother Melvin Smalls, president of the Ushers and Health Auxiliary, gave remarks on the planned work of the Ushers and Health Unit that will be brought to fruition at the annual session. This meeting was followed by the letter listed below from Secretary Haynes.

President Isaiah H. Henderson, Jr.	The Missionary Baptist State Convention of Missouri Organized in 1889	Treasurer A. M. Hudson
Vice President Victor H. Wells	5654 North Avenue Kansas City, MO 64130 (816) 363-2040	Auditor William Givens
Vice President Maceo Piggee		Statistician Haymond

Recording Secretary
Qunicy Keeble

Neal J. Haynes
Executive Secretary
159 East Kirkham Avenue
West Groves, MO 63119

May 28, 1977

Fellow Pastors, Auxiliary Presidents and Chairmen:

   Words alone are not adequate to fully express the sentiment of the Missionary Baptist State Convention's May Board Meeting held on the campus of Western Baptist College. If you missed it, you missed a blessing and the fellowship of the brethren. There are a few things that I trust you are mindful of, if not, I shall also share them with you at this writing.

Your receipt(s) is/are attached. The July Board Meeting will be held at the Washington Tabernacle Baptist Church, 3000 Washington Avenue, St. Louis, Missouri. Dr. Melvin Smotherson, Pastor, at 2:00 p.m., Wednesday, July 6, 1977.

1. Send now your gift FOR THE PRINTING OF THE HISTORICAL BOOK. We must have this book ready for distribution by October.
2. The Eighty-eighth Annual Session of the Missionary Baptist State Convention will be held at the Newstead Baptist Church, Dr. W. A. Scott, Sr., Pastor, 4374 North Market Street, St. Louis, Missouri, October 10-14, 1977 with the Congress Board Meeting, Saturday, October 15, 1977.
3. Remember the National Baptist Congress of Christian Education theme will be: "The Role of the Church in the Prevention of Crime" (This change in theme comes from the National Congress Office).
4. A special motion prevailed that all churches of this convention and friends of Christ share in helping the people in the Sedalia, Missouri area that were victims of the recent tornado that struck there. THE NEED IS GREAT AND IMMEDIATE!!! Send your contributions to the Office of President I. H. Henderson, 5654 Norton Street, Kansas City, Missouri 64130. Make checks payable to the Sedalia Disaster Relief Committee.

Your Secretary,
Neal J. Haynes

THE 1978 ANNUAL SESSION OF THE CONVENTION WAS CONDUCTED WITH NEWSTEAD BAPTIST CHURCH OF ST. LOUIS

   The Convention was convened by President Henderson on the 11th of October 1978. Executive Secretary Haynes presented the following report during the 1978 Annual Session.

Brother President, Fellow Presidents, Official Staff, Auxiliary Presidents, Delegates, Messengers and all: this is another occasion to make my Annual Report to you.

In coming to St. Louis in October 1977, we were the guests of the Newstead Baptist Church, Reverend Dr. W. A. Scott, Sr., Pastor. Without a shadow of doubt, Pastor Scott and the good members of the Newstead Baptist Church were very kind to us in making things very comfortable and convenient. From the beginning to the ending, the convention was in high gear. The Monday evening musicale was par-excellent; no other has surpassed it. As I view the love and the fellowship of the Lord Jesus Christ, I am delighted and thank the eternal God for the history of the convention. Time and space would fail me if I attempted to write all the exquisite and elegant receptions we received at the Newstead Baptist Church.

You already know, we are the largest Missionary Baptist Convention in the State of Missouri. Under the matchless leadership of our President, Reverend Dr. Isaiah H. Henderson, Jr., our convention continues to grow. Time and time again, he has presented to us new challenges. Each year, there is improvement over previous years. I continue to work in harmony with our president, Dr. Henderson, and all auxiliary presidents of the convention, even pastors and friends of the convention. Let me pause here to thank you for your prayers during my present illness that prevented me from attending the July Board Meeting in Kansas City, Missouri at the Paseo Baptist Church, Reverend Charles Briscoe, Pastor. While prayers were going up, healing grace was coming down. Again, let me say I thank you!

The Financial Budget of the convention is being understood by more of our pastors. Our records show an increase in the funds that help us to keep our commitments to other organized bodies. If any pastor desires detailed information concerning the financial plan of the convention, contact me and I delight in helping you. If you discover any mistake in this report, call my attention to it: an investigation will be made and rectified.

Have a good day and may the Lord bless you real good!!!

Your Secretary,
Neal J. Haynes

Fifteen Associations and one-hundred-twenty churches were represented. They were: Antioch with thirty-nine churches; Berean represented with twenty-five churches; Central represented with thirteen churches; Christian Liberty represented with seven churches; Friendship represented with eight churches; Greater Union represented with seven churches; Midwest represented with seven churches; Mt. Carmel represented with eight churches. Mt. Zion represented with six churches; New Era represented with twenty churches; North Missouri represented with four churches; Pemicott-Dunklin represented with two churches; Southwest District represented with six churches; and United Fellow District represented with one church.

The attendees at the convention provide major financial contributions for the World Youth Conference in Manila, the Prison Ministry Project, Home and Foreign Missions and Western Bible College. Major contributors to the Home and Foreign Mission work in the National Convention were Jerusalem Baptist Church, pastored by Rev. Joseph Morgan and First Baptist Church, Webster Groove pastored by Reverend N. J. Haynes.

Another highlight of the year was the release of *A History of Black Baptists in Missouri* written by Dr. and Mrs. David O. Shipley.

OFFICIAL DIRECTOR 1977-78

Dr. Isaiah H. Henderson, Jr.	President
Dr. Victor H. Wells	Vice President
Rev. Maceo Piggee	Vice President
Dr. Neal J. Haynes	Executive Secretary
Rev. Qunicy Keeble	Recording Secretary
Rev. A. M. Hudson, Sr.	Treasurer
Dr. W. A. Givens	Auditor
Rev. Haymond Fortenberry	Statistician
Rev. William Hobson	Editor
Sister Noimi Erickerson	Pianist
Sister Doris C. Nance	Chorister
Sister Rosemary Hunt	Sponsor State Oratorical Contest
Sister Marguerite Jones	Assistant Directress Christian Education
Dr. William Claiborne	Director Christian Education

AUXILIARIES

Sister V. O. Woods	Women's Home and Foreign Missions
Sister Ophelia Brown	Ministers' Wives Fellowship
Sister Ann E. Moore	Music Department
Brother Melvin Small	Usher
Brother Lyman Parks	Laymen
Rev. Fred John	Evangelistic Department
Dr. Daniel Hughes	Sunday School and Training Union

Spring of 1979 Board Meeting

The meeting was called to order by the President. The adoption of the agenda was the next item of business. The Convention's theme will be "Forward with Christ." Rev. J. Morgan, Rev. Peay, Sr., and Rev. Givens were asked to give a Scripture for the theme.

Vice President Morgan stated that he had visited the government hospitals and they had pictures of the President of the United States on the walls, and he thought it would be nice if each one of us had a picture of the President of the Convention in our homes. It was moved and seconded that at the Annual Session pictures of the President would be available as a tribute to the 90th year session. It carried.

Dr. William Givens reported on the Baptist Student Center. They received $3,600.00 missing our goal by $1,000.00. The National Baptist retreat will be in Memphis, TN. We have four students who will serve as summer missionaries from Lincoln University.

Dr. Haynes reported that the National Convention asked our convention for one thousand dollars, this money will go to Bishop College. Dr. Haynes moved, Rev. Hudson seconded the adoption of this item. It carried. President Henderson stated during the centennial celebration that Missouri will be called and we will give our money then.

Dr. Javis reported on the entertainment for the session, all things are in motion, you will be glad to come. Rev. Shipley gave the historian's report. He suggested that we establish a committee to get information. Dr. Haynes served as moderator's advisory. We need some women to serve on this committee: Mrs. Regina , Mrs. C. Hampton and Mrs. V. O. Woods. Rev. Hudson gave the names of Mrs. L. C. Glass and Mrs. Delois Miland. The names of board members to serve on the National Convention were given. Dr. Hughes objected; he stated that the name of a non-pastor and a pastor who is not a member of the association are on the board, and it should not be. It was suggested that we look through this and see what we come up with.

The Music Department stated that they will still have the salad supper. Dr. Hughes reported on the entertainment committee for the National Congress. Everyone is working and everything is going fine. Come and be with us. Pre-registration will be at Central Baptist Church. Rev. Dukes made the treasurer's report. Copies were passed out.

Dr. Briscoe asked a question about the money to Western. Rev. Hudson and Rev. Javis explained that this is a partial report and Western received sixty percent of the money. Dr. Javis stated that we need to help upgrade our churches, many of them are using Southern Baptist material and most of this is given to them. We want to help our churches through the State Congress.

President Henderson asked Dr. I. C. Peay, Sr. to come and give the balance of his report on foreign missions. This report was in print. Dr. W. A. Givens, campus minister, gave his report. V. O. Woods gave remarks and thanks to the pastor and church. Dr.

Hughes reminded everyone that the congress board was meeting on Saturday morning at 9:00 a.m. at the Missionary Baptist State Convention of Missouri, Spring Session March 1-4, 1980, Second Baptist Church, Jefferson City, Missouri.

The Executive Secretary made the following report from the Annual Session for November, December, 1979 and January—February, 1980.

Receipts

90th Year Celebration Contributions:

1. Churches	$5,652.56
2. Personal	2,937.64
3. Associations	1,105.00
4. Souvenir Ads and Sales (incomplete)	1,840.00
5. Banquet	9,309.00
6. Regular representation	18,683.52
	$39,527.72

Allocation to Western Bible College for this period: $10,508.21

Respectfully submitted,
Rev. A. M. Hudson, Sr.
Treasurer
Rev. McKinley Dukes
Assistant Treasurer

1980 March Board Meeting Held at Second Baptist, Jefferson City, MO

The Missionary Baptist State Convention of Missouri conducted its March Board Meeting at the Second Baptist Church in Jefferson City. Rev. David O. Shipley, pastor, on March 13, 1980. The meeting opened with singing. President I. H. Henderson, Jr., presiding. Issues for discussion were the retirement of Dr. Loren Belt, Southern Baptist Liaison; assistance for our association; the Annual Session; Baptist Student Union work; and a request from the National Baptist Convention, USA, Inc. to support Bishop College.

President Henderson stated that Dr. Loren Belt, a member of the advisory committee for National and Southern Baptist cooperation, is retiring. The president stated that Dr. Belt had been faithful and we want to be a part of it. We will send a resolution and monetary gift. We were assured of suggestions concerning his replacement would be forthcoming.

There was discussion concerning appointing someone to attend the district associations. We need the districts, and they need us. The names were called of the districts that had not responded. Dr. Briscoe asked if this would be a budgetary item. Only the expense to the meeting.

THE MESSENGER
March, 1981

GREATER FAIRFAX MISSIONARY BAPTIST CHURCH – 2941 GREER AVE., ST. LOUIS, MO.

REV. DR. HAYMOND FORTENBERRY, PASTOR

GREATER FAIRFAX IN CENTENNIAL CELEBRATION

The Greater Fairfax Missionary Baptist Church, located at 2941 Greer Avenue, St. Louis, Missouri will begin a centennial celebration with a pre-musical to be held at the church on March 1st, 3:30 p.m. featuring The Greater Fairfax Mass Choir.

Among the guests will be the West Side Baptist Church with exhortative remarks from the pastor, Rev. Moses Javis. Services will be held nightly, Monday thru Friday beginning at 7:30 p.m. at the church with many area churches participating.

On Sunday, March 8th, the guest speaker at 11:00 a.m. and 3:00 p.m. will be Dr. E. A. Freeman, pastor of the First Baptist Church, Kansas City, Kansas. Dr. Freeman also serves as Superintendent of Christian Education of the National Congress.

The final will be a banquet on Monday, March 9th beginning at 7:30 p.m. at the Sheraton St. Louis Hotel at Convention Plaza Downtown. The speaker will be Dr. Enoch H. Oglesby, Associate Professor of Theology and Social Ethics at the Eden Theological Seminary, Webster Groves, Mo.

A cordial invitation is extended to the public. For further information you may call 314/534-1998. The Reverend Dr. Haymond Fortenberry is pastor.

THE BIBLE AND THE TV GUIDE

On the table, side by side
The HOLY BIBLE and the TV GUIDE.
One is well worn and cherished with pride.
But it's not the BIBLE, it's the TV GUIDE.

One is used daily to help folks to decide–
No! it's not the BIBLE it's the TV GUIDE.
As they turn the pages, what shall they see?
OH! it doesn't matter, just turn on the TV.

Then confusion is started, for they can't all agree.
On what they shall watch on the TV.
So they refer to the book on which they all relied.

But it isn't the BIBLE--It's the TV Guide.
The word of God is seldom read.
Perhaps a verse before they fall into bed.
Exhausted and tired and as sleepy as can be–
Not from reading the BIBLE. But from watching TV.

Then back on the table side by side,
the Holy Bible and the TV Guide.
No time for prayer, no time for the word.
the plan of salvation is seldom heard.
Forgiveness of sin is full and free.
But the plans in the BIBLE–Not on TV.

...... COPIED

THE MESSENGER
OFFICIAL ORGAN OF THE MISSIONARY BAPTIST STATE CONVENTION OF MISSOURI
Rev. Otis L. Hawes, Jr., Editor
P.O. Box 431 – Poplar Bluff, Missouri 63901
SUBSCRIPTION RATES
$3.50 ANNUALLY — $3.00 BUDGET PLAN - 10 OR MORE — $1.25 PER SINGLE COPY
PUBLISHED
MARCH — JULY — OCTOBER — DECEMBER

THE GOD OF NEW BEGINNINGS

We begin the year of our Lord, 1981. Whatever might have been the experiences of our yesteryears, they have now been hushed in the quietude of the past. We live in our now — anticipating our future. While we say that our past is indeed past, the fact of the matter is, it is not simply past. We still have the consequences of mistakes, sins, and guilts of days gone by. The context of human existence so often means that a new year brings despair more than hope; more problems than solutions; more questions than answers. In and of itself, life grows older, and the newness of a new year is merely the superficiality of wishful thinking.

The Gospel of Jesus Christ is the human existence that does not have to be in and of itself. The Church proclaims that there is a new element available for life that will give it a new dimension, a new quality, a new meaning. This newness of life has been revealed and made possible in Jesus Christ. Because of Him, the new year is truly new — not because the page of the calendar has been turned, but because He has done something to the pages of the old calendar! Jesus Christ redeems human life, reclaims it from all the consequences of a sinful past, recreates it in truth and in love; in faith and acceptance. Life in Jesus Christ is real. He takes away the burden of the guilty past and says to all of us: "Go thy way and sin no more."

God in Jesus Christ means a new beginning in another significant way. He not only forgives us for the past, He makes a new life possible. 1981 can be different from any of our previous years. It can be different because God offers us His strength by which we can live a new life... "If any man be in Christ Jesus, he is a new creation: old things have passed away, and behold all things have become new." New strength, new guidance, new directions, new light — this is the type of newness we can have in Jesus Christ. We can lift our heads high, knowing that 1981 will not be the same as our previous years because God is creating our lives anew each and every day.

Lillian Glass

PROGRESSIVE BAPTIST CHURCH NEWS

The Progressive Baptist Church usher board recently held it's Annual program. The Rev. George Coleman of the Sugar Grove Baptist Chruch, Columbia was guest speaker.

The Progressive Baptist Church has planned to share in the Pastors Installation services of The Rev. Jewell D. Jones, Sr. on March 27. Rev. Jones is the former pastor of Second Baptist Church, Columbia. Also former Vice Moderator of Mt. Carmal District and has been called to pastor the Strangers Rest Baptist Church, Kansas City, Kansas.

The construction of a new sanctuary for the Progressive Baptist Church is well on the way and the pastor and congregation anticipates dedicatory services the first Sunday in April.

Reported by Mrs. Clara Coleman

Page 2 — THE MESSENGER — July, 1982

DAY BY DAY ACTIVITIES OF INTEREST FOR THE CONGRESS

Monday:
- 10:00 a.m. Registration and Classification
- 2:00 p.m. Executive Board Meeting
- 5:00-7:00 p.m. Doris Nance Memorial Tea
- 8:00 p.m. Pre-Congress Musical — Pleasant Green Music Dept.

Tuesday:
- Morning: The Congress will be called to order by Dr. Daniel W. Hughes, President.

Wednesday: Guest speaker will be the president of the Kansas City Branch NAACP Rev. Omni Nelms.

Thursday: The 7:15 service features the annual address by president Hughes.

Friday: Attend "Formal Evening with Christ." Please support our youth.

Music for the week will include Mt. Sinai and Memorial Choirs, Kansas City; and Prospect Hill and Eastern Star of St. Louis featuring the Children's Choir of Eastern Star.

HOUSING

For those seeking private housing call (816) 923-7751 or (816) 923-7814.

$10.00 per night one (1) person — $15.00 two (2). For Hotel accomodations make your own reservations. The Howard Johnson at 5 East 6th Trafficway is one for ideal location.

The theme for this year's Oratorical Contest remains the same as last year: "The Influence of the National Baptist Convention, U.S.A., Inc. on the Religious Life of America."

SPECIAL REMINDER

The guest lecturer will be Rev. Jewell Jones, Pastor of the Stranger's Rest M.B. Church of Kansas City, Kansas. Rev. Jones is the former pastor of the Second Baptist Church of Columbia, Mo. President Hughes is asking that "we do our best to make this the best session ever.

THE CONGRESS BANQUET

The Banquet chairperson reports that plans are finalized. The banquet will be Wednesday, July 7, 1982 — 5:00 p.m. at Linwood Multi-Purpose Center. For banquet reservations you may contact your district presidents or moderators.

ADEQUATE CLASS SPACE

Some classes will be held in facilities that are within a radius of a few blocks from Pleasant Green and Memorial Baptist Churches.

GOOD FOOD AT REASONABLE PRICES

Meal prices have been set as follows:
- Breakfast $3.00
- Dinner $4.00

Breakfast will be served beginning at 7 a.m.

YOUTH DAY ACTIVITIES

Youth Director, Mrs. Rosemary Hunt is asking that all entries for the Oratorical Contest, Intermediate Sword Drill be submitted no later than July 5, 1982. ABSOLUTELY NO last minute entries will be accepted.

ST. PAUL OF POPLAR BLUFF CALLS PASTOR

Rev. Henry D. Young of St. Louis, Missouri was called to the pastorate of St. Paul Missionary Baptist Church of Poplar Bluff, Missouri. Rev. Young is the son of Mrs. Carrie M. Young of Neelyville, Missouri and the late Rev. Moses Young, Sr.

EVANGELISTIC REVIVAL

The Rev. Charles L. Fairchild, pastor of the Greater Faith Missionary Baptist Church of Chicago, Illinois was the evangelist in a weeks revival at the St. Paul Missionary Baptist Church. Rev. Fairchild is the son of Mr. and Mrs. William Fairchild, 903 Garfield, Poplar Bluff, Missouri.

MISSIONARY BAPTIST CONGRESS OF CHRISTIAN EDUCATION

DR. DANIEL W. HUGHES, PRESIDENT
DR. WILLIAM H. CLAIBORNE, DEAN
DR. HAYMON FORTENBERRY, ASS'T. DEAN

JULY 5-9, 1982

PLEASANT GREEN BAPTIST CHURCH — KANSAS CITY, MISSOURI

STUDIES BEING OFFERED AT THIS SESSION

COURSE NO.	TITLE	INSTRUCTOR
104	EFFECTIVE BIBLE STUDY	Rev. Richard Pearson
131	THE ACTS OF THE APOSTLES	Rev. Don McNeal
209	BAPTIST DOCTRINE	Rev. Clarence Duvall
226	MISSIONARY EDUCATON IN THE LOCAL CHURCH	Dr. Carolyn Ealy
296.1	BECOMING AN EFFECTIVE DEACON	Mr. Allen Blewett
299.1	THE GROWTH OF THE LAITY	Mr. Lewis B. Parker
YOUTH	YOUTH FELLOWSHIP	
110.1B	HOW TO READ AND STUDY THE BIBLE	Rev. Chris Jackson
234	TEENAGE EVANGELISM	Mrs. Viola Howard
299	THE YOUTH DIRECTOR AND HIS/HER WORK	Mrs. Rosemary Hunt
	BIBLE FOR JUNIORS	Mrs. Annie Bullock

LABORATORY SCHOOL
Mrs. Dorethea Scott, Director — Mrs. Beverly Robinson, VCS Coordinator

219	CREATIVE ACTIVITIES	Mrs. Lucy Clark
222	RECREATIONAL LEADERSHIP	Mrs. Louise Aubrey
260	THE USE OF THE BIBLE WITH CHILDREN	Mrs. Edwynna Harris
262	WHEN CHILDREN WORSHIP	Mrs. Cora Wilson

SEMINARS

252 THE BLACK MALE AND FEMALE IN THE DEVELOPMENT OF THE FAMILY IN CHURCH — Dr. Mary L. Franklin

THE BAPTIST MINISTERS SEMINAR — Rev. F. W. Johnson, Director
Revs. Ronal Bridewell, Lawrence McKinney, A. L. Pryor

THE MINISTERS WIVES SEMINAR — Mrs. Ophelia B. Henderson, Dir.
Mrs. Ora Hughes, Mrs. Regina Nance

299.1 To impress upon the laity the fact that the work of the church is theirs and that the success of the church depends upon their growth and involvement.

226 How to build missions into the total education program of the local church.

104 How does one read the Bible? is the question to be dealt with in this study, the historical setting, the literature, and theological strata are the deminsions to be touched upon.

131 The student will be led to approach the study of the Acts of the Apostles as the first attempt of the early church to present a history of the Church. Special attention will be given to the contribution of two early church's foremost apostles, Simon Peter and the Apostle Paul.

THE DUKES PRESIDENCY 1983-1992 (A TIME OF TRANSITION)

A major power vacuum occurred in the convention following the death and twenty-two year tenure of President I. H. Henderson. Several individuals submitted their names for consideration as president. The names included Pastors McKinley Dukes, I. C. Peay, Sr. and Neal J. Haynes, to name a few. The election was conducted during the Ninety-eighth Annual Session at Palestine Baptist Church in Kansas City, October 14-19, 1993.

President Dukes was elevated from the rank of assistant treasurer to the rank of president. His tenure followed the peaks and valleys of Dr. Henderson's presidency. His tenure was indeed a time of transition for himself and the convention. He was elected to the presidency after having served the convention and congress in a number of capacities.

It was extremely difficult to gather information and literature to describe the nine-year tenure of President Dukes. The Convention presented an interesting paradox when he assumed office. The body was vibrant, and yet divided. Western continued to be a source of concern. There was a determination to end the six-year dialogue about tenure by enacting it. It also appears that the auxiliaries were struggling and not necessarily working together. There were factions that were not excited about his election. Some, even left the body and remained inactive for a variety of reasons. One might say that he inherited a can of worms that kept him in prayer.

These issues certainly had their impact on the president and the convention. He sought to bring harmony and unity back to the body. He sought to get clarification concerning the ownership of Western Bible College. It appears that there was a question about whether the school belonged to the Convention or the Board of Trustees. He encouraged the convention to help improve the quality of Western and to retire her indebtedness. The second hot issue was the matter of tenure in office. That issue was later resolved with the decision to enforced tenure.

The following individuals comprised his executive staff:

Reverend Fate White	Vice President
Reverend Maceo Piggee	Vice President
Reverend Fountebury	Vice President
Sammie E. Jones	Executive Secretary

President Dukes was born on December 8, 1918 in Magnolia, Arkansas to Zollie and Mattie Dukes. He is the younger of two children; his older brother Thomas Dukes died in 1918. Pastor Dukes' father died when he was one and a half years old. His mother, who is now deceased, cared for him and his brother by working for a white family in Homer, Louisiana, walking six miles each way, for five dollars a week.

He attended high school in St. John, Louisiana. Just before finishing high school, he was called into the ministry. He enrolled in the American Baptist Theological Seminary in Nashville, Tennessee, following his graduation from high school. He served as a waiter in local restaurants to finance his education. He received his Bachelor of Theology degree from the seminary. He later served as an associate minister to the Antioch Baptist Church in Shreveport, Louisiana under the late Reverend E. C. West from 1944 to 1946.

He married Jessie M. Dias on March 29, 1946. They are the proud parents of nine wonderful children. His beloved Jessie departed this life on September 9, 1983. They also have a son, Billy Wayne, who departed this life May 24, 1992.

Reverend Dukes accepted a call to pastor Greenwood Baptist Church in 1951 and has ministered there to the present. The membership has grown from 54 to over 300 members during his pastorate. He has provided them with dynamic and innovative leadership for forty-eight years. He has been very active in New Era and the state convention since acceptance of the call to Greenwood Baptist Church.

Pastor Dukes has been active in the religious and civic activities in Kansas City. He has served as president of the Baptist Ministers' Union of Kansas City, moderator of the New Era District Association, and treasurer and president of the Missionary Baptist State Convention. He presently is President Emeritus.

Pastor Dukes was awarded an Honorary Doctorate of Divinity degree from Central Theological Seminary of Monroe, Louisiana for his pastoral contributions to the betterment of society.

First Annual Address
Delivered at New Northside Baptist Church in St. Louis, Missouri

Mr. Presiding Officer, Officers of the Convention, Auxiliary Presidents, Moderators, Pastors, Christian Workers, Ladies and Gentlemen:

Once again, God has allowed us meet as messengers from churches throughout the state.

We gather here in St. Louis with the New Northside Baptist Church pastored by the Rev. Willis Ellis. He and his good people have invited us here; they have rolled out the red carpet for us, and doing all in their power to make us comfortable as we endeavor to worship our God.

We commend Rev. Earl Abel and the wonderful members of the Palestine Baptist Church, Kansas City, Missouri for the fine job in entertaining our convention last year.

We are all aware that our times during the 80s are times that are designed to try our faith. Our world is in a state of total unrest; nations are in competition with one another producing war materials and other devices of destruction. Yet, in the midst of these efforts, we who know God should stand the more for Him in daily witness.

Looking back twelve months ago, you made the choice of me as president. In accepting this task, I was definitely aware of the difficulty that was ahead, as well as the expected accomplishments. However, I felt and still feel sure that much good can and will be done as we work together for the advancement of the Kingdom of God. As President, I ask for your prayers and cooperation.

Our lives are written in three volumes: the past, the present and the yet to be. The first we have written and laid away. The second we are writing every day. The third of these three volumes is hidden from sight; God keeps the key.

Let us seek to preserve the past even though it is blighted with spoils and errors. We should study it carefully and use every possible means to place ourselves close in the past. Among the many things that possibly should not be done is to worship in the past.

Remember with deep appreciation and humbleness of heart those who have gone from us, who faithfully worked and served, and suffered in this moral vineyard of kingdom building. Much homage must be paid to those of yesteryears who sacrificed for the growth of this convention. Let us set our hearts and minds to the task of improving our convention. To help our convention is helping our race.

Remember that Christian ministers and Christian laymen are great blessings to any church or any society. While on the other hand, the church can suffer a tragic blow when pastors and people turn from their democratic fellowship and go to the civil courts of the land expecting to gain power.

It should be thoroughly understood that the best law firms in church disputes concern themselves with money and not unity.

We must continue as leaders to be servants of the people. As your President, I have been in attendance at all meetings including our last National Baptist Convention held in our nation's capitol. May I voice my thanks to the convention for their confidence placed in me. Thanks for the many pastors and laymen across the state for their loyal support.

Through the years, our State Convention has had within its ranks outstanding men and women who had left a legacy for each of us to follow. Those who have read the history of this convention can rejoice in the fact that through many dangers, toils and snares, we've already come. It was truly grace that has brought us safe thus far, and we definitely must depend on grace to see us through. Our broken harmony has been something to behold, together with the fruits of the past years. All have been rich and abundant.

**Annual State Banquet, Kansas City
President Dukes and leaders**

Christian Education in Our State

Our focus from the state has been and still is on Western, our school, not primarily in terms of genuine support, but in a casual way of maintaining. I call upon the entire state to take a hard look at the school and make her strong and debt free. This perhaps will set some of us in a lonely state. But I point you to the Master's lonely travel—forging His way, praying alone in Gethsemane, dying alone on Calvary.

Congress of Christian Education

In its Annual Session held with the Mt. Olive and Eastern Star Baptist Churches, the Congress realized its better session. We have reason to believe that the Congress is in good hands with Dr. Daniel Hughes and his staff. We pray not only for our Congress, but for all our auxiliaries. Many of them suffer for lack of full support.

Would you look with me now in the book of Matthew 17:21 and also 2 Kings 20:1. The theme: "The Church Identifying and Perfecting its Healing Ministry."

It must be thoroughly understood that there is no healing power in the church, but in the God of the church. The church must identify not only on mountain peaks when spirituality is exceedingly high and conditions are pleasant, but in the valley where faith is lacking, requests are serious, and hope is needed.

Identify, perfect, assume responsibility, claim the victory through Jesus Christ. If life is to make sense, yesterday's experience must have something to do with today's living. Behind every worthy spiritual victory lies many trials and defeats. God's victories come by the way of defeats.

MAY 16, 1990 BOARD MEETING OF THE MISSIONARY BAPTIST STATE CONVENTION OF MISSOURI, WESTERN BAPTIST BIBLE COLLEGE, KANSAS CITY

The Missionary Baptist State Convention of Missouri Board meeting convened at the Western Baptist Bible College in Kansas City, Missouri on May 16, 1990 at 10:20 a.m. The Meeting opened with singing, "Pass Me Not," led by Sister Viola Howard. The Scripture was read by Fate White from the 133rd and 134th Psalms. Prayer was offered by Rev. Culton Hamilton. There were opening remarks from President Dukes commenting on the fact that God knows just what to do and when as in the case of the heavy rains we are having. President Dukes also commented on the well-run machinery of the Women's Department. Everyone scheduled for reports in their session was ready with detailed and written reports. The President stated that his desire was to see the masculine sector get into that same frame of mind.

Rev. Fate White was asked to read the agenda and Reverend R. E. Miller was asked to distribute the agenda to those present. The President then asked for additions or corrections to the agenda. None were voiced. Rev. Givens moved and Bro. Melvin Smalls seconded the motion for the agenda's acceptance. The motion carried.

Rev. Harry Givens was asked to distribute copies of the minutes of the last meeting, and Rev. Fate White was asked to read the minutes. The President commented on the fact that we had a capable and conscientious executive secretary to make sure that the minutes were there and on time even though he was running late. After the reading of the minutes, Rev. Hamilton moved for acceptance with any necessary correction. The motion was seconded and several not-readies were noted.

Rev. Singleton asked that the minutes reflect the full name of the host pastor for Western's commencement services. The name should be Dr. W. H. White, Sr. Viola

Howard stated she was not the chairperson for the Western Centennial and the May 16th date given was not for the banquet, but for the commencement services.

In the call for unfinished business, Sister Peyton questioned what had been done by State Convention's personnel to get our act together (reference paragraph 3, page 2, March Board minutes). President Dukes stated that from October to March, we had given Western $5,500. The State Convention had also sent additional funds for the Centennial celebration and had made good on the promise to support Rev. Chris Jackson as he made his decision about Lincoln. The President said he felt these things were indicative of trying to get together.

Also, on unfinished business, Rev. Culton Hamilton questioned what had been done about getting a cost factor and plan of action to finance the President's trip to Korea to represent the state of Missouri (reference paragraph 1, page 2). There was much discussion on the varying packages and prices ranging from a basic cost of about $1,500 to $4,000.

The President stated that we have until August to get the fund together. During the discussion, it was indicated that some pastors felt that each church should donate a present amount. The Mt. Bethel Church had sent a check for $60 towards the President's trip. President Dukes said he felt more comfortable with freewill donations, rather than placing assessments on pastors and churches. At this point, Rev. Givens asked that anyone who had monies to turn in today would tell him at turn-in time what the funds are for if specifically earmarked so that he can keep the records straight.

The next item for consideration was the distribution of the newly revised constitution. He stated that Secretary Jones had the copies and would be responsible for distribution. The president added that because of the cost involved in printing the constitution, it was not feasible to mass distribute. The Women's Department had requested and received eighty copies of the constitution and had offered to give a donation of $1 each to help defray the cost. The President felt it good that other auxiliaries should follow the example. He asked that the moderators, auxiliary leaders, and presidents help with the distribution by making request for the number needed in their district or area and then distributing and collecting them for the copies and the monies turned back in to the Executive Secretary. The following distributions were made: Berean (J. Brown) 70, Antioch (S. Jones) 54, (R. Bridewell) 21, Mt. Carmel (H. Butler) 50, Friendship Consolidated (L. Glass) 25, Mt. Zion (R. Miller) 20, Midwest (F. White) 35, Southwest (H. Givens) 30, New Era (J. Miles) 50, State Ushers (S. Peyton) 51, Music Dept. (V. Howard), 20, Laymen (T. Jones) 30, total distributed 636.

The next item under consideration was upcoming activities. Rev. Harold Butler gave information on the upcoming Congress in July in Columbia. Activities will be held at the Calvary Baptist Church, 696 Ridgeway, just two blocks west of Progressive. Pastor Lloyd Reed had stated that we could use the facility free, but Rev. Butler stated he felt that the Congress should give a donation to offset utilities.

No lunch meals will be served at the church due to Calvary's involvement in a Meals on Wheels program. Continental breakfast will be offered at the church. The headquarters hotel will be the Drury Inn and the rate is $40 with up to four people allowed in a room. The Convention's Board Meeting will be held on Wednesday afternoon during the week of the Congress. The President asked that each person who had obtained a copy of the constitution take a look at the section that places emphasis on the activities of the auxiliaries coming under the heading of the convention. All activities, legislative actions, etc. must be ratified by the convention to become effective. All officers must be presented at the Convention's Annual Session.

Rev. Sam Jones, host pastor for the Convention's Annual Session in October, stated that Mt. Zion is in readiness for this event. The Holiday Inn Convention Center is to be used as the Headquarters and the location of the Banquet. Dr. Henry Lyons will be the speaker. There were accommodation forms made available for the room rates that were $45 for 1-2 people and $55 for 3-4 people. Rev. Jones also stated that Rev. Ray has been in touch with him and sent him banquet tickets for distribution in the St. Louis area. Meals will be available at the church and courtesy vans will be available also.

The President then asked that each district present would take a look at themselves as a district and discuss their support of the State Convention and Western. By general consensus, less than one-half support the state and the percentage for the school support was even less. The President stated that it might be advisable to send advisors or consultants to the districts to motivate the non-participating churches.

The President then commented on our State's support of the national work. President Woods added that some of our women try to bypass the state and go directly to the national. President Dukes stated that we need to get away from the club mentality and look at the full setup. He also noted that the Junior Matrons are being overlooked because of problems arising from children, husbands, jobs, etc. As a result of these conflicts, the older women are carrying on and the younger women are not being trained. We need to look closer locally to meet the needs of the practical side of training all our districts to strengthen the local church.

The president would like to request that each church obtain and display a photo of the Baptist World Center Building in Nashville, the headquarters of our Convention. This will be a legacy to our children rather than the photo of a white Jesus.

Dr. Singleton recounted Western's history from organization, stating that tonight's commencement exercises celebrate 100 years of service. He stated that we are living in a competitive age and the problems facing Western are ones relating to obtaining the wherewithal to do all that needs to be done. He gave a brief financial report stating that there will be $5,073.33 on hand after paying teachers $1,085.03. Many things are needed to get ready for the encampment. Rev. Jimmy Brown has volunteered to donate a cooling system for Goins Halls.

President Dukes commented on the Endowment Fund being underwritten by the State Convention. He stated that it should be clearly understood that the fund will not be exclusively for Western. At the present time, there is $3,103.00 in that fund. Sister Flora Hope questioned if the problem of ownership of Western had been cleared up. She said that she felt that cooperation and support would be more easily obtained if the problem was resolved. Rev. Schielle responded that it is like the church, the issue of ownership is not important. President Dukes said that while it has been said that the State Convention does indeed own the school, nothing has been put in writing or verified.

The question over insurance and the limits of coverage was brought up again as the roof is still in need of repair or replacement. It was determined that the age of the roof would more than likely make the insurance be of no effect with this problem. The statement was made that the convention was to do some renovations but had stopped due to the lack of money. The President stated the lack of funds was not the reason work had stopped, but the lack of cooperation from the Alumni group that had been collecting and raising funds for Western's renovation.

The state had proposed to do inside remodeling and updating but found that the roof leaked so extensively that it needed to be repaired or replaced before they could continue. The Alumni group that had the bulk of renovation funds refused to authorize and pay for the roof on the grounds they did not consider roofing to be renovation. Rev. Ellis stated that the same thing it takes to build churches is the same thing it will take to build Western, and that is money. It is a known fact that people will not give money without some information. Deeds need to be produced and questions answered. Brother Thad Jones stated that they had received six bids on the roof project ranging from $6,000.00 to $16,000.00. Because of the range in difference, a consultant had been secured to determine the true needs and cost. The consultant will report back to the trustees and they will in turn get back to the State Convention. Rev. Ellis commended Brother Jones' report and made a motion that this report be accepted. Rev. Jimmy Brown seconded, and the motion was carried. Rev. Sam Jones motioned that a written report of all regular meetings of the Trustee Board can be sent to the President and the Executive Secretary. Rev. Mallory seconded, and the motion carried. Rev. Schielle agreed to obtain and present deeds to Western.

Rev. Chris Jackson reported that this has been a good year at Lincoln and that he wished that some of these board meetings could be held at Lincoln so that the students could interact with the convention. He also reported that he is being led by God to move on. He will be going to Tennessee State University. He suggested that the Convention vote not to have a representative in the Commission to decide who his replacement will be. The question was raised if Southern Baptists supported the BSU at Lincoln and if so, how much? Rev. Jackson replied that they did support with $12,000 and the building. Rev. Jones suggested that something be done for Rev. Jackson in appreciation of the fine work he has done at Lincoln.

President Dukes commented that one day, Southern Baptists' support will run out and we should begin now to support ourselves. He further stated that he was organizing an advisory group to deal with discontent and problems within the state. The group will respond after notice from a pastor and/or church. One project may be a seminar in practical ethics. Rev. Daniel Childs, Pastor of Good Samaritan, had brief comments on his work with the Centennial Celebration of Western. A souvenir book is available and the cost is $5.00.

Rev. Jimmy Brown gave a report on the Moderators' Division and presented to the President a new listing of all the districts and churches within the districts. Rev. Sam Jones moved for adoption and Rev. Fate White seconded.

Rev. Harold Butler presented Rev. W. A. Finney, the new pastor of Second Baptist in Mexico. Rev. Finney gave words of greetings. Sister Woods gave a report on the WMU. She reported that she had ten district presidents present in the May Board meeting. They will be sending a check to the Executive Secretary for the constitution booklets. Funds collected today were $800 which includes Convention Representation $210; Western $100; World Center $50; and President's Trip $440. The meeting was closed with prayer from Brother Morris.

March 1991 Board Meeting, Second Baptist Church (Baptist Student Union-Lincoln University), Jefferson City, MO

The Missionary Baptist State Convention of Missouri's March Board met in Jefferson City at the BSU, Lincoln University at 10:00 a.m. The meeting came to order with singing. Mrs. Flora Hope led in a medley of songs: "Jesus The Light of the World," "Blessed Assurance," "Hold to God's Unchanging Hand."

President McKinley Dukes came with remarks. He stated that Dr. I. C. Peay would preside. He stated that we are having trouble in the Middle East with the school system. The congregation then sang "Keep On Believing."

Vice President Peay came with comments. He asked the congregation to sing "Amazing Grace." Rev. Harry Givens, moderator of Southwest District, came and presented the speaker. Rev. Rufus Kelley, pastor of Washington Avenue Baptist Church in Springfield, MO. Rev. Kelley came with comments. Amos 7:3-17 was the Scripture and sang, "There is a Fountain Filled with Blood." Rev. Givens extended the invitation. No one came. Dr. Peay had comments. We gave our gifts.

After the offertory prayer, Vice President Peay presented President Dukes. He called for announcements to come to the pulpit. Pastor Spencer gave words of welcome, Greetings from Councilman Halsey, William C. Clay, State Legislature, Peggy Maghee, Missouri Legislator. Pastor Roberts had comments and announcements.

Music was provided by Lincoln University's BSU Choir. Miss Priscilla Robinson came and presented a panel from the BSU. Rev. Sam Jones presented the panel from the convention. The topic was "Making it Through." After the panel discussion, music was presented by Second Baptist Church and BSU combined choirs.

President Dukes presented Dr. Singleton a check for the Western Bible College. The President also presented to Dr. Singleton a check from the convention. Secretary Jones thanked the Convention for what it did for BSU. Ushers will be in session.

Last Four Presidents of the Congress of Christian Education

Presidents Givens, Walker, Brookfield and Hughes

Dr. Sammie E. Jones ascended to the rank of president after serving the convention as executive secretary. He came to office with a burning desire to be creative and innovative. The minutes included in this section will provide an overview of those initiatives.

THE PRESIDENCY OF DR. SAMMIE E. JONES, 1992-PRESENT (A TIME OF ACTIVISM)

President Jones was born August 1, 1949 in Dodsville, Mississippi to Bessie Jones. They moved to St. Louis. He received his formal education in the city's public schools. He accepted Christ at an early age at the Olivet Baptist Church. He was actively involved in the church's ministry.

He served in the armed forces of the United States from 1966 until 1969. He rose to the rank of a Specialist 5 (Sargent) during that period and served as a Chaplain Assistant. He served a tour of duty in Viet Nam before the completion of his three years of service.

He worked for Union Electric following his return from the army for over eleven years.

He was called to his first pastorate in 1976. He commuted from St. Louis to Columbia for three years as he pastored Friendship Baptist Church.

He was rewarded for his faithfulness in 1979 as a call was extended to him to pastor the historic Mt. Zion Baptist Church in his hometown of St. Louis in 1979. The church's history described him as an energetic young visionary for Christ. They were amazed by his organizational skills, tenacity and commitment to a comprehensive approach to ministry.

He has seen the hand of the Lord move in an awesome manner during his twenty-year pastorate at Mt. Zion. The Mt. Zion Church has experienced phenomenal success during his tenure. The congregation moved into a new ministry complex that has a worship/educational center and child development center. Plans have been designed for a senior citizens housing complex.

Pastor Jones has continued to expand his educational background. He received an Associates of Arts degree from St. Louis University in 1976. He also completed his Bachelor of Arts degree from Lindenwood College in St. Charles in 1992. He was awarded an honorary Doctorate of Divinity degree from Western Bible College in 1993.

Pastor Jones has worked in a number of capacities in the Mt. Carmel and Antioch District Associations, the State Convention and National Convention. He has served as moderator of Antioch; executive secretary of the State Convention, associate director general and third vice president of the National Convention.

He has served on several Boards and Task Forces to include Boy Scouts, St. Louis Urban League; NAACP; National Black Council of Churches; National Baptist Convention, USA, Inc.; School of Preachers at Morehouse College; Western Baptist Bible College and the Governor's Task Force on Crime.

He is married to Sandy and they have a son, Shawn.

DECEMBER 1992 BOARD MEETING, SECOND BAPTIST CHURCH, COLUMBIA

The meeting of the Convention was called to order by President Jones. Scriptures were read and prayer was offered. President Jones read Matthew 28:19-20 to the body. He stated that he would like to use that Scripture this year and that the theme be "Forward Through Ministry." He stated that it was his prayer that the State Convention take on the image of ministry through Jesus Christ (all auxiliaries, forward through ministry).

PROPOSAL FOR THE DOE

The Rev. Patterson presented the report. The mission statement of the DOE and its goals for the first year were given, which included but were not limited to the following: (1) it will be a working entity of the Convention, managed by a Director appointed by a President to accomplish the mandate of Matthew 28:19-20; (2) develop evangelistic activities for each meeting of the Convention and sponsor activities that will enhance local churches in their efforts in evangelism; (3) its goals is to develop an organizational structure that would embrace the entire state; (4) for each Moderator to establish a

District DOE made up of a director and two assistant directors and (5) to communicate with local churches, to encourage in policy and trust. After the presentation, President Jones asked for questions pertaining to the DOE. The Rev. Patterson's name and address was requested. It was asked if representatives of the DOE would be visiting all of the local churches, both active and non-active. The Rev. Dawson stated that he would address the last part of the question in the executive secretary's report. President Jones stated that the Convention was concerned about all the churches.

The Rev. Patterson indicated that it was the goal of the DOE to embrace all the churches in a special way, to help in their evangelistic activities in order to reach the mandate of the Director. The Rev. Jimmy Brown halted the motion. He indicated that in the mission statement, the President would appoint the Director, therefore, the body did not need to approve the appointment. He recommended a substitute motion, to accept the revised proposal for the DOE with the President empowered to appoint a director. The motion was seconded.

He also stated the need for the names of the director and two assistants from each Moderator immediately. It was also noted that Brothers Young and Morris would be working with him.

Proposal for Western Baptist Bible College

President Jones asked Vice President Miles, Rev. Jones and Rev. Mallory to stand while Secretary Dawson presented the proposal, that the Convention established a Christian Academy within the structure of Western Baptist Bible College. The Academy would provide quality Christian and secular education for urban youth. It would be open to all children of the Metropolitan Kansas City area, especially to families who attend or work at Western Bible College.

Initially, the Academy would operate a day care center. Secretary Dawson emphasized that the day care center will not interfere with the normal operations of Western Bible College, but will operate adjacently to the ongoing of Western. The short and long-range goals of the Academy are (1) the evolution of the Academy to a full school (K-6) and eventually become a Full Academy (K-12); (2) quality instructors sought to provide a comparable educational opportunity for both young and adults; (3) proper city and state licenser and (4) appropriate accreditation. Areas pertaining to licenser and accreditation, insurance, income, benefits and preliminary needs were also presented.

After the presentation of the proposal, Brother Thad Jones reported the findings of the Western Committee, in regard to licenser requirements of a Christian Academy to the body. The licensing of the day care centers does not fall within the jurisdiction of the City of Kansas City, Jackson County, but the Missouri Division of Family Service of the Missouri Department of Social Services, issues licenses, sets standards and makes investigations of day care center in Kansas City, Jackson County. The standards do not apply to churches, many churches in Kansas City are not licensed by the state and do not conform to state rules and requirements.

Western Bible College could operate a day care center until capital improvements are made, designed to facilitate an area for this type of operation regardless of whether it is state regulated or not. The Committee proposed the following recommendations: (1) officers of the Convention, alumni and Board of Trustees re-define the purpose and usage of the Western facility; (2) develop a capital improvement plan; (3) appoint an oversight committee selected from the three groups; (4) acquire capital and (5) develop a self-supporting revenue plan. President Jones thanked the Committee for doing an excellent job.

In response to President Jones' request for comment, it was agreed that the proposal was meaningful, with lasting benefits. It would also add to Western a new sense of direction and fit in with "Forward Through Ministry."

The Rev. Hamilton asked if this plan had been discussed with the Board of Trustees of Western. The President stated that the proposal was presented to the body of the Convention first and it is his intent to discuss it with all parties involved. He also stated it would take a year to put the plan in place. The Rev. Hamilton also asked how many board members were members of the convention, and for them to stand so others could see who they were. It was noted that about a third of the Board of Trustees were members of the Missionary Baptist State Convention of Missouri.

Brother Morris asked if the proposal was to establish the day care center on campus, if so, was there a structure and/or land within close proximity of the campus? President Jones replied that there were two buildings in question and there was ample land.

The report was accepted and the Committee was again commended for its work.

BAPTIST WORLD CENTER

President Jones informed the body that he would be attending the Board Meeting in January in Nashville, Tennessee. He also asked for continued financial support of the Center and stated that a letter had been sent out to this effect. He requested those who had checks/money for the Center to bring it forward. The Rev. Miles inquired as to the amount requested of the districts. Districts are to give $200 and individual churches $100.

Support of Lincoln University Baptist Student Union

The President stated that the Convention needed to decide if it was going to support Lincoln or not. The Rev. Patterson indicated that supporting Lincoln was in line with what the President had said in his opening statement about focusing on ministry and that if the Convention did not support Lincoln, it would be contrary to the statement. A motion was made and seconded to support Lincoln. The President reiterated that the Convention was agreeing to support Lincoln financially and approximately $900 per month was required to meet this obligation. He wanted to be sure the body understood what it was agreeing to. The Rev. Hamilton halted the vote. He offered a substitute motion to study the project before making a commitment because a previous commitment had been made and was not met. The previous motion passed with one opposed.

Rev. Patterson asked if the President had a method to support this particular ministry in an orderly way, so that at such meeting, this money would not have to be requested. At the present time, a plan had not been developed and approximately $2700 was needed immediately. President Jones appointed a committee made up of the Reverends Mallory, Davis and President Johnson to study this issue. After some discussion, the Rev. Patterson suggested that each District give $100 a month (this would bring $1300 monthly) and would provide the money to meet the obligation. The body agreed to do this. The President, Harold Butler, pointed out that even though the districts were to give $100, that did not eliminate the individual churches from giving donations.

Congress of Christian Education

The Rev. Jimmy Brown, President of the State Congress of Christian Education, stated that the basic plan for the 52nd session had been made. It will be held at Central Baptist Church, 2843 Washington Avenue, St. Louis, Missouri 63103. Arrangements are being made with Holiday Inn. More information would be available at the March Board meeting.

Women's Missionary Union

The report was presented by Sister Ruthie Sanders with greetings from President Woods (still sick and shut-in). Youth Camp Western will be held August 8-13. The date was moved up one week because of Western's 50th Anniversary.

The Regional Youth meeting will be April 22 in Evansville, Indiana. Sister Sanders informed the body that Mrs. Clayton (her husband a former moderator of Mt. Zion) and the Western Regional Director's father had passed away and asked that their families be remembered in prayer. President Jones asked that he or the executive secretary be notified of sickness or deaths so they can let the families know that the

Convention cares. Members of the Convention asked for the addresses of Mrs. Clayton and the director, in order to send cards. They are: Cecil Clayton, 39143 E. 72nd Terrace, Kansas City MO 64132 and Dr. Benicia Toms, 6573 3rd Avenue, Los Angeles, CA 90043.

Department of Music

Sister Cherie Jones stated that the Music Department was planning a spiritually enriched year. The objectives are to build a spiritual music department with God first; to physically increase their number; to financially increase their budget, to better support the Convention; to encourage individual, church and district representation and musically to provide good, wholesome music theoretically, biblically and spiritually.

It is the focus of the Music Department to provide workshops in different areas throughout the year to prepare for the Convention in October. The first workshop was held on March 6, 1993, which included North Missouri, Central and Mt. Carmel Districts. The Department circulated a newsletter throughout the year so the entire state would know of their activities. Classes within the workshop included (but were not limited to) instrumental music, vocal music, choral conducting, children's music, hymn and spiritual preparation. A team was formulated to travel to the various areas to work with the various music ministries. It is the department's desire to build a great music department from the cradle to the seniors. Sister Jones asked for the cooperation of all ministers, pastors and moderators in providing the names and phone numbers of musicians and choir members in their districts. Sister Jones also asked those districts that are not active in the music ministry to contact her so the teams may help develop its music department. The music department is preparing to publish a booklet this year; it is anticipated that the booklet will be completed for the Annual Session in October. It is the desire of the music department to build and to do God's will, that they might be the best state music department in the National Baptist Convention, U.S.A. Inc., by teaching, praying and practicing what they have learned.

Laymen's Auxiliary

Brother Ernest Johnson stated that the Laymen would support the president in whatever he asked them to do. The 1992 Annual Session was a disaster, everyone had gone home when the Laymen presented their program. He has discussed this with the president. On April 3, 1993, the State Laymen held their Annual Workshop and Banquet at the Executive Holiday Inn, Columbia, MO. The theme was "Survival of the African American Male."

The Southeast Laymen's Conference will be held in Kansas City, MO. Brother Johnson asked for the help of the Convention to host the conference. The Laymen will have to finance the majority of the conference. A budget has been developed which is approximately $68,000. The visiting states will pay about one-third of it and Missouri will have to pay the remaining balance (about $40,000). More information about this will be forthcoming. President Jones stated that Missouri must support the Five State Workshop. He asked the Laymen to let the Convention know what was needed and the Convention would do what it could to help.

Ushers and Health Unit

The Ushers pledged their support to the State Convention and Congress and want to be a working part of it. The ushers plan to conduct workshops throughout the state. They have asked for the support of the pastors and moderators. It was noted that the ushers would like to continue with the program as usual in annual session, if possible. The Friday night slot for the Junior Ushers would also remain the same.

Moderators

The Rev. Lofton pledged the support of the moderators. The Rev. Lofton stressed the need for seminars to train moderators. The seminars would prepare them to deal with some of the problems that they will be confronted with.

The Rev. Lofton stated that the moderators should be informed of the installation of pastors and other activities in their districts. He also asked that the moderators be contacted before a church within their districts elects a pastor. They want to be available to assist churches in their districts, but they cannot force their way in. The communities should respect the moderators and call them to help with things that need to be done in the communities.

The President agreed with the Rev. Lofton and stressed the importance of contacting the moderators about various activities within the communities. It was asked if the seminars would be limited. Only to the moderators, the classes will not be closed sessions.

March Board Meeting

The March Board meeting was discussed and the times, auxiliaries' sessions and the guest speakers were appointed.

Home Missions

President Jones received a letter from Dr. Moore concerning the earthquake in California. We were asked to give assistance and a person to serve as the Missouri representative. President Jones appointed Rev. D. Burch to serve as chairperson of the Home Mission Board. He will be the representative from Missouri serving on the

National Home Mission Board. President Jones is asking all churches and auxiliaries of the Convention to set aside a Sunday to collect monies to help the earthquake victims and send the funds collected to Secretary Dawson.

Reverends Hamilton and Butler questioned the avenue for sending monies to the National Home Mission Board. President Woods stated the WMU sends monies on a regular basis. President Jones asked Mrs. Woods and Rev. Burch to coordinate their work, and that all monies should flow through the new department. He further stated that Rev. Burch would not only be working with the WMU, but with all of us in the state.

President Jones stated that Rev. Burch and his department would develop further plans, such as Health Care, Housing and other considerations concerning the Home Mission program. Rev. Burch presented printouts on the Home Mission program and asked that each church send $5.00 per month or $60.00 a year to further the work of the Home Mission program. If there are additional questions, Rev. Burch can be reached at 314-6845 or 868-6927.

WESTERN BAPTIST BIBLE COLLEGE

Brother Thad Jones, President of Trustee Board, stated that the work is progressing on the rest rooms at Western.

THE ANNUAL LOYALTY BANQUET

The date was April 15, 1994, and the cost of the tickets were $30; the location being the Pentecostal COGIC, 800 Meyer Blvd., Kansas City, Missouri.

REV. WILLIAM SINGLETON'S RETIREMENT

The celebration was held during the annual session in St. Louis, in October 1994. Rev. Adrian Jones was selected as chairperson. President Jones sent letters to each church concerning the gift (monies) for the retirement of President Singleton. The President requested that each church donate $300 and the monies are to be in the Congress meeting by July 1994.

Rev. Fate White asked if other conventions would be involved in the retirement celebration, and Rev. Jones replied, "If they want to." Also, the Baptist Ministers' Union, Kansas City, Missouri asked churches to donate.

HEALTH CARE

Rev. Patterson reported on the State's group insurance health program, and shared information at the March Board Meeting. Also the insurance will be open to all church workers; i. e., secretaries, janitors, musicians, etc. He distributed forms regarding the insurance.

Department of Evangelism

The evangelist meeting scheduled for Columbia was cancelled. Rev. Patterson reported the DOE has completed four seminars in the state. He also stated that the program's success would depend on the information being shared in the districts. A Street Ministry will be considered in the March Board meeting and that Monday and Tuesday nights have been set aside for evangelism. The DOE will be sharing plans in the March Board meeting regarding assessments to support the work.

Credit Union

Rev. D. Hunter, the chair, sent a letter that was read to the group by Rev. Hamilton regarding the State Credit Union. Rev. Hunter and committee will present a formal report at the March Board meeting. A representative of the State Credit Union will be present during the meeting.

Ushers

Sister Titus reported that a State workshop would be held on April 23, 1994 at West End Baptist Church, Sikeston, Missouri. Rev. R. Williams, Pastor. Sister Titus requested that all members be present at the ushers' program in October. She also requested that a first aid room be provided at the October session.

Laymen

President Johnson reported that an Annual Workshop would be held in Columbia, Missouri. Also, the Junior Laymen are working on the presentation of several workshops around the state.

President Jones spoke concerning the Foreign Mission project in Africa. Presently, we have Alfred White, Curtis Reed and Carl Allen in Africa. Laymen from across the country are working on this project and need items such as typewriters, robes, etc. Brother Johnson will present a formal report at the March Board meeting.

Special prayer was requested by Brother Johnson for his son, Damen Toombs, who was injured in an auto accident. Sister White led the group in prayer.

President Jones reported that the Annual State Convention will be held with the Hopewell Baptist Church, Rev. George McFoulon, pastor. The President called for adjournment.

Dr. Sammie Jones, Convention President
Rev. Kenneth Ray, Assistant Executive Secretary

Rev. Jones thanked Rev. Culton Hamilton for the fine job he is doing as academic dean and Brother Thad Jones as acting president of Western. Brother Jones reported that there were 26 students for the first semester and that the school year began in a very positive way.

Also, there have been several capital improvements: ceiling in the chapel, P. A. system and vestibule, Johnson Hall and security. Rev. Hamilton reported that the committee is still receiving applications for the presidency of Western, and requested continued support of the convention as they prepared their budget for 1995. A special request was made that this support be on a monthly basis if possible.

AUDIT OF WESTERN

Rev. Manuel Dillingham reported that the books are in proper order and all books and records were returned. He further recommended that the school consider purchasing a computer to store data because it is labor intensive to do it manually. Motioned by Rev. Bobo to accept report, seconded by Rev. Givens.

CREDIT UNION

Rev. Phillips gave an update on the credit union. He had only received 100 survey forms and needed 900 more in order to start the credit union. The committee met and discussed policies and budget for the new credit union. He answered several questions regarding the establishment and running of the credit union. Also, he made an appeal to have survey forms to his office by November 1, 1994.

ASSESSMENT

The President presented a new table of assessment for churches and convention auxiliaries (see attached budget). The Moderators were still working on their assessment amount for their district association and would report at a later date. Motioned by Rev. Harry Givens that assessment be adopted, seconded by Rev. Ray, motion carried.

THE MISSIONARY BAPTIST STATE CONVENTION OF MISSOURI, SECOND BAPTIST CHURCH, COLUMBIA, MO, DECEMBER 3, 1994.

The evaluation meeting was called to order by President Sammie Jones. The devotion committee led the body in singing "Near the Cross." The Scripture was read and Rev. C. Hamilton offered prayer. Rev. Kenneth Ray, Assistant Executive Secretary, read the agenda for the meeting; there was an addition under old business. Commitment to President Lyons, motioned for adoption with addition by Rev. E. Clark, seconded by Rev. F. White. Rev. Ray read the minutes of the previous meeting, motion for adoption by Rev. E. Clark, seconded by Rev. F. White.

President Jones stated that Dr. C. W. Dawson, Pastor of Second Baptist, Columbia, gave his verbal resignation from the job of Executive Secretary. The President stated that according to the constitution, the Treasurer was next and that the Assistant Executive Secretary was not listed as an office. He requested permission to change this particular section and allow the Assistant Secretary to be moved to the office of Executive Secretary until election during the annual session. Rev. Morgan made a motion to the same, and Rev. Harry Givens seconded, motion carried.

BUDGET

President Jones stressed that monthly assessment is very important to carry out the ministry of the convention. He asked that all churches send their assessed amount to the Treasurer, Rev. Harry Givens.

COMMITMENT TO DR. LYONS

The President stated that many pledges were made during the annual banquet and that he had received only $11,500.00 of the $21,000.00 to date. Dr. Lyons made a request that all monies be brought only to the Winter Board meeting in January. Rev. Ray read all pledges and President Jones reemphasized that he wanted Missouri to be represented and he could not do this without the cooperation of all state workers. President Lyons was scheduled to be in St. Louis in 1996.

I. H. HENDERSON BANQUET

The treasurer was given an additional $100 from the Mt. Carmel district. No other monies to be reported.

BUENOS AIRES, ARGENTINA TRIP

The trip was for Convention President and Mrs. Jones and Congress President and Mrs. Brown and their deposits were due by December 31, 1994. This trip cost approximately $12,000 and a transportation committee was appointed to raise the needed funds. The committee consisted of Rev. F. White, Chairperson, Rev. J. Miles, Rev. A. Jones, Rev. O. K. Patterson, Rev. H. Givens, Sister Parker and Brother Walker.

ANNUAL SESSION

Second Baptist Church, Columbia, Missouri, Dr. C. W. Dawson, Pastor, was the scheduled host church and the Holiday Inn Executive the host motel. If they were not available, the session was scheduled to be held with the Palestine Baptist Church, Kansas City, Missouri, Rev. Earl Abel, Pastor. The dates were October 9-13, 1995. The continuing theme was "FORWARD THROUGH MINISTRY."

Executive Meeting

The Executive Board met at the Mt. Olive Baptist Church, Springfield, Rev. John McGlaun, Pastor, on February 18, 1995 at 10:00 a.m. During the meeting, the programs for the Spring Board and Annual Session were totally revised and final plans were made for the Spring Board.

President Jones requested the executive secretary to read a letter from Brenda Catlin, who is disabled. She praised the convention for making the annual session at Hopewell available for people like herself and pray that we continue the good work that we are doing.

Credit Union

Rev. Phillips reported that no additional surveys had been received since the annual session. He appealed for additional surveys and reported that he could go no further until he received the 1000 survey forms. President Jones had copies made of the survey forms and appealed to the pastors and auxiliaries to complete and mail to Rev. Phillips as soon as possible.

Western Update

Brother Thad Jones reported that the board supported the audit committee and the recommendation to use a computer in the future. He stated that they were presently using Dr. Askew's personal computer. Brother Jones apologized to the president because he was unable to attend the meeting with Dr. LaFayette. There had not yet been a selection for president of Western. The Search Committee was still gathering information and was to make a recommendation to the convention some time in the future. Also, there had been several capital improvements: the chapel, rest room project near completion and vestibule, office space and classrooms were next on the list.

The National Laymen were on the Western campus in May 1995 doing many repairs. An appeal was made for local laymen to come and join in the work.

Dean Hamilton reported the enrollment for the first semester was 28 students. Sixteen attended night classes. The Topeka Satellite had 15 students enrolled. The second semester enrollment began January 24th and he encouraged all pastors, especially those in the Kansas City area, to come and see the school for themselves. The students were elated about the improvements at Western. However, additional financial support was needed to hire the best staff to teach our young people. Presently, the tuition is $35 for auditing a class, $60 per accredited hour or $260 per semester. Western is expanding and plans to come to the St. Louis area and also have correspondence courses.

President Jones presented Brother Jones and Dean Hamilton a check for $2,500 from the convention to further the work at Western.

Congress of Christian Education

The State Congress was held with the Mount Zion Baptist Church, St. Louis, Missouri, Rev. O. K. Patterson, Pastor. The Holiday Inn Plaza was selected to be the host motel. Dr. Issac Peay was the lecturer. The theme was "REDISCOVERING FAITH," Hebrews 11:6; Congress Board meeting March 14, 1995 at 5:00 p.m. The mini congress will emphasize "Church Growth Through the Sunday School."

Ushers

Sister Sallie Titus reported that there are usually 40 members in attendance at the state sessions; however, she would encourage each pastor to support the Ushers' Board and hopefully more would attend. She pledged to meet the assessment goal for the ushers. Rev. Jimmy Brown will be their lecturer.

The ushers have planned future workshops with the Pleasant Hill Baptist Church, Poplar Bluff, Missouri; Rev. Quincy Keeble, Pastor; Jerusalem Baptist Church, St. Louis, Missouri and Skylight Baptist Church, Kansas City, Missouri. Sister Sallie requested prayers for the Ushers & Health Unit and her spouse who was in a serious accident.

Music

Sister Sherry Jones reported growth in the department this past year and planned the following workshops: Mt. Carmel District, March 10-11, 1995, Second Baptist Church, Columbia, Missouri; Southwest District, April 7-8, 1995, Mt. Olive Baptist Church, Springfield, Missouri. All Districts Workshop, June 2-3, 1995, Morning Star Baptist Church, Kansas City, Missouri and Western Regional Conference, April 27-29, 1995, all young people ages 14-27 and all children ages 6-13.

WMU

Dr. Woods stated she had been in office for 27 years, had enjoyed it and needed support of the convention and field workers to carry out the missionary work. Sister Auvelia Arnold stated the Young People's Department is progressing; however, there is still much work to be done. The young people are requesting the support of the convention for the 5th Annual Western Region Conference to be held in St. Louis. The host motels were Holiday Inn and Howard Johnson near the airport and I-70. The Eastern Star Baptist Church (and satellite churches) was selected to be the host church. Mt. Olive Greater Fairfax and 5th Baptist were selected to host classes.

President Jones presented a $300 check to Ms. Arnold to show that the convention supports the young people's efforts in the 5th Annual Western Conference.

Home Mission

Rev. Burch was absent. However, he left his report that Home Mission Rallies were scheduled for Mt. Sinai Baptist Church, Kansas City, Rev. Fate White, Pastor and New Northside Baptist Church in St. Louis. The laymen are responsible for the devotion and the WMU to provide the mistress of ceremonies. The music was presented by the Antioch and Berean Districts in St. Louis and two districts in Kansas City, and the speaker to be announced later. Scheduled dates were December 17th and 18th.

Laymen

Brother Ernest Johnson stated the Laymen had made progress the past year. He further stated that the Laymen need to do more to help pastors and the laymen in their churches. He gave the November and December assessment amounts to the treasurer.

Moderators

Rev. Lofton pledged continued support and stated that it is his desired hope that all moderators would be present at the Spring Board meeting.

Ministers' Wives and Widows

Sister Lofton gave a partial report. She stated they had spirit-filled sessions all week and the Fellowship breakfast had over 30 in attendance. Seven of the thirteen districts registered with a total of 53 registering for the annual session. The Lady of Distinction was a success this year and we will be able to meet our assessment of $1000.00 and donate $300.00 to Western. All ministers were encouraged to register with the Ministers' Wives and Widows and provide addresses for future mailings.

The President called for the sick and prayer lists. Rev. Charles Brown offered prayer and the meeting adjourned at 12:10 p.m.

Rev. Kenneth Ray/ Dr. Sammie E. Jones
Executive Secretary/President

Mt. Olivet Missionary Baptist Church, Springfield, Missouri, February 18, 1995

The planning meeting was called to order by President Sammie Jones. The meeting was held at the Mt. Olivet Missionary Baptist Church, 1616 Robberson Street, Springfield, Missouri, Rev. John McGlaun, host pastor. Rev. Michael Phillips read Psalm 122 and Rev. Jimmy Brown offered prayer.

The minutes of the previous meeting were not read, but will be read during the Spring Board Meeting. In attendance were: President Jones, Mrs. S. Titus, Mrs. A. Wilson, Mrs. F. Chatman, Mrs. V. O. Woods, Rev. R. Mallory, Rev. E. Clark, Rev. K. Ray, Rev. H. Givens, Rev. & Mrs. J. Brown, Rev. & Mrs. M. Phillips, Rev. J. McGlaun, Rev. D. Burch, Rev. C. Brown and Mrs. V. Brown.

President Jones asked for an update of the transportation committee for the Buenos Aires trip. Rev. F. White, chairman not present. However, Rev. Given reported that approximately $6000 in so far. He also asked that all checks be sent to him by the end of March and please earmark checks for trip instead of assessment.

The President reported that the annual session (October 9-13, 1995) will be held with the Palestine Baptist Church of Jesus Christ, 3619 East 35th Street, Kansas City, MO instead of the Second Baptist Church in Columbia. Rev. Earl Abel is the host pastor. The committee is presently working on a contract for the Marriott-Downtown as the host motel.

President Jones asked if any auxiliary had a brief report that they would like to share regarding the upcoming meeting. Rev. Jimmy Brown reported that all classes for the mini congress will be held at the motel. He stated that the program being offered would work in every church if the pastor, superintendent of Sunday school and one other worker would attend. The president asked several ministers present to make available their busses to bring people to the Spring Board Meeting. Rev. Burch will be coordinator for the St. Louis area. Reverends McGlaun and Givens will coordinate efforts in the Springfield area and handle public relations for the entire meeting. The secretary will send letters to the moderators requesting them to spread the word about the state work in their area.

The President asked about the status of early registration and Rev. Givens reported that most of the rooms in the host motel were taken. President Jones asked Reverends Givens and Ray to work on a secondary motel for the week and to place information in the letters that will go in them two or three days to all state workers.

Rev. Michael Phillips reported that he has received the 1000 survey forms and that he would accept any others. Also that this information for the Credit Union would be labor intensive and that most information would need to be computerized.

Rev. Duane Burch reported that plans were made to form a Home Mission Board and that he would be contacting pastors to submit the name of one individual that would be willing to work.

President Jones reemphasized the importance of sending assessments on a monthly basis for the church and that auxiliaries may send or bring assessments during the Spring Board Congress of the Annual Session.

The President appointed Reverends Abel and Mallory to work on the Residential Health Care Facility project (323 HUD) at Western. President Jones adjourned the meeting at 12:30 p.m.

>Dr. Sammie Jones
>President
>Rev. Kenneth Ray
>Executive Secretary

THE MISSIONARY BAPTIST STATE CONVENTION OF MISSOURI
SECOND BAPTIST CHURCH COLUMBIA, MISSOURI, DECEMBER 7, 1996

The Board Meeting opened officially at 9:00 a.m. by President Sammie E. Jones. Devotion was led by Sister Verdell White and Sister Wilma Herbert with singing, "Joy to the World." The Scripture, St. John 17:7-11 was read by Rev. R. Anderson with Rev. F. Morris offering prayer.

An official welcome was brought by the President, who called for the reading of the agenda by Executive Secretary Ray. President Jones offered the following additions to the agenda: report of the One/Church Recruit/One Family Program, discussion of Solidarity Day, the Freedom Wall and Roster Program. The motion carried with the necessary additions to the agenda.

The President called for the reading of the last minutes by Secretary Ray. The president commented that the minutes mentioned Mt. Calvary and it should be Calvary Baptist Church, St. Louis, Missouri. A comment was made on the reading of new officers. Several individuals were listed for more than one office. President Jones stated that at the Executive Planning meeting in February, we would sit down and take a look at the list and discuss it further at the March Board meeting. President Jones stated that there is enough work to go around so that no one person would need to hold more than one major office. A motion to adopt the minutes was made by Reverend Charles Brown and seconded by Rev. Fate White, Jr. The motion carried.

President Jones stated that the Executive Board meeting will be held on February 15, 1997, at the Best Western Coach House Inn in Sikeston, Missouri. The meeting will begin at 9:00 a.m. Plans for the March Board meeting will be discussed at this meeting.

President Jones called for the reading of the revised section of the State Constitution by Sister Vernestine Bounds.

The report of the Western Bible College was brought by President Jones in the absence of Brother Thad Jones. President Jones stated that it is the intent to open extensions across the state. The first extension will be in St. Louis. Rev. Butler will be the campus dean for this site. Popular Bluff and Columbia have also requested sites in these areas. President Jones stated that if we are going to help Western, it must be available to all brethren across the state. The first extension will reopen January 27, 1977, at the Pleasant Green Baptist Church, St. Louis, Missouri. The President read the classes that will be offered and stated that if anyone was interested in attending, the applications are available at this meeting. Rev. Butler is available to work with anyone else who wants to open an off-site extension.

The President asked Sister Sherry Jones and the Music Department to work with him as it relates to Western. A scholarship fund had been established. Sister Jones will work with St. Louis and the President has asked Rev. J. Miles to work with the Kansas City area in planning musicales in both areas. The musical proceeds will be divided between the convention and the scholarship fund. After Kansas City and St. Louis have finished their musicales, other areas will be visited. The goal is $10,000.00 for the special effort. The future plans are to present scholarships during the annual session. Qualifications for recipients will be developed.

President Jones requested that Rev. Miles be the co-chairman with Sister Sherry Jones in pulling together the musical fundraiser for the scholarship fund. He would like to see this happen in April or May 1997.

The question was raised as to when the computer classes will be available through the Convention. President Jones stated the computers have been loaded with certain programs and are sitting in his church. He has been waiting on word from Dean Butler and President Brown about when the classes will be added to their schedule. This will be looked into.

Be in prayer for Rev. Ronald Packnett, along with Rev. James Davis, Rev. McKinley Dukes, who took sick at the Board meeting and Sister V. O. Woods. Auxiliary heads are not to forget to bring your programs to the February meeting for the March planning session. Rev. O. K. Patterson made a motion to accept all reports. Second by Adrian Jones, and passed.

President's 5th Annual Address
Mt. Sinai Missionary Baptist Church
Kansas City, Missouri
October 17, 1997

Mr. President, Officers and State Vice President, Dr. Ronald William and my District Moderator, Dr. George McFoulon, who also rendered that wonderful introduction: thanks to both of you. To the other State Vice Presidents, Rev. Fate White, our host pastor and Rev. John Miles.

To each member of the Missouri State Convention Executive Staff; Congress President Dr. Jimmy Brown, Ministers' Wives President, Sister Ollie Lofton; Music Department President, Sister Sherry Jones, Ushers President, Sister Ruthie Sanders; Laymen's President, Brother Alfred White, Moderators President, Rev. Charles Brown, Home Mission President, Dr. William Boone, Foreign Mission President, Dr. Ronald Bobo, and Department of Evangelism President, Dr. Oliver K. Patters: Congratulations to Sister Sallie Titus who is now elevated to National Ushers' and Health Unit President. Continue in the service of the Almighty King.

Special thanks and recognition to our most loyal and efficient administrative staff; Dr. Ray, Sister Bounds, Rev. Adrian Jones and Dr. G. B. Roberson. They have given total support to the president and to the work of the State Convention.

Special guests and delegates of the Missionary Baptist State Convention of Missouri, I greet you in the matchless name of Jesus Christ, our most High Priest and King.

Rev. White and the Sinai Missionary Baptist Church complex, thanks for giving support and allowing me to serve as both your pastor and the State Convention President. In whatever capacity I may ask you to serve, Mt. Zion, you always support in the utmost manner.

And especially to my beloved wife Sandra, and son Shaun for their love and encouragement, I Love You. No matter what situation or condition in which we find ourselves, we remain a loving family with the help of Jesus Christ.

Reflections

Let us give a gracious amen and applause to Dr. James Brown and the Mercy Seat Family for the extraordinary courtesy and care extended to us last year. Everything we needed or desired was provided above expectation, and the last was a great session because of their untiring hospitality.

Prayer

Let us pause now in silent prayer as we remember the committed souls who have gone from labor to reward. I thank the Lord for their work in the Convention and the opportunity to have known and worked with them during their stay here. May the eternal joy of God be theirs forever. Amen.

Looking Ahead

This past year has brought us many opportunities for growth and positive change. We are all aware that change for only the sake of changing is futile. However, if we are going to meet the needs and the demands of a progressing age, we must be willing to move forward with positive aggression. With this in mind, we must take another look at the mission, our ministry and its budget needs, from each auxiliary to each state activity to our schools, yes, even Western Baptist Bible College. We must ensure that our total focus is on Jesus and our mission is to win and cultivate souls for Him at every opportunity He affords us. Paul instructs in Philippians 2:1-5 (NIV), "If you have any encouragement from being united with Christ, if any comfort from his love, if any fellowship with the Spirit, if any tenderness and compassion, then make my joy complete by being like-minded, having the same love, being one in spirit and purpose. Do nothing out of selfish ambition or vain conceit, but in humility consider others better than yourselves. Each of you should look not only to your own interests, but also to the interests of others. Your attitude should be the same as Christ Jesus."

It is not just Western Baptist Bible College that needs our combined support, but each ministry of this Convention is equally important: Home and Foreign Mission, Laymen's, Music, Evangelism, Ushers and Health Unit, as well as Christian Education. No work of the body is more important than the other. Paul tells us in Ephesians 4:11-13(NIV), that "It was he who gave some to be apostles, some to be prophets, some to be evangelists, and some to be pastors and teachers, to prepare God's people for works of service, so that the body of Christ may be built up until we all reach unity in the faith and in the knowledge of the Son of God and become mature, attaining to the whole measure of the fullness of Christ."

With this in mind, I am appointing Dr. Oliver K. Patterson as Fifth Vice President in charge of budget and special projects to help design and recommend programs to better ensure opportunity for progressive movement. He is to fulfill the duties of the office vacated by Dr. Ronald Packnett.

We have shared with pastors and members of the Convention around the state to encourage the churches of our Convention to strive for the cause of Jesus Christ. It has been my intent, as I follow the leading of the Holy Spirit, to carry out the mission of the Father as described in Matthew 28:18-20 (NIV), Then Jesus came to them and said, "All authority in heaven and on earth has been given to me. Therefore go and make disciples of all nations, baptizing them in the name of the Father and of the Son and of the Holy Spirit, and teaching them to obey everything I have commanded you. And surely I am with you always, to the very end of the age." We have tried to provide aid in all areas of the state to assist in developing strong ministries.

I believe that if the collective black churches in Missouri are to stand in these challenging times with which we are faced, the State Convention must take on a new aggressive look at what is being done and the reason for each activity. When individual church families are more successful in evangelism and outreach than all of our collective work, something is wrong! When new pastors say they have no need for District, State, or National Convention, it says to me that we have lost our focus. Somewhere along the lines, we have lost our purpose. Why?

We need to identify and reset the priority for the real reason that we are here. That priority is a resurgence of World Evangelism and Discipleship, beginning here in Missouri. We need a strong mission statement that identifies the critical path. What is our purpose, our reason for existence? Can we help them? Should our school's only purpose be for the training of preachers who cannot attend other universities because of financial status? We are empowered, each of us as individual members of the State Convention, to become a part of the evangelistic thrust and be lights in the local communities.

We can learn about the work Jesus has assigned us to do, work in the fields and train others in the work, replicating ourselves as lights for Jesus. I believe that we can educate our own under the guidance of the Holy Spirit. If we really love our own, we should not embark upon change with a half-full measure. We must move forward toward a goal that our churches and our school, yes, even Western Baptist College, can send forth preachers, AND teachers AND journalists AND politicians that have a love and zeal for God. We want to send forth Christians regardless of their professional choices, who will always allow the Holy Spirit to work in their lives as they move out into the world. Through these means, these individuals can reach the masses, men of every birth, preaching and teaching that Jesus is the key to salvation. This is how we can change the cities, the counties, the states, the country and the world.

The Gospel according to Matthew 6:33 (NIV) states, "But seek first his kingdom and his righteousness, and all these things will be given to you as well."

We go about performing our daily tasks, accomplishing what we see as our goal for the day with the reasons we have specified previously, either by our plan or by fitting someone else's plan in ours. What guidelines are we using to set our priorities? What are we accomplishing? Why have we taken on these tasks as our priorities? As a rule, do we seek God's guidance for the day before it begins, or after we have entered into it? Solomon reminds us to seek and acknowledge the Lord in everything. In Proverbs 3:5-6 (NIV) he says, "Trust in the LORD with all your heart and lean not on your own understanding; in all your ways acknowledge him, and he will make your paths straight." We mentioned earlier that we must identify the priority, as established by the Lord Jesus Himself. Secondly, we must determine and state the real reason why we are here.

Last year, we focused on three areas of priorities: (1) In the Word of God, (2) In the Spirit of God, and (3) In the Service of God. As we expand on the theme, "Setting Priorities" and seek a deeper understanding of the Word, let us turn our minds and hearts now to discuss the mission and the reason. Before we can move forward, we must first define these two words that so fully determine our purpose here.

What is mission? The *Holman Bible Dictionary* defines a mission as "a task which God sends a person He has called, particularly a mission to introduce another group of people to salvation in Christ. This person is charged with the task of spreading the Gospel of Jesus Christ to people whom He is sent." This reference further states that "The term mission is found in this Scripture, yet the concept of mission permeates the entire Bible."

Let us look at the Christian's ultimate example. Jesus Christ was sent to each:
(1) to help us know God, His Father
(2) to glorify God
(3) to bring His Father's kingdom to each
(4) to seek and save the lost
(5) to reveal God's love and mercy for the world

Throughout His mission here, He made it known that His mission was to continue; i.e., through those He empowered to carry out the work that He could not complete during His tenure. Jesus tells us in John 14:12 (NIV), "I tell you the truth, anyone who has faith in me will do what I have been doing. He will do even greater things than these, because I am going to the Father." Jesus crossed all barriers, He reached out to all ethnic groups, social classes and cultures AND HE empowered the church to do these and greater things because He was going back to the Father.

What is this mission? Again, we reiterate Matthew 28:18-20 (NIV). Then Jesus came to them and said, "All authority in heaven and on earth has been given to me. Therefore go and make disciples of all nations, baptizing them in the name of the Father and of the Son and of the Holy Spirit, and teaching them to obey everything I have commanded you. And surely I am with you always, to the very end of the age."

Laurie Beth Jones, author of *"Jesus, CEO,"* establishes the following about a mission statement:

(1) it should be no more than a single sentence.
(2) it should be easily understood by a twelve year old.
(3) it should be able to be recited by memory at gun point.

According to these elements, let us dissect the mission in this context:

"No more than a single sentence."

Go and make disciples of all nations baptizing them in the name of the Father and of the Son and of the Holy Spirit, and teaching them to obey everything I have commanded you.

"Easily understood by a twelve year old."

It is simple! Children younger than twelve years of age have been called into the ministry. They, being called disciples. It is simple to grasp and therefore easily understood by adults also.

"Able to recite by memory at gun point."

It is essential that we understand the sense of urgency this mission dictates. Jesus will not return until the message has been carried to and heard by people in the uttermost parts of the world. The sense here is not necessarily that we are held at gun point, but that we must live and breathe this mission as though our lives depend on it. John says to us, "This is how we know what love is: Jesus Christ laid down His life for us. And we ought to lay down our lives for our brothers."

Christians, this mission of evangelism is not a choice, it is a requirement. It is not stated in the relative "If you have time" mentality, but it is mandated. We have to carry out the mission. Just as the disciples were commissioned to go forward and make disciples, we are also expected to carry out this mission daily. Wherever we are, Christians, we are expected to be obedient in every sense. However, we cannot go forth on our own authority and understanding, for we are indeed powerless apart from the Spirit of God.

John 14:25-26 (NIV) reiterates to us what Jesus told the disciples when He promised the Holy Spirit. "All this I have spoken while still with you. But the Counselor, the Holy Spirit, whom the Father will send in my name, will teach you all things and will remind you of everything I have said to you." Empowered by the Holy Spirit, the church is to preach and teach, "Jesus" and His gospel only. The Lord says to us in Acts 1:4b, 5 and 1:8a, (NIV) "But wait for the gift my Father promised, which you have heard me speak about. For John baptized with water, but in a few days you will be baptized with the Holy Spirit...you will receive power when the Holy Spirit comes on you; and you will be my witnesses."

The mission is clear! It has already been defined by Jesus. It is to be fulfilled by His witnesses. The authority through the Holy Spirit is the enabling power. In order to be effective witnesses, we must know the Lord and His saving power. This is not something we receive second-hand or think about because we have established grandiose theories. We must know the Lord in order to be a witness for Him.

Backtrack for a moment. There has been an accident and you were on the scene when it occurred. However, you did not see the events leading up to the accident, just the fender bender itself. How can you tell anything about the behavior of the driver who struck the car ahead? You did not see anything. The only thing you can safely say is that you saw the first vehicle hit the second. You cannot tell that the driver was suffering a heart attack or losing control of the car because he was stung by a bee inside. You cannot contribute any details because you do not know any details prior to the accident.

The same is true about witnessing about the Lord. If you do not know Him, you cannot testify to the fact that "His mercy endureth forever." You cannot tell anyone that you "heard" somebody else say "You may ask anything in my name and I will do it." The Bible is the only reference and the Holy Spirit is your guide in your efforts to get to know the Father. You cannot say to a dying world that "If you really knew Jesus, then you would know the Father as well."

Understanding the full measure of the mission and what it is to us, let us now explore the reason why we are sent to fulfill this mission. Jesus said to His disciples in John 15:9-13, (NIV) "As the Father has loved me, so have I loved you. Now remain in my love. If you obey my commands, you will remain in my love, just as I have obeyed my Father's commands and remain in His love. I have told you this so that my joy may be in you and that your joy may be complete. My command is this: Love each other as I have loved you. Greater love has no one than this, that he lay down his life for his friends." Love is the reason we are compelled to carry out the mission: love for Jesus and love for each other.

What is love? As it is used in this context, the understanding is "agape." As defined by the *Holman's Bible Dictionary*, love is "unselfish, loyal and benevolent concern for the well-being of another." Christian love is not associated with an emotion for another person for who they are or what they have done for you. Christian love is a relationship of self-giving which results from God's activity in Christ. Paul renders a benediction of love in these words, "May the Lord make your love increase and overflow for each other and for everyone else, just as ours does for you" (1 Thessalonians 3:12, NIV).

Where are we? Why are we driven to help people the way Jesus did? Have we lost that burning desire to tell the world about Jesus because of our preoccupation with ourselves and our world? Can we share the power of God within us to help others? Have we lost the sincerity of what it means to truly love one another as Christ has loved us? In Revelation 2:1-5 (NIV), John writes to the church of Ephesus these words: "To the angel of the church in Ephesus write: These are the words of him who holds the seven stars in his right hand and walks among the seven golden lampstands: I know your deeds, your hard work and your perseverance. I know that you cannot tolerate wicked men, that you have tested those who claim to be apostles but are not, and have found them false. You have persevered . . . and have not grown weary. Yet I hold this against you: You have forsaken your first love. Remember the height from which you have fallen! Repent and do the things you did at first."

The Evangel Speaks

VOLUME 3, ISSUE 1   JANUARY 1998

Missourians On The Move

Our President, Dr. Sammie E. Jones, has been appointed 3rd Vice President for the National Baptist Congress of Christian Education.

Dr. Jones has worked for the National Congress for over twenty-two years. He has served in numerous positions.

After the death of Dr. Samuel Austin and the appointment of Dr. Robert G. Brown, President of the National Congress, Dr. Jones was selected by Dr. Brown. This is a wonderful opportunity for Dr. Jones. It is also a wonderful opportunity for Missouri. Many more Missourians will have an opportunity to serve because of Dr. Sammie E. Jones.

Dr. Jones has been assigned the responsibility as liaison to the Finance Committee, Public Relations, and Transportation. We are very proud of our State President and his new responsibility.

God Exalts Those Who Are Faithful!

Our 4th Vice President, Oliver K. Patterson, was appointed Program Director for Christ Alive, of the National Baptist Convention's Evangelistic Campaign by Henry J. Lyons, with the recommendation of President Sammie Jones and Dr. E. J. Jones, chairman of the National Board of Evangelism.

Patterson's responsibilities will include Ways and Means along with recruitment and training of SWAT participants. In Missouri, he is responsible for budgets, special projects, and the Department of Evangelism.

Christ Alive has a goal of winning 200,000 new souls for Christ in 1999. The victory celebration will be held June 25, 1999 in Louisville, Kentucky (Pray for these Missourians in their new roles).

Convention Officers

President	Dr. Sammie E. Jones
Vice Presidents-at-Large	Dr. Fate White, Jr.
	Revs. Ronald Williams,
	George McFaulon, John Miles,
	Oliver Patterson

General Secretary	Revs. Kenneth Ray, Adrian Jones, Mrs. Eloise Dukes
Treasurer	Revs. Culton Hamilton, James Brown
Special Assistants	Mrs. Vernestine Bounds, Rev. B. G. Roberson

Auxiliary Presidents

Congress	Dr. Jimmy Brown
Ministers' Wives & Widows	Mrs. Ollie R. Lofton
Moderators	Rev. Charles Brown
Laymen	Rev. Alfred White
Ushers	Mrs. Sallie Titus
Music	Mrs. Sherry Jones
Women's Missionary Union	Mrs. Ruby Sanders

THE MISSIONARY BAPTIST STATE CONVENTION OF MISSOURI
SECOND BAPTIST CHURCH, COLUMBIA, MO, MARCH 9-12, 1998

The Missionary Baptist State Convention of Missouri's Spring Board Meeting opened on Tuesday, March 10, 1998, at 2:00 p.m. with singing, "Hold to God's Unchanging Hand," led by Sis. Flora Hope and committee. The Call to Order was brought by Vice President-at-Large Fate White, Jr. Scripture reading, Psalm 133; by Rev. O.K. Patterson and prayer offered by Rev. Walter Harper. The Devotional Message was brought by Rev. IBS Groves, Pastor of the Mt. Olive Baptist Church, Marshall, MO.

Dr. Dillingham came forth with a report on Western. He shared a picture of the new Western that cost $5 million dollars to build. Dr. Dillingham is looking for 200 entities to give $5,000 each which will be $1 million dollars from the Convention. Rev. Patterson has already pledged $5,000 and Dr. Dillingham's church is also giving $5,000. Dr. Dillingham would like to start the construction of the new Western in 1999 and have it completed in the year 2000. Rev. Kenneth Ray has personally pledged to build the swimming pool for the facility. The school will house sleeping rooms, banquet room, etc. Dr. Dillingham states that individuals should look at leaving something to Western when they have gone on. The Western Baptist Bible College's banquet will be held on April 24, 1998 in Kansas City. The donation is $30. Several individuals have pledged $1,000 toward the banquet. Prince of Peace has pledged $5,000. Vice President White requested that anyone who wanted to pledge toward the new Western should see Dr. Dillingham. The Convention did not vote on the $1 million dollar pledge in the absence of President Jones.

SCHOLARSHIP FUND

Vice President Patterson came forth to discuss the president's vision for scholarships to be given for young people to attend college. President Jones desired to have a banquet at this session to help raise money for the scholarship fund. The University of Missouri-Columbia has agreed to host this banquet that will be held on Wednesday evening. All proceeds from the banquet will go toward the Scholarship Fund. There are only eight tickets sold at this time. The University is expecting at least 100 persons. Busses will be sent to the hotel to pick up those attending the banquet. The ticket cost is being reduced from $25.00 to $15.00.

Report on Africa

Laymen in Africa
Far Right: President Alfred White and father, VP-at-Large Fate White

Vice President-at-Large Fate White brought a brief report on the trip to Africa. President Jones preached on Tuesday night, Rev. Fate White preached on Wednesday night and Rev. Alfred White preached on Thursday night. There were 60-70 souls that came to Christ. On Thursday night, there was a revival at the school outside. Even in the rain, 30-40 souls came to Christ. Another highlight of the trip was meeting some Muslim young men who were selling clothes. After witnessing to them, they both accepted Christ. One of the young men was baptized in the pool at the Holiday Inn by President Jones and Rev. White. School supplies were passed out to the students. A special thanks to the Convention for sending President and Mrs. Jones.

Rev. Ricky Anderson, Pastor of the Prince of Peace Baptist Church, Sikeston, Missouri, came forth to introduce the speaker for the afternoon. The afternoon message was brought by Vice President Ronald Williams, Pastor of the Western Baptist Church, Sikeston, Missouri. His theme: "The Purpose of the Church" (Matthew 5:13-16). Announcements were brought by Executive Secretary Ray. Vice President White stated that the reports will begin tomorrow morning. The evening session of the Spring Board meeting began on Tuesday, March 10, 1998 at 7:00 p.m. The Devotional Message was brought by Rev. W. A. Finney. His theme: "The Beauty of Our God" (Psalm 90:17). The welcome program was brought by the Second Baptist Church. Introduction of the evening speaker was brought by Executive Secretary Ray. The message was delivered by Rev. William Matthews, Pastor of the Mt. Zion Baptist Church, St. Charles, Missouri. His theme: "The Christian's Role in Society" (Matthew 5:13-17).

The Wednesday morning session of the Board Meeting was held at the University of Missouri-Columbia campus. During the scholarship banquet, information about the university was shared in the hope that more individuals would consider sending their children to the school. The evening speaker was Dr. George McFoulon.

The Thursday morning session opened at 9:40 a.m. by Vice President-at-Large White, with the Convention singing, "Jesus, Keep Me Near the Cross." The Devotional Message was brought by Rev. Lemon Hope, Pastor of Bethany New Life Baptist Church, St. Louis, Missouri. His Scripture reference was First John 4 and his emphasis was on the importance of showing love to one another.

Vice President White called for the names of those persons who need to be lifted up in prayer. Executive Secretary Ray came with remarks and thanks to those who attended the scholarship banquet on Wednesday night. There were 92 tickets sold at $15 each. There were 37 churches represented in this Board meeting.

The Convention had a moment of silent prayer in memory of Sister V. O. Woods.

Rev. John Miles came forth to speak briefly about the National Baptist Convention that will be convening in Kansas City, September 7-13, 1998. Those who have not yet done so need to get their housing forms in as soon as possible. There are a certain number of rooms dedicated to Missouri. Send your housing forms to Morning

Star Baptist Church. The Mayor of Kansas City has pledged $100 to help with the Convention. Rev. Sam Nero is the chairperson for this year's banquet. Dr. Miles is asking Missouri and Kansas to help us bring our attendance to 2,000 persons. The goal for the baptism for Friday night is 200 souls.

Vice President George McFoulon came forth to introduce the speaker for the closing of the Board meeting.

The message was brought by Dr. Earl Miller, moderator of the Antioch District. His theme: "Your First Love." Scripture reference was Revelation 2:4.

Dr. Miles came with the closing prayer. The meeting closed at 11:15 a.m.

Some Congress and Convention workers

Mrs. Eloise Dukes — Convention
Mrs. Vernestine Bounds — Convention
Mrs. Jackie Jackson — Congress
Mrs. Irene Carr — Congress

Rev. Adrian Jones — Convention
Rev. George McFoulon — Convention
Rev. Ronald Williams — Convention
Rev. John Mims — Moderator, North Missouri Baptist Association

The Western Baptist Bible College
RECORDER
A New Era, Door of Opportunity
Called to Faithful Stewardship

Thad Jones, Chairman Board of Directors

Dear Friends,

The table is set and the meal is about done as we prepare to feast on the goodness of God in regards to our beloved school Western Baptist Bible College in what I call "A New Era, A Door of Opportunity, and a Call to Faithful Stewardship."

Dr. Manuel Dillingham has been named as the 19th president of our school. We congratulate him on this appointment and special calling.

Our support and prayers are with Dr. Dillingham in this new era for Western as he has brought stability and permanency to our school. He also brings a great amount of zeal and energy to the administration. He and the Board will be challenged to have our school equipped, accredited, attractive and appealing to the 21st century student.

With a clear direction charted and the Board and Dr. Dillingham working together, this provides for a great door of opportunity for all the friends and supporters of the school to rally around this spirit of cooperation and cohesiveness to make ready all necessary resources to bring the new era to fruition.

Dr. Dillingham in the short time he has been president, has already developed relationships that will be beneficial to the school. The Board, Convention, staff, faculty and friends must take advantage of this opportunity.

Everything that God does that involves man has a purpose. Many times man is given things and placed in situations to test his love and accountability to God. This is called stewardship. God asks us to be faithful stewards, managers, trustees or caretakers. He has called Dr. Dillingham along with you to be a faithful steward.

Western is a talent in the parable of talents. We are called to take care of and enhance it. We need to build upon what the founders started and what Dr. Singleton managed so faithfully while the owner is away.

I believe we are up to the challenge. If it were not so, God would not have entrusted it to our care.

It is my prayer that we will rise up and meet this New Era, this Door of Opportunity and Call to Faithfulness with conviction in that we do all things when we are unified and are reaching for the same goals and objectives.

Thad Jones, Chairman of the Board

CHARACTER IN THE LIFE OF WESTERN BAPTIST BIBLE COLLEGE

Dean's Message

My enthusiasm has reached another notch as I watch with great anticipation the development of curriculum, and school activities emerge into genuine and great possibilities with the purpose to serve people in our community and churches. Western takes another step in its long history to provide quality education for its student body and those who are going to be served in the community.

We have improved our staff, and over ninety percent of this year's staff has a Master's degree level education. Our student body has increased as our campus has expanded to St. Louis, Missouri and Topeka, Kansas. Presently, we have fourteen departments and department heads whose main ambition is to provide an opportunity for discipline and major core courses for our degree program.

Presently, we offer a certificate program that allows lay persons and ministers to receive a discipline without having to go through the rigors of a degree program. We also offer an Associate of Arts degree that requires sixty hours in one of fourteen disciplines we offer at Western.

BUILDING EDUCATION WHILE BUILDING QUALITY

Our last degree program is our Bachelor's program that affords the student who completes one hundred twenty hours in specialized areas of training the opportunity to move on to a graduate program. Successes will only be measured in the opportunities the school provides for students to achieve their goals and share their skills with others. We commend the staff and student body who have entered our program for the 1997-1998 academic school year and pray that they will succeed in their efforts to achieve a quality education.

Let Western provide you with an opportunity to improve your skills as you take the call to ministry seriously and allow us to enhance your commitment to achieve the greatest good in the service of our Lord.

Dr. Robert Baynham

The Western Baptist Bible College
RECORDER

Vol. 3 No. 2 – Main Campus: 2119 Tracy, Kansas City, MO 64108 – 818-842-4195 – Winter 1999

President's Message
Dr. Manual Dillingham

Thanks to Mrs. Georgia Covington and added staff member who have efficiently managed this edition in time for our annual state convention here in Kansas City.

Since our last edition, significant events have occurred here at Western including two additional extension campuses: Popular Bluff, Missouri and Wichita, Kansas. Thanks to Dean Baynham for his overseeing and implementation of these two campuses.

Student enrollment at the main campus, beginning this fall, is approximately 45 students. Our total enrollment from all campuses is close to 100 full-time students. In comparison to many Bible schools and seminaries, this number is at least equal. The hiring of Ms. Covington has enhanced our efforts to increase monthly contributions from churches and organizations. She also assists the president with public relations events and activities.

Mrs. Singleton, the wife of our former president, Dr. Singleton, has established a "Hall of Fame" concept for former students and graduates of Western. Her goal is to encourage these former students to contribute on a consistent plan to Western's future. Thank you Mrs. Singleton for your continued support as we are often reminded of your husband's longevity here at Western. The Alumni Association will spearhead the implementation of this program.

A recent study of restoring our building has been completed and the cost estimate will be presented to our Board of Trustees during the Convention meeting. We continue to be blessed with monthly and regular contributions from loyal alumni, churches, individuals and our own State Convention under Dr. Sammie E. Jones. Sister Ruthie Sanders continues to motivate our sisters to give every month for which we are truly grateful. Mrs. Sanders, along with Mrs. Auvelia H. Arnold and her staff, completed another Youth Encampment with outstanding results. The presence of and sermon by our President, Dr. Sammie E. Jones and the contribution that they left to Western was greatly appreciated. The youth seemed to enjoy themselves tremendously as they were taught the many facts of the Christian experience.

In pondering our present state at Western, I am constantly inspired by the loyalty and generosity of our staff members, the hope and aspiration of the student body and supportive contributors whether they be great or small. I am convinced that there is a committed few determined to carry Western into the new century and beyond. Please know that this President, and all who work for the good of Western, appreciate your time, talent and treasures.

The future state of our existence depends upon all our efforts by this administration and the goodwill of so many people who are committed to Western. The prudent use of our time and talent will assist in bringing about restoration, a new building, accreditation and increased student enrollment.

As President, my own personal health has been a factor in delaying some of the goals originally stated. But God is restoring me daily, through your prayers and patience. The school and I will always need your help and support.

Please pray for us, lend us your talents, resources, contacts and whatever you might give or do to keep this great institution alive and well.

Western Baptist Bible College Welcomes
The Missionary Baptist State Convention of Missouri
Dr. Sammie E. Jones, President

Friendship Baptist Church will host this 11th Session from October 11-15th. The week will be busy with informational and inspirational sessions and events. During this time, be sure to include attending the Western Baptist Bible College Banquet, Tuesday, October 12th at 5:00 p.m. at Morning Star Baptist Church, 2411 E. 27th Street. Donation is $15.00. Please see Mrs. Erma Eason, New Era District President, for tickets.

Western Baptist Bible College Faculty

Kansas City Campus
Dr. Robert L. Baynham
Rev. L. Henderson Bell
Ms. Janice Blackmon
Dr. Stanly Counts
Mrs. Viola Howard
Rev. Floyd Knight
Rev. Thomas McDormick
Dr. Ellis C. Robinson
Mrs. Ruth Walker
Rev. Larry B. Williams
Rev. J. J. Woods
Dr. Lemuel Wynn

St. Louis Campus
Rev. John Anderson
Rev. Keeland Atkinson
Rev. Julius C. Bonner, IV
Mrs. Marva F. Butler
Rev. Mike Emory
Rev. Dwight Jackson
Mrs. Gwendolyn Packnett
Rev. David Rice
Rev. Ed Schneider
Mrs. Anita Stevens-Watkins

Topeka Campus
Rev. Arnold Fitzgerald
Rev. Michael Moore
Rev. Delmar White

The Evangel Speaks
Volume 3, Issue 4, October, 1999

The State President Speaks

As this week began, we assemble to celebrate another year of service to our God. Dr. Manuel Dillingham and the Friendship Baptist Church family have planned for our arrival in Kansas City for this session. We are looking forward to a great week. There is much business we must conduct. The musicale held on last night was wonderful. Some of the highlights planned for the week are:

Monday, we open registration at 9:00 a.m.

Tuesday from 8:00 a.m. until 10:00 a.m., a Ministers' Seminar will convene. Our guest speaker will be Dr. Michael William of Houston, Texas.

Tuesday at 11:00 a.m., a special Women's presentation. Sister Regina Spear of Boston, MA is our special guest.

Wednesday at 6:30 p.m. until 10:00 p.m., our State Banquet will be held at the Adam Mark Hotel. Dr. Harry Blake, our new Executive Secretary, will be our special guest.

Thursday night at 7:00 p.m., we will hear our President's Annual Address.

Friday night at 7:00 p.m., our State Youth Parade and Evangelism Program.

As President, I salute Pastor E. Stanley Howlett and the True Light Baptist Church of St. Louis for an excellent job of hosting our Annual Session last year. Dr. Howlett and his staff are to be commended for their concern and generous hospitality.

As you know, Dr. William J. Shaw is our new National President. Several changes are coming. Several new people will be serving in various roles in our national work. We will address this issue as our annual session unfolds and as we get more information. Our National Convention needs our prayers. Our new National President and his family need our prayers, encouragement and support.

I believe the most important agenda item for us as Missionary Baptist Christians is to make sure we line up behind our new president as he reveals to us our new national program. Satan would have us sit on the sideline and not be supportive. The election is over! The majority has spoken. Now let us get on with the work. **We have been and we will continue to be supportive of the National Baptist Convention.**

We are at war against the forces of evil. We must win. Since our mandate, our divine imperative is to "Go, make disciples," we must not allow anything to dilute our energy. Only through the winning of more "Souls" for Christ can we build the true kingdom of Jesus. We must preach, teach, sing and witness. In the words of another, "By any means necessary!" We must do our part and leave the result to the Lord. This is our job!

Officer of the Missionary Baptist State Convention of Missouri are as follows:

President	Dr. Sammie E. Jones
Vice President-at-Large	Dr. Fate White, Jr.
Vice Presidents	Rev. Ronald Williams
	Rev. George McFoulon
	Rev. John Miles
	Rev. Oliver K. Patterson
General Secretary	Rev. Kenneth Ray
	Rev. Adrian Jones
	Ms. Elouis Dukes
Treasurer	Rev. Culton Hamilton
	Rev. James Brown
Special Assistants	Mrs. Vernestine Bounds
	Rev. B. G. Roberson
Auxiliary Presidents	
Congress	Dr. Jimmy L. Brown
Ministers' Wives & Widows	Mrs. Ollie R. Lofton
Moderators	Rev. Charles Brown
Ushers	Mrs. Sallie Titus
Choir	Mrs. Sherry Jones
WMU	Mrs. Ruthie Sanders

President Jones and Convention Leadership Team

Epilogue

President Jones' Seventh Annual Address
Delivered at Friendship Baptist Church
Kansas City, Missouri
October 14, 1999

I thank God for my son, Minister Shaun Ellison Jones, for that touching and heartfelt introduction. A son to follow in a father's footsteps is a precious thing.

To our most able Vice Presidents: Dr. Fate White, Dr. Ronald Williams, Dr. Oliver Patterson, Dr. George McFoulon and Dr. John Miles:

I offer much thanks and appreciation to each of our supportive auxiliary presidents and workers: Sister Ruthie Sanders and the WMU, Sister Sallie Titus and the Ushers and Health Ministry, Sister Ollie Lofton and the Ministers' Wives, Reverend Alfred White and the Laymen, Dr. Charles John Brown and the Moderators, Sister Sherry Jones and our Music Department, Dr. Oliver Patterson and the Department of Evangelism, Dr. Jimmy L. Brown and the Congress.

To my staff of committed and loyal workers: General Secretary Kenneth Ray and Dr. Adrian Francis Jones, Special Assistants, Dr. Bobby Roberson, Sister Vernestine Bounds, Sister Elouise Dukes, Treasurers, Dr. Culton Hamilton and Dr. James Brown and to all delegates and messengers from across this state:

To our special guest, Dr. Harry Blake, General Secretary of our NBC: I greet you in the name of our Lord and Savior Jesus Christ who has given to us an abundant life through faith in Him.

Last year, we were blessed to have been at the True Light Missionary Baptist Church, St. Louis where the Dr. E. Stanley Howlett serves as pastor. He and the True Light family treated us royally. Many thanks to them for a job well done.

Now we meet this week at the Friendship Baptist Church under the leadership of Dr. Manuel Dillingham. We can from firsthand experience say that here at Friendship, you can really find some friendly people. With the support of the pastor, his loyal staff, and the special work of Georgia Covington and her band of workers, we are being entertained well.

This year has been a year to remember, we have seen much happen across this vast country of ours, from killings of children by children, wars and rumors of wars in Teman and other Third World countries, men and women displaced by major companies moving from the inner cities of America across the borders into Mexico and other areas where the pay is cheaper, hate crimes of racism on the rise and as the song says, "The band plays on."

Yes, we do face uncertain and bleak days ahead, and as people from all walks of life look to the Y2K's mystery to come, questions are in the minds of many as to what may be in our future: questions from the White House, to the State Mansion, and to the seats of Government in each city, questions from our economist who tells us whether we are financially sound or leaning on one leg. All these leaders we look to seem to be caught up in this depressive state of mind.

One day we're up, the next day we're down, depending on what newspaper you read or news telecast you turn on. And the band plays on.

Presidents, religious leaders, and politicians, both major and minor, keep failing the test of personal and public accountability, and the band plays on.

Y2K is coming and the new millennium troubles many that wonder if tomorrow will be any better. The prognosticators of future happenings keep proclaiming doom and gloom. Those of us who are planning to fly on January 1st to the Baptist World Congress in Australia have been urged to postpone until the next day for fear of computer problems causing planes to fall from the air. Banks and government agencies are quickly moving to restructure their computer systems. Hospitals are worried about surgical rooms and support systems failing.

Everybody is talking about the chip that's causing the technology that runs the brains of the computers to not recognize the New Year, thus throwing everything back to 1900. Governments are talking, financial institutions are talking, Wall Street is talking, and yes, even the church has joined in the conversation.

Should we be concerned? Should we prepare for what might happen? Is it possible that the end is near? Is Christ preparing us for the rapture? Are there any signs to the Second Coming of Christ in the midst of all this speculation of doom?

I must confess, I do not know what tomorrow is going to bring. The next two months are a mystery to me. Yes, I do believe we should look at it all. We should make some preparations for the failure of man's planning for the toys of his invention (computers).

The Bill Gates of the world have given us some useful gadgets to help make life and work easier for mankind. Even I have learned to use my PC to help in my sermon preparation. The worst typist and speller can look good by the assistance of these mechanical brains. My son and my church secretary have taught me how to turn it on and off and not let it intimidate me. But as far as tomorrow is concerned, that's in God's hand.

Should we worry? I think not. If the God of our salvation is still Savior of those who trust in the blood of Jesus; and if the Lord's Word is true, that no man knows the day or the hour when the Son of Man will return, it is not about fear, but readiness. People who fear His return or the end of the world as we know it have not the Spirit of Christ.

They forget that the Word of God has already declared that we as a world will become wiser, but weaker. We will learn more about our brainpower and the use of genes. We will have in every home personal computers and cell phones we will carry in our pockets that can not only hear, but see the ones we converse with. We may even return to the moon through space travel, and possibly beyond to Mars. All this and more I believe will happen, but only those who have Jesus as the Christ and have traveled in their hearts and minds to heaven will be at peace.

I offer this to all here; that the problem is not what Y2K will bring. The problem is in not remembering what Y2K brought to us. Jesus said, "I have come that you might have life and have it more abundantly." The stage for the saved has already been set. The scene has been written, there is no need for a rewrite.

And who can rewrite what God has put in place? We need not fear what will happen next year, or ten thousand years from now; it's all in His hands. If you have faith in His power to do exceedingly abundantly above all that we ask or think, according to the power that works in us, then know that Y2K is still in His hands.

We ought not to be afraid of what will come: we are safe in the hands of God. Romans 5 says, "Therefore being justified by faith, we have peace with God through our Lord Jesus Christ: By whom also we have access by faith into this grace wherein we stand, and rejoice in hope of the glory of God. And not only so, but we glory in tribulations also; knowing that tribulation worketh patience; and patience, experience; and experience, hope: and hope maketh not ashamed; because the love of God is shed abroad in our hearts by the Holy Ghost which is given unto us. For when we were yet without strength, in due time Christ died for the ungodly."

Should I be afraid? No. The Lord your God and my God has promised to meet us in our dying hour. And if He chooses to let us live, Jesus said, "Lo, I am with you, even to the end of the world." But if not, fine. Heaven is a better place than this world. No! No! No! Do not fear and don't be afraid. Put your trust in your living God. Keep your eyes on Jesus, our Leader and Instructor. He was willing to die a shameful death on the cross because of the joy He knew would be His afterwards; and now He sits in the place of honor by the throne of God.

What do I say about Y2K? If you want to keep from becoming fainthearted and weary, think about His patience as sinful men did terrible things to Him, and how He took our sins upon Him to the cross. Died for us. Paid the penalty for our transgressions. Was buried with the stench and smell of sinful death. Walked among the dead for three days and then just as He declared, rose from the grave with all power in His hand. Face Y2K with the knowledge of a new day, a new opportunity.

"I heard the voice of Jesus say, come unto me and rest; Lie down thy weary one lie down, thy head upon my breast. I came to Jesus as I was, weary, worn and sad, I found in Him a resting place and He has made me glad."

Concluding Words

This work has covered twenty-two years of a marvelous journey that has kept Missionary Baptists across the state of Missouri on the "Edge of Adventure." We have looked at the contributions of a noble people in quest of becoming all that God has given them the potentials to become. We have seen God work through three men, Drs. I. H. Henderson, McKinley Dukes, and Sammie E. Jones to bring this dynamic ministry into a new millennium: each of them with different abilities, visions and constituencies. Yet, they all had one thing in common. They had an undying commitment to their Creator, the spread of the Gospel through preaching and teaching, and a desire to see our Convention become all that God has intended it to become.

The Missionary Baptist State Convention of Missouri has had its good days and bad days. There have been many hills to climb. There have been many valleys to cross. There have been years of great support. There have been years of waning support. Yet, we have learned not to complain. For after all, God has been good to us. We have come a long way. We have come from the shores of Africa. We've come from Kansas, Arkansas, Nebraska, Illinois, Tennessee, Mississippi, Oklahoma, Kentucky, Iowa and across the nation to be blessed and to become a blessing. We have come to continue the legacy that was commenced one hundred and eleven years ago in Chillicothe, Missouri when our founding fathers were concerned about the evangelization of the race, Christian education and the betterment of our people in every area of life.

We cannot and will not forget the sacrifices that were made for us to be where we are today. We cannot and will not sell that heritage at any price. We must do all within our power to continue to build upon the foundation that was laid for us. We must not grow weary in well doing for we will reap if we faint not. We must be vigilant daily, steadfast, immovable, always abounding in the Word of God, knowing that our labor will not be in vain.

Yes, we have a story to tell. It is a story of men and women overcoming the degrading and debilitating institution of slavery. It is a story about a group of people who were determined to survive and thrive in a land of racism and oppression. It is a story of people who chose to view themselves as victors rather than victims. It is a story of a people who took the gospel message and created institutions that empowered them to live creative and productive lives. It is a story about the grace and mercy of God that has resulted in our being where we are today. We must continue to tell the story to our children and their children and their children's children.

Yes, we can say with jubilance: "This is my story. This is my song. Praising my Savior all the day long." For Jesus is truly our joy in the time of sorrow. He is our hope for today and tomorrow.

We face a new millennium, trusting the God of our fathers who has never failed us yet. We do not know about tomorrow. However, we have utmost confidence in the God who holds tomorrow in His hands.

Moderator Charles Brown and some of the association moderators

Bibliography

Bennett, Lerone. *Before the Mayflower.* Penguin Press: New York, 1962.

Butcher, Margaret Just. *The Negro in American Culture.* Alfred Knopf, Inc: New York, 1971

Cone, James H. *Liberation, A Black Theology of Liberation.* J. B. Lippincott Company: Philadelphia, New York, 1970.

Dodd, Linda. *History of Mount Zion Baptist Church,* 1998. *History of the Mt. Zion Baptist Association,* 1998.

Drake, St. Clair. *The Redemption of Africa and Black Religion.* The Third World Press: Chicago, 1970.

Ellis, Carl F. *Beyond Liberation, The Gospel in the Black Experience.* Inter Varsity Press: Downers Grove, Illinois, 1983.

Felder, Cain Hope. *The Original African Heritage Study Bible.* Word Bible Publisher: Iowa Falls, Iowa, 1993.

Fitts, Leroy. *History of Black Baptists.* Broadman Press: Nashville, 1985.

Franklin, John Hope, Moss, Alfred A. Jr. *From Slavery to Freedom.* Alfred A. Knoff, Inc.: New York, 1988.

Jackson, John G. *Introduction to African Civilization.* Citadel Press: New York, 1970.

Jordan, L. G. *Negro Baptist History, NBC.* Sunday School Publishing Board: Nashville, 1930

Busy Pastors Guide. NBC, Sunday School Publishing Board: Nashville, 1929

Kremer, Gary R., Holland, Antonio F. *Missouri Black Heritage.* New York, 1988

Lincoln, C. Eric. *The Black Church in African American Experience.* Anchor Press: Garden City, N.Y.,1974

The Black Church Since Fraiser. Schochen Books: New York, 1974

Mbiti, John S. *African Religions and Philosophies.* Anchor Press: New York, 1970. *Concepts of God.* S.P.C.K: London, 1969.

McNeil, Donald R. "*History of Mt. Carmel District,*" 1978.

Powell, C. D. "*History of North Missouri Baptist Association,*" 1996.

"*History of 18th Street Baptist Church,* Hannibal," 1996.

Scott, C. S. "*History of New Era District Association,*" 1979.

Shipley, David O, Alberta D. *History of Black Baptists in Missouri.* 1977.

Woodson, Carter G. *History of the Negro Church*, Associated Publishers: Washington, D. C. , 1921

INDEX

Antioch District Association   120
Arnold, Sister Auvelia H.   19
Berean Missionary Baptist District
   Association   107
Bobo, Dr. Ronald   20
Booker, Pastor James Monroe   19
Bridgeton Baptist Church, Bridgeton   65
Brown, Dr. Jimmie Lee   21
Brown, Sister Johnnie Howard Franklin   21
Calvary Baptist Church, Fulton   87
Central Baptist Church, St. Louis   58
Central Baptist District Association   115
Claiborne, Dr. William H.   22
Dillingham, Pastor Manuel   22
Dukes, Dr. McKinley   145
Eighth and Center Streets Baptist
   Church, Hannibal   60
Ellis, Pastor Willie J. Jr.   23
First African Baptist Church,
   St. Louis   52
First Baptist Church, Baldwin   55
First Baptist Church, Chesterfield   70
First Baptist Church, Webster Groves   87
Fortenberry, Pastor Haymond   24
Friendship Consolidated Baptist
   Association   121
Galilee Baptist Church, St. Louis   96
Givens, Pastor Harry   25
Greater Union Baptist District
   Association   106
Griffin, Brother Dan 25
Hawes, Pastor Otis Landon   26
Henderson, Dr. Isaiah H. Jr.   128
Howard, Sister Viola   26
Hughes, Dr. Daniel   27
Hunter, Pastor Donald   28

Jones, Mrs. Marguerite   28
Jones, Deacon Thaddeus   29
Jones, Dr. Sammie E.   155
Keeble, Pastor E. C.   30
Log Providence Baptist Church,
   Columbia   86
Lofton, Sister Ollie   30
Mallory, Pastor Raymond   31
Martin, Sister Betty Jean   31
Matthews, Pastor William Z.   32
McDowell, Sister Westly Mae   32
Meachum, Pastor John Berry   17
Middle Passage   3
Midwest Baptist District Association   122
Miles, Pastor John Modest   33
Morgan Street Baptist Church,
   Booneville   56
Morning Star Baptist Church,
   Kansas City   98
Mount Nebo Baptist Church,
   Rocheport   86
Mount Zion Baptist Church,
   Chillicothe   66
Mount Zion Missionary Baptist Church,
   St. Louis   70
Mt. Carmel Baptist District Association   117
Mt. Zion Baptist Association of Missouri   112
Musick Baptist Church, Maryland Heights   49
Nero, Pastor Samuel W.   34
New Era District Association   118
North Missouri Baptist District Association   104
Packnett, Pastor Ronald Bradnax   34
Patterson, Pastor Oliver K.   35
Peay, Dr. I. C.   36
Pittman, Sister Ann   37
Pleasant Green Baptist Church, Kansas City   93

Pleasant Hill Baptist Church,
    Poplar Bluff 90
Prairie Grove Baptist Church, Tipton 95
Sanders, Sister Ruthy 38
Scott, Rev. Corneleus S. 38
Scott, Dr. William Albert, Sr. 39
Second Baptist Church, Independence 80
Second Baptist Church, Jefferson City 74
Second Baptist Church, Kansas City 80
Second Baptist Church, Mexico 88
Second Baptist Church, Moberly 88
Second Baptist Church, Neosho 91
Second Missionary Baptist Church,
    Columbia 84
Second Missionary Baptist Church,
    Lexington 83
Shipley, Dr. David Oliver, Sr. 39
Singleton, Dr. William M. 40

Skylight Baptist Church, Kansas City 96
Southwest District Association 114
St. Francis Baptist Temple, St. Joseph 77
Titus, Sister Sallie 41
True Light Missionary Baptist Church,
    Kinloch 100
Unity Baptist Church, Joplin 98
Walker, Brother Everett T. 42
Ward Memorial Baptist Church,
    Sedalia 92
Western Baptist Bible College 126
Washington Avenue Baptist
    Church, Springfield 89
White, Pastor Alfred 43
White, Pastor Fate, Jr. 43
Wood Street Baptist Church,
    Lebanon 92
Woods, Sister Vivian O. 44